GEORGE J

A MINDSET FOR T.

—— BOOK ONE ——

MILLENNIAL
SAMURAI

Millennial Samurai—Book One—
A Mindset for the 21ˢᵗ Century. George J. Chanos.
First printing. Manufactured in the United States of America.
ISBN-9781688563339. Millennial Samurai is a trademark of George J. Chanos.

For information about special discounts for bulk purchases, please contact George J. Chanos at gjchanos@gmail.com

Book cover and interior book layout and design by Uri Schwarz.
Copyediting by Tiffany Pace and Ricadonna Uy.

TABLE OF CONTENTS

RELATIONSHIPS...138

About the Author

⟊

George J. Chanos, Esq. served as Nevada's thirty-first Attorney General. He administered Nevada's Department of Justice and acted as the state's chief legal officer and advisor. While serving as Nevada's Attorney General, he successfully argued (9/0) the case of *Whorton v. Bockting*, 549 U.S. 406 (2007) before the Supreme Court of the United States.

Prior to serving as Nevada's Attorney General, Mr. Chanos had a distinguished legal career representing individual and corporate clients on all matters relating to the growth and management of their businesses. He is an author, speaker and business consultant. He has served on numerous boards, both civic and corporate and for the last ten years has served as Chairman of Capriotti's Sandwich Shop Inc., a rapidly growing one-hundred-plus-unit QSR franchise whose Millennial owners—his partners—he continues to advise and mentor.

Mr. Chanos is a father and an uncle. His daughter, Alexandra, is currently attending the University of Nevada, Las Vegas and his nephew, David, is a graduate of San Diego State University. They are both Millennials and are the inspiration for this book. For more information on the subjects covered in this book and on related topics, visit GeorgeJChanos.com and MillennialSamurai. com.

Dedicated to Alex and David

FOREWORD

In 1995, astrophysicist Carl Sagan published a book called The Demon-Haunted World, which warned against the dangers of pseudoscience and scientific illiteracy. In it, Dr. Sagan predicted a future that is eerily similar to what we are seeing today and he encouraged all of us to engage in critical and skeptical thinking.

One passage that now seems more relevant than ever reads as follows:

"I have a foreboding of an America in my children's or grandchildren's time—when the United States is a service and information economy; when nearly all the manufacturing industries have slipped away to other countries; when awesome technological powers are in the hands of a very few and no one representing the public interest can even grasp the issues; when the people have lost the ability to set their own agendas or knowledgeably question those in authority; when, clutching our crystals and nervously consulting our horoscopes, our critical faculties in decline, unable to distinguish between what feels good and what's true, we slide, almost without noticing, back into superstition and darkness."

Millennial Samurai is intended to encourage and facilitate that critical and skeptical thinking by exploring and explaining many of the most important issues, concepts and technologies that will redefine life as we know it during the 21st Century.

INTRODUCTION

Millennial Samurai Introduction

C hange is coming. The next five years will create significant disruption. In ten years, artificial intelligence (AI) will exceed human intelligence. And in less than thirty years, AI will redefine life as we know it, in a way that is beyond our ability to even comprehend.

America is at a tipping point, with radical changes already under way. These changes will test our competency, our sense of community, our beliefs and our resolve. And yet today, the vast majority of us are unprepared for these tectonic changes.

At a time when we should be planning and preparing, we are instead divided by race, age, sex, religion, economics and identity politics. And we are paralyzed by political dysfunction.

Millennials will be at the vanguard of this change and the decisions that they make will affect all of us.

Dates used to define Millennials range from 1978 to 2004. Some classify those born in the United States between 1978 and 1997 as Millennials. Others use 1980 to 2004 to identify their period of birth. They are defined here as the over 85 million people born in the United States during the above time frames.

While *Millennial Samurai* speaks directly to Millennials, it wasn't written exclusively for them. It's dedicated to my children (who are Millennials) but I wrote it for anyone and everyone who wants to get more out of their one and only life and for everyone who understands that change is coming and wants to be part of that change - the leaders of tomorrow.

The opportunities available to Millennials are beyond extraordinary. Some of these opportunities will radically transform life as we know it.

In 2014, Stephen Hawking said that success in creating AI would be "the biggest event in human history." Hawking believed that in the coming decades, AI could offer "incalculable benefits and risks."

Advances in areas like AI, genomics, biotechnology, nanotechnology, space travel, renewable energy, 3-D printing, cloud computing and the Internet of things promise a future unlike anything we can currently even comprehend.

The challenges that this generation will face are equally significant. They include social, political and economic instability and uncertainty; increased

4

unemployment and the inadequacy of education; racial, social and economic inequalities and injustice; environmental threats and resource limitations; cultural and religious tensions; an absence of political accountability, vision and leadership; and the opportunities and dangers of technology - to name just a few.

ALL OF THIS IS COMING MUCH FASTER THAN WE REALIZE OR ARE ACCUSTOMED TO EXPERIENCING.

In *21 Lessons for the 21st Century*, Yuval Noah Harari says, "In the nineteenth century, the Industrial Revolution created new conditions and problems that none of the existing social, economic and political models could cope with. Feudalism, monarchism and traditional religions were not adapted to managing industrial metropolises, millions of uprooted workers, or the constantly changing nature of the modern economy. Consequently, humankind had to develop completely new models—liberal democracies, communist dictatorships and fascist regimes—and it took more than a century of terrible wars and revolutions to experiment with these models, separate the wheat from the chaff and implement the best solutions…"

THE CHALLENGES THAT WE WILL FACE IN THE 21ST CENTURY ARE MUCH BIGGER THAN THE CHALLENGES POSED BY THE INDUSTRIAL REVOLUTION.

And given the destructive power of our current civilization, we cannot afford more failed models. Harari says, "This time around, failed models might result in nuclear wars, genetically engineered monstrosities and a complete breakdown of the biosphere."

What will the world look like in 2050 when machines do virtually everything faster, cheaper and more efficiently than humans and the world no longer needs cheap, unskilled labor? Some suggest that America may not even exist as a sovereign nation—that a "United World Government" might be making decisions for us, providing for our "basic income" or "basic services" and controlling our daily lives. That may sound improbable but it is by no means inconceivable. Nationalism is clearly in decline and its most vocal advocates are its biggest liability.

Will the freedoms we take for granted today still exist in thirty years? Will our relationships with each other be marked by collaboration or conflict? Will governments be more or less efficient and/or accountable? These are just some of the questions that each and every one of us should be thinking and talking about.

Most of us believe that we can't afford the luxury of thinking about these things. We're far too busy dealing with the challenges of daily life. We have to pay the rent, feed the kids, get to work and care for our parents.

Unfortunately, we now find ourselves at a tipping point with a tsunami of technological change on the horizon. The future of humanity will be decided by the course we chart—or the one that is charted for us—over the next thirty years. And the disturbing reality is; you and your children won't be immune from the consequences of those decisions just because you're too busy feeding and caring for your family.

YOU DON'T HAVE THE LUXURY OF NOT THINKING ABOUT THESE THINGS.

As Benjamin Franklin, author, scientist, statesman and diplomat said, "By failing to prepare, you are preparing to fail."

To make matters even more urgent, scientists, corporations and governments are now learning how to hack the human brain. Over the next thirty years, scientists believe that we will learn not only how to hack brains but how to design them and to create or terminate thoughts at our discretion. This creates unprecedented opportunity *and* risk, yet none of these issues are even on the political radar, let alone on the political agenda.

We are being told that immigrants are going to take our jobs, not that computers are going to take our jobs. And yet computers *are* going to take our jobs—millions of our jobs.

If government continues to fail us, history has taught us that the public will eventually rise up and demand change. But government control of the media, including attempts to control social media, obscures the truth and keeps people distracted.

As Harari says;

"THROUGH ITS MONOPOLY OVER THE MEDIA, THE RULING OLIGARCHY CAN REPEATEDLY BLAME ALL ITS FAILURES ON OTHERS AND DIVERT ATTENTION TO EXTERNAL THREATS— EITHER REAL OR IMAGINARY... IF THE NATION IS FACING EXTERNAL INVASION OR DIABOLICAL SUBVERSION, WHO HAS TIME TO WORRY ABOUT OVERCROWDED HOSPITALS OR POLLUTED RIVERS?"

Ted Turner, founder of CNN, has also expressed concern over the role of the media, saying, "The media is too concentrated, too few people own too much. There's really five companies that control ninety percent of what we read, see and hear. It's not healthy."

Both Harari and Turner are right.

The media is no longer a source of objective information—if it ever was one. And this only serves to amplify the need for critical thinking and discernment.

Millennial Samurai is intended to stimulate thought and discussion, to promote critical thinking and discernment, to help us participate in the discussions that will shape our future and to help us understand what to teach our kids. It is intended to provide the guidance, encouragement and direction that can inspire transformative, life-changing action—action that can change and improve our lives. And it is written in the hope that it may inspire and empower new leadership.

I certainly don't claim to have the answers to the world's problems. I believe, as Aristotle and Socrates did, that "the man who thinks he knows everything knows nothing at all." The only thing that I know for certain is that there is a great deal that I do not know.

We don't require all the answers, but we do need to start asking the right questions. And we do need to be having a dialogue surrounding all the important issues of our age—now rather than later.

Millennial Samurai is intended to contribute to and facilitate that dialogue. How we think and how we act influences every aspect of our lives. *Millennial Samurai* provides insights, examples and suggestions on how to successfully overcome obstacles, seize opportunities and advance your objectives, all of which are extremely relevant to leveraging the opportunities and navigating the challenges ahead.

If it helps even a small group of readers to improve their lives, it will have been well worth the effort.

The following 182 chapters are intentionally short. The limited discussion of each subject is intended to alert, inspire and encourage you to learn more.

The subjects chosen for Book One are intended to identify and introduce important foundational concepts, subjects and resources. It is not a complete guide to everything you need to know but it's a good and empowering start. Books Two and Three, which will be written over the next several years, will offer further guidance and direction.

Think of *Millennial Samurai* as a resource—a combination of guiding principles, essential tools and useful reconnaissance. Those who want to seize the phenomenal opportunities ahead, while avoiding a myriad of potential threats, will need to adapt to a rapidly and radically changing environment. They will need to leverage their strengths while mitigating their weaknesses. They will need to embrace the ancient core values that have allowed prior generations to succeed while developing their own moral compass—one that will allow them to navigate the moral and ethical challenges that the technological revolution is certain to present. They will need to engage in a process of lifelong learning and critical thinking. They will need to pivot, adapt and persevere while traversing an ever-evolving landscape that can't even be imagined, let alone predicted—one that we can scarcely even currently comprehend. Those who are able to do this will be the Millennial Samurai - who will lead their generation and future generations through the 21st Century.

Millennials

"**M**illennials" or "The Entitlement Generation" may be the most misunderstood and maligned generation in modern history. Many have been characterized as having a delusional sense of entitlement. While some Millennials may deserve this characterization, the majority clearly do not. Millennials are the most educated, technically advanced, socially networked, ethnically diverse and globally oriented generation in human history. And what some see as their weaknesses may actually be the very strengths that will allow them to survive and thrive in a future that will look nothing like our past.

The Pew Research Center's reports on Millennials reveal a highly intelligent and complex generation. Millennials have been taught to value individuality and see themselves as independent thinkers. They are not defined by their jobs. Instead, they want to define their jobs. Most have no interest in working in a cubicle; they believe that advances in technology and mobility should allow them to work anywhere there's a Wi-Fi connection. They have high expectations and won't stay at jobs they find unfulfilling.

Millennials are the first generation to question work as a priority. In contrast to prior generations, they place quality of life first and work second. They believe in working smarter, not harder. They use technology to multitask and to find shortcuts to accomplishing tasks. Advances in technology and its ubiquitous nature have created the potential for Millennial workers to be more competent and efficient than any prior generation.

Yet despite these inherent strengths, some managers find them challenging to work with. The reason for this is twofold: failures in communication and priorities that are not aligned.

Millennials are different from their Baby Boomer managers. According to an Intelligence Group study from 2014, 64% of Millennials said they would rather make $40,000 a year at a job they love than $100,000 a year at a job they think is boring. Money alone doesn't motivate them. This creates a disconnect between Millennials and their Baby Boomer parents, managers and employers who are, to a greater degree, motived by money and who believe that their path to success was facilitated and enhanced by that motivation.

The disconnect between Baby Boomers and Millennials arises out of differing mindsets and priorities.

MONEY IS NOT HOW MILLENNIALS KEEP SCORE; THEY'RE SEARCHING FOR SOMETHING MORE.

Perhaps they're smarter than their Baby Boomer parents and they want to make the most of their one and only life, which causes them to prioritize experience over money. Perhaps their mindset is influenced by an awareness that they may not have the same economic opportunities that their parents had and they're simply adapting to a shifting landscape. Perhaps they see the dramatic increases in economic inequality and recognize that these changes are morally indefensible and ultimately unsustainable. Perhaps it's all of the above or something else. One thing is certain: their priorities are generally very different from those of their parents, their managers and their employers.

MILLENNIALS ARE MORE ACCEPTING OF DIFFERENCES NOT JUST AMONG WOMEN, MINORITIES AND THE LGBTQ COMMUNITY—BUT IN EVERYONE.

Many don't go to church because they don't identify with big institutions. In fact, one-third of adults under thirty—the highest percentage ever—are religiously unaffiliated. Millennials are also financially responsible. Although student loans have hit record highs, they have less household and credit card debt than any previous generation on record and they save more than prior generations. They love their phones but rarely talk on them. They're earnest and optimistic. They're pragmatic idealists and they have no leaders.

WHAT EMERGES IS A COMPLEX GENERATION THAT HAS SIGNIFICANT STRENGTHS AND WEAKNESSES.

As Baby Boomers get older, they will become increasingly less productive. Once a major source of innovation and contribution, they will eventually become unproductive liabilities. During this period, advances in technology will literally redefine life as we know it.

Since 2016, Millennials have become the largest generational employee group. One only needs to look to Google to see that millennial influence is already substantial and growing. On November 1, 2018, 100 employees walked out of Google's offices in Tokyo to protest the company's handling of sexual harassment claims. 25 hours later, 20,000 Google employees in 50 cities around the world had joined the protest. Employee resistance has also caused Google to cancel at least two major projects: one was project Maven (which uses artificial intelligence to help analyze drone footage for the United States Department of Defense); another is a project code-named Dragonfly (a censored search engine that was being developed for China). In response to employee pressure, Google announced that it would not renew its contracts for project Maven or Dragonfly.

Companies like Amazon, Facebook, Microsoft and Salesforce are also seeing push-back from Millennial employees on projects and practices that involve climate change, immigration, sexual harassment and diversity.

The Millennial Generation, regardless of how anyone may choose to characterize them, will be at the tip of the generational spear as humanity encounters unprecedented opportunities and risks during the 21st Century. How the future of humanity will be defined and experienced over the next thirty years will, in large part, be the opportunity and responsibility of Millennials.

Therefore, society as a whole needs to be focused not on ridiculing and denigrating Millennials—but on educating and empowering them.

Samurai

――――――――――*Ꭿ*――――――――――

S amurai were the military elite of pre-modern Japan. They dominated Japanese politics, economics and social policies between the twelfth and nineteenth centuries. Samurai initially rose to power as warriors. They were experts in archery, swordsmanship and horseback riding. Samurai employed a range of weapons such as bows and arrows, spears and guns, but their main weapon and symbol was the sword. The art of war was by no means their only strength. Samurai were also known for their political, financial and cultural acumen.

Many were highly educated and devoted patrons of the theater and the arts. They were accomplished poets and calligraphers. They amassed impressive art collections and built beautiful temples and gardens. Their massive temples became the central symbols of the age and they were responsible for creating many uniquely Japanese arts such as the tea ceremony and flower arranging, which continue today.

Samurai led their lives according to the ethical code of "bushido" (the way of the warrior). Confucian in nature, bushido stressed concepts such as loyalty to one's master, self-discipline and respectful, ethical behavior.

COURAGE, LOYALTY, VERACITY, COMPASSION AND HONOR WERE REVERED ABOVE LIFE ITSELF.

Bushido also emphasized frugality, kindness, honesty and care for one's family members, particularly one's elders. The samurai was equated with the Confucian "perfect gentleman" and taught that his essential function was to exemplify virtue.

The Soul of Japan by Inazo Nitobe is a study of the way of the samurai. These are what Nitobe describes as Bushido's Eight Virtues:

I. RECTITUDE OR JUSTICE

Rectitude, or justice, is the strongest virtue of Bushido. A well-known samurai defines it this way: "Rectitude is one's power to decide upon a course of conduct in accordance with reason, without wavering; to die when to die is right, to strike when to strike is right." Another speaks of rectitude in the following terms: "Rectitude is the bone that gives firmness and stature.

Without bones the head cannot rest on top of the spine, nor hands move nor feet stand. So, without rectitude, neither talent nor learning can make the human frame into a samurai."

II. COURAGE

Bushido distinguishes between bravery and courage: courage is worthy of being counted among virtues only if it's exercised in the cause of righteousness and rectitude. In his *Analects*, Confucius says, "Perceiving what is right and doing it not reveals a lack of courage." Essentially, courage is doing what is right.

III. BENEVOLENCE OR MERCY

A human invested with the power to command and the power to kill was expected to demonstrate equally extraordinary powers of benevolence and mercy. Love, magnanimity, affection for others, sympathy and pity are traits of benevolence, the highest attribute of the human soul. Confucius said the highest requirement of a ruler of men is benevolence.

IV. POLITENESS

Politeness should be the expression of a benevolent regard for the feelings of others; it's a poor virtue if it's only motivated by a fear of offending good taste. In its highest form, politeness approaches love.

V. HONESTY AND SINCERITY

True samurai, according to Nitobe, disdained money, believing that "men must grudge money, for riches hinder wisdom." Thus, children of high-ranking samurai were raised to believe that talking about money showed poor taste and that ignorance of the value of different coins showed good breeding. Bushido encouraged thrift, not for economic reasons so much as for the exercise of abstinence. Luxury was thought the greatest menace to manhood and severe simplicity was required of the warrior class.

VI. HONOR

The samurai was born and bred to value the duties and privileges of his profession. Fear of disgrace was like a sword hanging over the head of every samurai. To take offense at slight provocation was ridiculed as short-tempered. As the popular adage put it: true patience means bearing the unbearable.

VII. LOYALTY

The samurai believed that true men remain loyal to those to whom they are indebted. Loyalty to a superior was a distinctive virtue of the feudal era and was of paramount importance.

VIII. CHARACTER AND SELF-CONTROL

Bushido teaches that men should behave according to an absolute moral standard, one that transcends logic. What's right is right and what's wrong is wrong. The difference between good and bad and between right and wrong are givens, not arguments subject to discussion or justification and a man should know the difference. Finally, it is a man's obligation to teach his children moral standards through the model of his own behavior.

The first objective of samurai education was to build up character. Bushido ultimately became the basic code of conduct for much of Japanese society. Zen Buddhism held natural appeal for many samurai. Its austere rituals, as well as the belief that salvation would come from within, provided a natural philosophical background for the samurai's own code of conduct.

The sword also had great significance in samurai culture. A man's honor was said to reside in his sword.

A study out of UC Davis found that even today, 140 years after the samurai gave up their swords, their descendants (people carrying surnames associated with Japan's feudal ruling class) still enjoy a privileged status in Japanese society. Many are the successful lawyers, doctors, architects, artists, entrepreneurs and government officials that remain a driving force in modern Japanese society.

Millennial Samurai

Millennial Samurai will be those who rise to the challenges of the 21st Century. They will be the century's elite class of social, political and economic warriors. They will be highly intelligent, technologically advanced, socially networked, globally oriented and fundamentally grounded in both ancient and modern core values.

Their elite status will not be born out of privilege but will be earned as a result of performance and virtue. Millennial Samurai will be those who are committed to developing and maintaining expertise in emerging technologies and leveraging those technologies to advance social, political and economic objectives that serve not only their own interests but those of their family, their community and humanity.

They will employ a wide range of weapons (an open mind, an ability to think for themselves, an ability to communicate effectively, an understanding of the inherent limitations of bias and perception to name only a few), but their main weapons—their "swords"—will be their minds and they will be committed to sharpening those "swords" through a process of lifelong learning.

They will be revered not only for their political, financial and social acumen but for their authenticity, honor, integrity, inclusiveness, empathy, generosity, humility, gratitude and compassion.

THEY WILL COME TO EXEMPLIFY
STRENGTH, WISDOM AND VIRTUE.

This special class of Millennials will not look for safe spaces or hide from problems. Instead, they will seek out new challenges, overcome obstacles and when necessary, provide safe spaces for others while leading their generation and future generations through the promise and perils of the 21st Century.

It is my hope and intention that this book, together with subsequent editions, will guide and inspire this and future generations of Millennial Samurai.

Book One is step one. It will empower you by exposing you to a wealth of information that can be life changing for you, your family and for those that you may one day be called upon to lead.

Book One shows you how to develop a healthy and empowering mindset. It explains the significance of core values and identifies the core principles that can help you to design, enhance and lead your one and only life. It explains how your brain (your sword) operates and shows you how to improve your cognitive function and increase your intelligence. It explains the significance of your relationships and shows you how to improve them. It teaches you why action is magic, shows you how to understand and overcome your fears and explains how and why your opportunities are virtually unlimited.

In sum, *Millennial Samurai* shows you how to design and lead an exceptional life—a life of purpose, passion and contribution—in what promises to be the most extraordinary period in human history. However, knowing how to do something is not the same as doing it. In the end, your choices and your actions will, in large part, determine the life that you lead. *Millennial Samurai* will inform those choices and inspire that action.

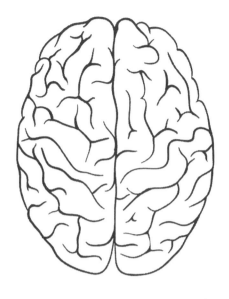

THE RIGHT MINDSET

A mindset for the 21st Century requires that you learn to engage in critical thinking, control your thoughts, set clear intentions, believe in yourself, think for yourself, have an open mind, search for the truth, maintain a positive attitude, show empathy, practice gratitude, be optimistic, have hope and embrace life with passion.

1

CRITICAL THINKING

*The 21ˢᵗ Century will be driven by information and
technology. To survive and thrive will require an
ability to adapt to a rapidly and radically changing
environment. It will require an ability to accurately
analyze information while guarding against false or
misleading information.*

Success and survival will require an ability to acquire, analyze and
integrate diverse sources of knowledge to solve problems. And this will
require critical thinking. Critical thinking is the ability to think clearly,
rationally and deeply about what to do and what to believe. It includes the
ability to engage in reflective and independent thinking. Someone with critical
thinking skills is able to understand the logical connections between ideas.
They are able to identify, construct and evaluate arguments. They are able
to detect inconsistencies and common mistakes in reasoning while solving
problems systematically. They are able to identify the relevance and weigh the
relative importance of competing ideas. And they are always conscious of how
their own beliefs, biases, perceptual limitations and values may influence their
perception.

A CRITICAL THINKER APPROACHES PROBLEMS WITH AN INSATIABLE THIRST FOR INFORMATION AND A CRITICAL, CREATIVE AND CURIOUS MIND.

Thinking critically requires that you actively seek to acquire information
and to improve your understanding in your search for the truth. Critical
thinking includes "outside-the-box" thinking.

IT REQUIRES CONSIDERING ALL FORMS OF INPUT INCLUDING INTUITION AND EMOTION.

It may also require challenging consensus and pursuing less popular views.

Thinking critically plays an important role in cooperative reasoning and collaborative problem solving. It complements creativity by evaluating new ideas, selecting the best ones and modifying them if necessary. Finally, it provides the tools for self-evaluation and reflection, allowing us to recognize and overcome our inherent biases and prejudices.

A liberal democracy requires citizens who can think critically about social, political and economic issues. Critical thinking will allow you to make informed judgments about those important issues.

In January 2016, the World Economic Forum issued a report titled The Future of Jobs, which says, "The Fourth Industrial Revolution, which includes developments in previously disjointed fields such as artificial intelligence and machine-learning, robotics, nanotechnology, 3-D printing, genetics and biotechnology, will cause widespread disruption not only to business models but also to labor markets *over the next five years*, with enormous change predicted in the skill sets needed to thrive in the new landscape."

According to the World Economic Forum, we will experience "widespread disruption" over the next five years and that's just the beginning.

OVER THE NEXT THIRTY YEARS, WE WILL WITNESS A TECHNOLOGICAL TSUNAMI WHICH WILL CAUSE SOCIAL AND POLITICAL SEA CHANGES.

Millennial Samurai will need to be prepared to lead society into those uncharted waters and that will require critical thinking.

According to the World Economic Forum, the top ten skills that are expected to be most relevant going forward are:

1. Complex Problem Solving
2. Critical Thinking
3. Creativity
4. People Management
5. Coordinating with Others
6. Emotional Intelligence
7. Judgement and Decision Making
8. Service Orientation
9. Negotiation
10. Cognitive Flexibility

Millennial Samurai should strive to be adept in all or most of these areas.

2

CONTROL YOUR THOUGHTS

"There is nothing either good or bad
but thinking makes it so."

—Shakespeare, English poet, playwright and actor.

Y ou have the ability to control and influence your thoughts. This is a power you can cultivate and develop. Your mind is your sword. Learn to use and control it. Learn to master it through lifelong learning, mindfulness, meditation, practice and repetition. If you find yourself thinking negative thoughts, pause to recognize and acknowledge your thoughts for what they are: transitory packets of sensory information that may or may not represent "truths" or "facts."

Simply pausing to reflect upon and examine your thoughts shifts the brain's processing of them from the amygdala (the emotional and reactive portion) to the prefrontal cortex (the region responsible for conscious and deliberate thought), allowing you to see your thoughts more clearly, less emotionally and more objectively.

TRAIN YOUR BRAIN TO THINK POSITIVE THOUGHTS.

You do this by making a conscious effort to think about positive things. You do it by looking at positive images and by remembering positive events. You do it through self-talk and through positive affirmations: "I can do this." The more you do this, the greater and more lasting the impact. Embracing gratitude as a core value and repeatedly engaging in positive affirmation can actually rewire your brain and allow you to live a more positive and self-affirming life. Make these positive thought processes a daily habit, a way of life.

THE QUALITY OF YOUR LIFE DEPENDS ON THE QUALITY OF YOUR THOUGHTS.

To control your destiny, you must first control your thoughts. Remember, your sword (your mind) is your weapon. It is the only weapon that you will always have with you and, if sharpened properly, the only weapon that a Millennial Samurai will ever need.

Millennial Samurai control their thoughts.

3

SET CLEAR INTENTIONS

*"Our life always expresses the result of
our dominant thoughts."*

—*Soren Kierkegaard, Danish philosopher.*

You are responsible for the energy you bring into every moment, every interaction, every conversation and into every room you enter. Intention is an important part of mindset.

**WHEN YOU SET A CLEAR INTENTION, YOU WILL BE
MORE LIKELY TO ACT IN WAYS, RESPOND TO SITUATIONS,
CREATE OPPORTUNITIES AND MAKE CHOICES
THAT SUPPORT YOUR INTENTION.**

Essentially, you will be more likely to have the experience that you consciously determine is important to you.

Intention is at the spiritual core of Indian religious and philosophical teachings. The classic Vedic text known as the Upanishads states, "You are what your deepest desire is. As your desire is, so is your intention. As your intention is, so is your will. As your will is, so is your deed. As your deed is, so is your destiny."

**WHEN YOUR INTENTIONS ARE BASED ON YOUR HIGHEST
VALUES, YOUR LIFE BECOMES MORE PURPOSEFUL BECAUSE
YOU UNDERSTAND WHAT'S IMPORTANT TO YOU.**

Your intentions are not only important for your broader goals in life, they're an important part of your day to day existence. They determine your direction in all things and ultimately, the results you achieve.

What is your intention when you wake up in the morning, when you go to work, when you greet a customer, or when you play with your children? How might your life change if you woke up every morning with the intention of having an incredibly productive, happy and healthy day? What would happen if your intention was to go to work with a positive, energetic, grateful, purposeful and enthusiastic attitude? How might having the intention to greet every customer with a smile, a cheerful attitude and a sincere desire to serve impact customer relations? How might playing with your children with the intention of creating loving, mindful and memorable experiences change their lives and yours? What are your goals? What results do you hope to achieve? Do you begin these engagements with intention? Or do you just go with the flow or operate on autopilot?

Your intention upon entering into any engagement will profoundly impact the nature and the consequences of that engagement. Setting clear intentions is a key to obtaining your personal and professional goals.

Millennial Samurai set clear intentions.

4

BELIEVE IN YOURSELF

"Whether you think you can or you think you can't—
you're right."

—Henry Ford, *founder of Ford Motor Company.*

You need to believe in yourself. Not in some delusional, unrealistic way but in a rational, optimistic and courageous way that inspires you to action. From there, add determination and commitment and you will be on your way to realizing your dreams.

The life you lead depends more on you than on anything else. How you think determines how you act—belief in yourself is therefore critical. It will guide every action you take. It will influence everything you say and do. For those who believe in themselves, anything is possible and for those who don't, nothing is possible. Use positive affirmation to build your self-confidence.

Wake up every morning saying, "I can do this." Believe it. Internalize it. Trust in it.

Millennial Samurai believe in themselves.

5

THINK FOR YOURSELF

"The individual has always had to struggle to keep from being overwhelmed by the tribe—if you try it you will be lonely often and sometimes frightened. But no price is too high to pay for the privilege of owning yourself."

—*Friedrich Nietzsche, German philosopher.*

D o you control your thoughts, or do you allow your thoughts and the thoughts of others to control you? In his bestselling book *Principles*, Ray Dalio's very first principle is, "Think for yourself." Dalio says, "If you can think for yourself while being open-minded in a clear-headed way to find out what is best for you to do and if you can summon up the courage to do it, you will make the most of your life. If you can't do that, you should reflect on why that is, because that's most likely your greatest impediment to getting more of what you want out of life."

Let's break Dalio's advice down and pay attention to each element of that advice:

1. Think for yourself
2. While being open-minded
3. In a clear-headed way
4. To find out what is best for you
5. And summon the courage to do it

This is especially critical at a time when social and political media is being manipulated by undisclosed interests, mainstream media has lost all objectivity and groupthink is increasingly the norm.

Groupthink is the refuge of a lazy mind. It's a short term solution for those who are unwilling or unable to think for themselves. And like all short term solutions, it fails to address our long term needs—which include the need to develop our ability to think critically, the need to develop and improve our minds and the need to make intelligent, well informed choices.

A failure to think for yourself weakens you by allowing these critical skills to atrophy. It leaves you with a sword unworthy of a Millennial Samurai.

Millennial Samurai think for themselves.

6

OPEN YOUR MIND

"A mind is like a parachute.
It doesn't work if it isn't open."

—Frank Zappa, American musician.

We all have blind spots and biases that cloud our perspectives. Alternative perspectives allow us to see the complete picture, inform our opinions and increase the probability that we will discover the truth.

HUMILITY AND OPEN-MINDEDNESS OFFER UNIQUE INSIGHTS THAT EGO AND OPINION PRECLUDE.

When searching for answers, don't be concerned with where the answers come from—be concerned that the answers are right. Surround yourself with the smartest people you can find, people who have alternative viewpoints and perspectives, people who can point out what you might be missing. Solicit, explore and evaluate other people's opinions and judge those opinions based on their merits.

Devour information and alternative opinions, not in a quest for validation but in a passionate search for the truth. And know this: the only certainty in life is that there will always be a great deal you do not know.

Millennial Samurai have open minds.

7

INTUITION

Psychologists define intuition as "immediate understanding, knowledge, or awareness derived neither from perception nor from reasoning."

Intuition is essentially the brain processing information without your conscious awareness—it is unconscious thinking.

Brainstorming is a powerful technique to discover solutions. Brainstorming encourages all suggestions—including those based on nothing but intuition—for good reason. Try the Brainstorming Rules from www.IDEO.org to achieve maximum results.

SOME OF THE MOST REMARKABLE DISCOVERIES, LIKE PENICILLIN AND TEFLON, HAVE BEEN BASED ON LITTLE MORE THAN INFORMED INTUITION.

However, not all intuition is equal. Bruce Kasanoff, cofounder of Park City Think Tank, says, "You might say that I'm a believer in the power of disciplined intuition. Do your legwork, use your brain, share logical arguments and I'll trust and respect your intuitive powers. But if you merely sit in your hammock and ask me to trust your intuition, I'll quickly be out the door without saying goodbye."

Kasanoff believes that for those who have been rigorous in using their conscious brain, intuition can sometimes provide the highest form of intelligence. He says, "Sometimes a corporate mandate or groupthink—or your desire to produce a certain outcome—can cause your rational mind to go in the wrong direction. At times like these, it is intuition that holds the power to save you."

Intuition can be cultivated and encouraged by setting aside time to reflect, taking walks, spending time in nature, clearing your head and practicing mindfulness and meditation. Engaging in creative activities also quiets the cognitive mind and allows your intuition to flourish.

Your intuition is a powerful tool especially when it is informed by due diligence and consistent with your core values.

Millennial Samurai understand the power of informed intuition.

8

SEEK THE TRUTH

"The illiterate of the 21st Century will not be those who cannot read and write but those who cannot learn, unlearn and relearn."

—Alvin Toffler, American writer and futurist.

To discover the truth, we must first recognize the need to discover it and that requires an understanding that our minds are filled with false ideas and conceptions. Unfortunately, the very idea that we cannot trust our own thinking is a very difficult thing to accept—maybe one of the most difficult. We resist unlearning and relearning just as we resist many kinds of change.

OUR EGOS HATE BEING TORN DOWN, EVEN TO BE REBUILT.

Carl Jung, Swiss psychiatrist and psychoanalyst, said, "People will do anything, no matter how absurd, to avoid facing their own souls." We don't welcome truth or change that interferes with our existing beliefs and worldview. We resist it.

WE PREFER COMFORTING LIES OVER HARSH TRUTHS.

More importantly, when confronted with harsh truths, our brains unconsciously deploy what are essentially self-defense mechanisms that challenge competing thoughts and ideas and often prevent us from seeing the truth.

The truth often conflicts with what we believe. It may conflict with our career, our associations and/or our relationships. It may threaten our status or our public image. We may be attacked and ridiculed for speaking the truth as others may not want to hear it. Instead, they may prefer to hear comforting and inspiring confirmation of that which they already believe.

The theory of cognitive dissonance also explains why we often have an aversion to the truth; our brains instinctively resist information that causes dissonance. Our brains unconsciously adjust competing facts to relieve dissonance. This phenomenon works alongside a complimentary phenomenon known as confirmation bias. Confirmation bias is the tendency to accept and remember information that confirms our existing beliefs and ignore information that contradicts those beliefs.

SOMETIMES THE TRUTH IS HARD TO RECOGNIZE.

It may go against everything we've been told and taught by society and governments. It may go against what we see, hear and read in the media. It may go against what we believe and what our friends, family and coworkers believe.

In an age where "fake news" has become more prevalent and where the ability to manipulate our thoughts and actions has become an emerging skill set and sought-after trade-skill, truth has become more elusive than ever. To find the truth, we must first understand that there are those who don't want us to find it. Some will even go to great lengths to conceal the truth from us.

Unfortunately, a lack of candor is increasingly becoming more common. A seller of a car or a home may conceal defects to secure a sale. A journalist or media personality may omit certain facts from a story that conflict with their preferred narrative. A prosecutor might withhold exculpatory evidence or treat people differently based on any number of criteria.

LIES ARE OFTEN MIXED WITH TRUTH TO AVOID DETECTION, NECESSITATING INCREASED ATTENTION, CRITICAL THINKING AND DISCERNMENT.

It is not always a lack of information or the quality of information that prevents us from seeing the truth. More often, it is the "barriers to entry" that our brain imposes on new ideas that threaten our existing beliefs— barriers that prevent us from seeing the truth. Rather than accept certain information at face value, we often bend, twist and disassemble information to fit our preconceptions, making it all the more difficult to recognize that our preconceptions are false.

WE WANT CERTAIN THINGS TO BE TRUE
MORE THAN WE WANT TRUTH ITSELF.

We want the candidates that we voted for to be the best candidates. We want the choices that we make to be the right choices. We want our worldview to be the right view. We want validation. Consequently, we unconsciously assess information that conforms to our preconceptions more favorably. We will accept a questionable source of information that confirms our existing beliefs while challenging a far more credible source that contradicts those beliefs.

TO FIND THE TRUTH, OUR PRIMARY GOAL
MUST BE THE TRUTH, NO MATTER WHAT IT IS.

This process requires a commitment to self-examination and critical thinking. "Social etiquette" and "political correctness," while well-intentioned, are often the enemies of truth. By not wanting to say anything "bad" and avoiding taboo subjects, we often avoid the truth in order to be spiritually or politically correct. This sometimes prevents us from seeing the world more clearly, honestly and objectively.

OUR NEED TO BE RECOGNIZED AND PRAISED FOR
WHAT WE SAY OR BELIEVE CAN FORCE TRUTH TO TAKE
A BACKSEAT TO AMBITION, STATUS AND OUR NEED
FOR ACCEPTANCE AND ADMIRATION.

Having good intentions is not enough. As T.S. Eliot, poet, essayist and playwright, said, "Half the harm that is done in this world is due to people who want to feel important. They don't mean to do harm, but the harm does not interest them. Or they do not see it, or they justify it because they are absorbed in the endless struggle to think well of themselves."

Don't allow yourself to be distracted by the political circus, the side shows masquerading as nightly news, or the priorities of the well-intentioned. Be open and sensitive to the views of others but make truth your priority. Educate yourself and attempt to see fraud, lies, distortion and deception for what they are, regardless of the consequences.

The more we engage in a joint search for the truth and work together to discern and act upon the truth, the greater our chances for mutual success and survival.

Millennial Samurai seek and are committed to the truth.

9

ATTITUDE

*"Nothing can stop the man with the right mental attitude
from achieving his goal; nothing on Earth can help the
man with the wrong mental attitude."*

—*Thomas Jefferson, 3rd President of the United States.*

Attitude is one of life's most powerful concepts. How you perceive the world and the way the world perceives you is, in large part, determined by your attitude. Your attitude will have an immense impact on your life. The good news is you control your attitude. Your actions are influenced by your attitude which in turn influences the resulting attitude of others toward you. A negative attitude invites failure and a positive attitude invites success. Enthusiasm is one of the most empowering and attractive qualities you can have.

SUCCESSFUL PEOPLE USE AFFIRMATIONS, REPEATED SEVERAL TIMES EACH DAY, TO REPROGRAM THEIR SUBCONSCIOUS WITH POSITIVE THINKING.

They choose to think positive thoughts. They visualize positive results. They create their own positive reality by thinking positively and visualizing their success. Studies have shown that these practices actually rewire our unconscious brains and increase our opportunities for success.

Nelson Mandela used visualization to maintain a positive attitude while being imprisoned for twenty-seven years. "I thought continually of the day when I would walk free. I fantasized about what I would like to do," he wrote in his autobiography.

Oprah Winfrey, American media owner, talk show host, actress and producer, tells us;

"THE GREATEST DISCOVERY OF ALL TIME IS THAT A PERSON CAN CHANGE HIS FUTURE BY MERELY CHANGING HIS ATTITUDE."

We are all influenced by our respective environments. We all encounter difficulty and disappointments—some are more severe than others. We may have had to endure intense physical or emotional pain or the loss of a loved one. When thinking about your personal trials, tragedies and disappointments, remember that no matter how bad you think your experiences may be, many people face challenges and disappointments that are far worse than yours.

Habitual bad attitudes are often the product of past experiences and events. Common causes include low self-esteem, stress, fear, resentment, anger and an inability to handle change. It takes work to examine the roots of a harmful attitude but the rewards of ridding yourself of this emotional baggage can last a lifetime.

Life is about choices. It is not what happens to you that matters—it's how you choose to respond and how you choose to think about it; how you choose to allow it to affect you. These are the things that matter and they are entirely within your control. Your attitude can become a habit.

DO YOU THINK THAT WHAT YOU WANT IS POSSIBLE? IF SO, IT CAN BECOME YOUR REALITY.

One of the best ways to move to a more positive and motivated frame of mind is to exercise. A regular exercise routine can provide relatively quick positive feedback in the form of weight loss, muscle development and a sense of doing something positive for yourself.

If, for whatever reason, a positive attitude seems like a bridge too far, then you need to examine why that is. Carl Jung, Swiss psychiatrist and psychoanalyst says, "Depression is like a woman in black. If she turns up, don't shoo her away. Invite her in, offer her a seat, treat her like a guest and listen to what she wants to say."

Engage in self-examination. Try to understand the root causes of your attitude. And then summon the courage and make the choice to move past them. Seek professional help if necessary. If you can't approach life with positivity, don't expect life to be positive. Life is what you make it. Begin by seeing and embracing all that is positive in yourself. You have greatness in you; find it, embrace it and allow it to flourish.

Millennial Samurai have a positive attitude.

10

10

EMPATHY

*"Empathy is a quality of character
that can change the world."*

—*Barack Obama, the 44th President of the United States.*

E mpathy is the ability to understand and share the thoughts and feelings of another. It may be the most critical 21st Century skill. Empathy builds character and develops leadership skills. It promotes trust, creative thinking, contribution and collaboration. It is essential to brainstorming and the design process. It is critical in negotiations and an essential part of raising capital.

People won't collaborate or offer their ideas if they feel that their views will be ignored or ridiculed. Understanding the needs, wants, perspectives and interests of the other side is essential to successful negotiations. And raising capital from investors begins with understanding their needs and objectives.

As Oprah Winfrey, the American media owner, talk show host, actress and producer, said;

"LEADERSHIP IS ABOUT EMPATHY."

Empathy is an important part of the hiring process both for employers and applicants. Employers need to understand what will motivate and strengthen an employee's contribution, collaboration and commitment. And employees need to have a clear understanding of their employers' needs and objectives.

Empathy is essential to sales, customer service and teaching. Knowing what a potential customer wants and needs allows you to tailor your offering. Responding to your customers' needs and concerns builds trust, allowing you to retain your customers. The relationship between a teacher and student also requires mutual understanding and shared goals. Teaching without empathy is like taking horses to water without caring if they drink.

Empathy exists when a manager understands the struggles of his team, when a husband understands the stress his wife may be experiencing, when a parent remembers what it was like to be a teen and when a child understands how much his parents care and why they think and feel the way they do. But we don't always have or show empathy. Sometimes we find it hard to understand another person's failings or weaknesses.

Psychologists Daniel Goleman and Paul Ekman break down the concept of empathy into the following three categories:

Cognitive empathy is the ability to understand how a person feels and what they might be thinking. Cognitive empathy makes us better communicators because it helps us relay information in a way that best reaches the other person.

Emotional empathy is the ability to share the feelings of another person. This type of empathy helps you build emotional connections with others.

Compassionate empathy moves us to take action, to help however we can.

Maya Angelou, the American poet, said, "I think we all have empathy. We may not have enough courage to display it."

Empathy takes time and effort and we don't always show empathy or our empathy is limited. We may find it hard to understand another person's feelings or we may understand those feelings but don't share them, or we may understand and share their feelings but fail to take any action.

We build cognitive empathy by paying attention, by understanding that we may not see the whole picture, by looking for subtle cues and by learning more about those we interact with, which may help to create understanding.

We develop emotional empathy by listening carefully, by resisting the urge to judge and by trying to remember when we had similar feelings about something that happened in our lives.

We engage in compassionate empathy by asking the other person what we can do to help. If they can't or won't tell you, think about what helped you when you felt a similar emotion. Don't minimize what someone else is feeling or suggest that you have the solution. Just offer to help and do what you can.

EMPATHY ALLOWS US TO ADD GREATER MEANING AND PURPOSE TO OUR LIVES.

It allows us to build teams and engender trust, collaboration and commitment. It allows us to solve problems and develop solutions. It allows us to lead.

Millennial Samurai have empathy for others.

11

GRATITUDE

*"Cultivate the habit of being grateful for every
good thing that comes to you and to give thanks
continuously. And because all things have
contributed to your advancement, you
should include all things in your gratitude."*

—*Ralph Waldo Emerson, American essayist, lecturer, philosopher and poet.*

Gratitude is one of the most important and least understood of all the great core values. It can turn an ordinary day into one of joy and fulfillment. It is a gift that you bestow on others, which enriches yourself.

IT CAN NOT ONLY TRANSFORM THE WAY YOU EXPERIENCE LIFE—IT CAN LITERALLY REWIRE YOUR BRAIN.

The antidepressant Wellbutrin boosts the neurotransmitter dopamine and the antidepressant Prozac boosts the neurotransmitter serotonin. Gratitude boosts both. Feeling grateful activates the brainstem region that produces dopamine, while trying to think of things you are grateful for increases serotonin production in the anterior cingulate cortex.

Moreover, gratitude doesn't just make you happy, it can also create a positive feedback loop in your relationships. Gratitude contributes to a reciprocal process of relationship maintenance whereby each partner's behaviors feed into and influence the other's.

Be grateful for everything you have no matter how small and seemingly insignificant. Life is, in large part, a matter of perspective and gratitude creates one of the healthiest and most ideal perspectives possible. Make gratitude a habit.

MAKE IT PART OF YOUR DAILY LIFE AND PRACTICE IT LIKE YOU WOULD A SKILL THAT YOU HOPE TO MASTER.

Wake up every morning with gratitude and be grateful every night, especially for the person next to you.

Millennial Samurai practice and understand the importance of gratitude.

12

12

OPTIMISM

"The pessimist sees difficulty in opportunity.
The optimist sees opportunity in difficulty."

—*Winston Churchill, former British Prime Minister.*

O ptimism is a critical concept. It's infectious and has a magnetic quality of attraction, drawing people to you. It permeates every aspect of your life and touches the lives of all those around you.

Optimism is an incredibly powerful force. Researchers have found that when they induce a positive mood, by whatever means, people are more likely to interact with and help others. Those who feel good about themselves are more cooperative in bargaining situations and are more likely to find constructive solutions to their conflicts and challenges. They are better problem solvers, more motivated to succeed and more likely to persevere in the face of obstacles.

As you confront life's challenges—whether it's losing a job or a loved one, dealing with poor health, spending years in school to obtain a degree, starting a new business, getting a divorce, going bankrupt, starting a new job, writing a blog, or climbing a mountain—optimism is the life preserver that keeps you afloat.

Millennial Samurai are optimistic.

13

HOPE

*"It is in our darkest moments that
we must focus on the light."*

—Aristotle Onassis, Greek shipping tycoon.

H ope is what inspires us to overcome our challenges and change our
condition. It's what comforts us in times of distress. It's the light at the
end of the tunnel that guides and sustains us.

Hope is directly related to our sense of possibility. By visualizing what you
want and imagining positive outcomes, you unconsciously structure your
behavior to create those outcomes.

If your present circumstances are difficult or unpleasant, the thought of
a positive future can lessen your stress. It can reduce the impact of negative
events or disappointments.

HOPE BRINGS PERSPECTIVE.

It allows you to view your circumstances by thinking beyond what's
currently happening.

Instead of focusing exclusively on the negative things happening in your
life, see the world how it could be.

Surround yourself with positive people who encourage you to become the
person you want to be. And distance yourself from negativity.

Volunteer with local organizations where people are taking care of one
another. Focus on how other people are caring for each other and improving
the lives of those around them. Doing this will restore your faith in human

nature and help you realize that everyone has challenges—it's not just you.

Meditation, physical exercise, breathing exercises, travel, recreation and spending time in nature can all reduce stress and inspire hope.

Millennial Samurai always have hope and inspire hope in others.

14

14

PASSION

*"There is no passion in playing small—
in settling for a life that is less than the
one you are capable of living."*

—Nelson Mandela, revolutionary, President of South Africa.

The movie *Serendipity* contains the following lines, "The Greeks didn't write obituaries. They only asked one question after a man died: did he have passion?" This ancient Greek philosophy, which regarded passion as critical to a well-lived life, is attributed to Aristippus of Cyrene (c. 435 - 356 B.C.). Thousands of years later, passion is still considered a foundational principle that guides people's lives.

PASSION DOESN'T SIMPLY CREATE EXCITEMENT; IT ALSO FUELS ENDURANCE.

Steve Jobs, co-founder of Apple, Inc., said, "You have to be burning with an idea, or a problem, or a wrong that you want to right. If you're not passionate enough from the start, you'll never stick it out."

We don't always have passion before we act. Sometimes our engagement, planning, decisions, or experiences ignite our passion. French philosopher Jean-Paul Sartre said, "We must act out passion before we can feel it."

Success also fuels passion. If you have one hundred followers on social media, you might not be very passionate about it. On the other hand, if you had one hundred thousand followers, that might make you more passionate about growing your followers to one million. If you're working at a fast food restaurant, you might see it as a job with no future. But if you knew that mastering the business of managing a franchise could result in a future opportunity to own one, you would approach it with a different intention, which would yield an entirely different result.

What is passion and how do you find yours? There are different ways of looking at passion.

PASSION IS SOMETHING THAT MOTIVATES YOUR ACTION AND COMMITMENT. IDEALLY, IT IS SOMETHING YOU LOVE AND ENJOY.

Some people are motivated by money; they want the things that money can buy. They may want to use the money they make to pursue their passions for art, travel or philanthropy. That's fine if that's what motivates you. Other people may not care about money. They may choose instead to pursue their passion for art, even by being a "starving artist," if necessary. These are individual life choices and there are no right or wrong answers. What's right is what's right for you.

The key is that passion must motivate your action and commitment. Don't expect your passion to identify itself in an epiphany moment. It is more likely to come to you over time through a series of discoveries resulting from varied experiences. To find your passion, broaden your experiences as much as possible. Over time, you will come to identify your true passion.

Our lives are cluttered with emotional baggage, busy schedules, obligations and physical possessions. These obligations and distractions can overwhelm or paralyze us and prevent us from having clarity, energy, time and focus. They can inhibit us from creating a passionate life.

Feelings of depression, anxiety, anger or fear can sabotage any effort to find or follow your passion. You can address these issues by blocking out a small amount of time every day or week and using that time to explore your potential passions. Use exercise, meditation, walking in nature, spending time with supportive friends and practicing positive affirmations to rid yourself of emotional baggage.

We each have a passion that awaits us and we each have only one life.

FIND YOUR PASSION AND YOU WILL MAKE THE MOST OF YOUR ONE AND ONLY LIFE.

And whatever you choose to do, do it with passion.

Millennial Samurai lead passionate lives.

15

LIFE ISN'T FAIR

"Life is not fair—get used to it."

—*Bill Gates, founder of Microsoft, philanthropist.*

Throughout our lives, we are taught to be fair. We are taught to share and told not to lie, cheat or steal. The games we play have rules that are designed to create fairness. Many of our laws and traditions are built upon principles of fairness. This is how the world should be. Unfortunately, things are not always as they should be.

LIFE ISN'T A GAME AND THERE ARE NO GUARANTEES.

Things don't always work out the way we would like and not everyone plays fair. Some people don't care about you, your rules or your opinions. As you make your way through life, you are certain to come into contact with some of these people. Some will lie, cheat and/or steal. Avoid these people while remaining alert to their existence. And by all means, don't follow their lead. In the long run, things won't work out for these people.

Choices have consequences and if you lack character, you will ultimately live a very empty, lonely and miserable life. Cowards make this choice. They fear failure and their fear drives them to "succeed" at all costs. That's not success.

To achieve true success, you must accept the world for what it is while working to make it what it should be. And while striving for fairness, accept occasional unfairness and disappointment as a natural and inevitable consequence of life. In other words, life isn't fair but you should be. I know— that's not fair.

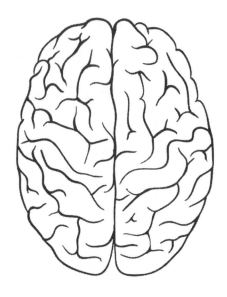

MINDSET RECAP

I n developing your mindset for the 21st Century, learn to engage in critical thinking, control your thoughts, set clear intentions, believe in yourself, think for yourself, have an open mind, search for the truth, have a positive attitude, show empathy, practice gratitude, be optimistic, have hope and embrace life with passion. For some of you, that may seem like a lot. It is. Life isn't easy or fair. It requires effort.

CORE VALUES

L eading a happy, successful and meaningful life requires that you embrace the core values that have allowed every generation before you to succeed. They include character, courage, commitment and compassion.

16

CHARACTER

"It is not by muscle, speed or physical dexterity that
great things are achieved but by reflection, force of
character and judgment."

—*Marcus Tullius Cicero, Roman statesman, orator, lawyer and philosopher.*

C haracter consists of the unique qualities that define each one of us. It guides our responses to any situation or circumstance. It determines why we do the things we do and how we do them. It is the sum of the qualities built into an individual's life that determine his or her choices regardless of circumstance.

GOOD CHARACTER IS PERHAPS THE SINGLE MOST ESSENTIAL QUALITY NECESSARY FOR SUCCESS.

Without it, no one will want to hire you, do business with you or have a relationship with you. In fact, a flawed or weak character will eventually cause others to avoid having anything to do with you.

Character includes multiple traits. Some traits that can lead to a happy, successful and meaningful life include honesty, integrity, honor, truthfulness, dependability, diligence, humility, punctuality, sincerity, tolerance and generosity. I sometimes refer to these positive character traits as "core values."

- **Honesty** is broader than truthfulness. It extends beyond what you say and includes all your actions and dealings with others. It's being fair, just, forthright and truthful at all times, in all circumstances.

- **Integrity** means being true to your word. It means honoring your commitments and being dependable and trustworthy. A person who has integrity is a person you can count on. Have integrity and surround yourself only with people who have integrity.

- **Honor** means taking personal responsibility to uphold what is pure, right, true and just. A person with honor always does the right thing regardless of consequences. A person of honor is a beautiful and enlightened individual. Of all the great values, honor is perhaps the most important and rare. If you have honor, you are—simply by virtue of that quality—already successful. Be honorable.

- **Truthfulness** means never lying or withholding information. Even a small lie can ruin an individual's career, destroy a marriage, or end a lifelong friendship. Be truthful in all your dealings and accept nothing less from those with whom you associate.

- **Dependability** means doing what you agree to do, even if it means making unexpected sacrifices. It means showing up for work on time, doing your job well, meeting your deadlines and supporting others. It is a cornerstone of success. You cannot be successful without it. Be dependable.

- **Diligence** means perseverance, hard work and constant effort to accomplish a given task. It means using your best efforts to overcome obstacles and achieve your objectives. It means doing whatever is required to meet your goals. Success requires diligence. Be diligent.

- **Humility** means being modest and selfless. It means giving credit where credit is due. It is the opposite of being boastful. It includes being willing to undertake unglamorous tasks and graciously accepting the sacrifices involved. Having humility is a sign of strength. Be humble.

- **Punctuality** means showing respect and esteem for others by showing up on time and meeting deadlines. Not being punctual is extremely inconsiderate and disrespectful. Successful people pride themselves on being punctual and expect others to be punctual. Be punctual.

- **Sincerity** is authenticity. It means being who you are, saying only what you believe and meaning what you say. Sincerity is extremely persuasive and compelling because it is real and comes from the heart. Be sincere.

- **Tolerance** means accepting others for who they are. It means being open to new ideas, people, cultures and customs. It means being open to alternative points of view. It means understanding the value of diversity. Be tolerant.

- **Generosity** means treating all people with respect even when they can't do anything for you. It means being gracious and kind to everyone you meet. It means recognizing that every human being, regardless of status, deserves respect, consideration and happiness. It means helping and caring about others. Be generous.

COURAGE

"Courage is rightly esteemed the first of human qualities ... because it is the quality which guarantees all others."

—*Winston Churchill, former British Prime Minister.*

Nelson Mandela, the former President of South Africa, said, "I learned that courage was not the absence of fear, but the triumph over it. The brave man is not he who does not feel afraid, but he who conquers that fear."

The capacity for courage lies within all of us. Courage can be cultivated and acquired. You develop courage by taking action that is inconsistent with fear and consistent with courage. Developing courage is a process.

YOU CAN OVERCOME YOUR FEARS AND DEVELOP COURAGE BY SETTING CLEAR GOALS, GATHERING INFORMATION, DOING RESEARCH, PLANNING THOROUGHLY AND CREATING A PLAN OF ACTION.

Action is magic. Success requires action. With each success, we become more confident and our courage grows. As our confidence and courage grow, we begin to take on new and greater challenges. When we develop courage, a new world of possibilities opens up to us. Be courageous.

COMMITMENT

*"The quality of a person's life is in direct proportion
to their commitment to excellence, regardless of their
chosen field of endeavor."*

—*Vince Lombardi, American football player and coach.*

B eing committed isn't easy. It takes time and effort. Commitment always involves choice and intent.

Commitment is never random or accidental. True commitment also demands passion. Without passion, our actions lack urgency and intensity.

Integrity is also tied to commitment. Our commitment demonstrates our integrity and our integrity often motivates and drives our commitment. Commitments are critical especially in a team environment where each team member needs to be able to depend on their teammates to achieve the team's goals.

MAKING A COMMITMENT SHOULD
NEVER BE TAKEN LIGHTLY.

Many of the things we want won't come quickly or easily. These things require commitment. Saving a down payment for a car or a house, losing weight, getting an education, or a promotion at work, maintaining an important relationship, staying married—all these goals require commitment, as does everything worth doing.

WHATEVER YOU DO, COMMIT TO DOING IT WELL.
OR DON'T DO IT AT ALL.

Be committed to your family and friends, your partners and spouse, your job, your business, your community, your education and your goals.

COMPASSION

*"I have found that the greatest degree of inner
tranquility comes from the development of love and
compassion. The more we care for the happiness of
others, the greater is our own sense of well-being.
Cultivating a close, warmhearted feeling for others
automatically puts the mind at ease. It is the ultimate
source of success in life."*

—His Holiness, the 14ᵗʰ Dalai Lama

What is perhaps most remarkable about compassion is not just what it does for those who receive it but what it does for those who practice it. Scientific studies indicate that people who practice compassion produce one hundred percent more DHEA—a hormone that counteracts the aging process and also decreases the stress hormone cortisol.

An experiment that was published in *Science* by Michael I. Norton, a professor of business administration at the Harvard Business School, shows that people tend to be happier when they give money to others than when they spend it on themselves. In a representative sample of more than six hundred Americans, the amount of money individuals devoted to themselves was unrelated to their overall happiness. What did predict happiness was the amount of money they gave away.

THE MORE THEY INVESTED IN OTHERS,
THE HAPPIER THEY WERE.

Elizabeth W. Dunn, an associate professor of psychology at the University of British Columbia who worked with Norton, found a similar phenomenon in children as young as two years old.

In *The Descent of Man*, Charles Darwin, English naturalist, geologist and biologist, argued that sympathy is our strongest instinct, sometimes stronger than self-interest. He argued that "the most sympathetic members would flourish best and rear the greatest number of offspring."

It appears that he was right. In a study examining the trait most highly valued in potential romantic partners, with 10,000 people surveyed in 37 countries, the single most important requirement for both men and women was kindness.

Practicing compassion has been found to improve your health by strengthening your immune system, normalizing your blood pressure, lowering your stress and depression, improving your recovery from illness and even extending your life.

THE TRUE POWER OF COMPASSION IS FAR GREATER THAN MOST OF US CAN IMAGINE.

Practice compassion by doing something small each day to help others. Offer a smile or a kind word, do an errand or chore for someone in need, or just listen to another person talk about a problem. Practice mindfulness while practicing compassion. Mindfulness means being present in the moment. Try to make compassion and mindfulness daily, lifelong practices. The more compassionate you are and the more mindful and authentic you are, the more you and others will benefit.

Neil deGrasse Tyson, American astrophysicist and author said, "For me, I am driven by two main philosophies: know more today about the world than I knew yesterday and lessen the suffering of others. You'd be surprised how far that gets you."

CORE VALUES RECAP

C haracter, courage, commitment and compassion are the cornerstones required for a happy, successful and meaningful life. A successful mindset for the 21st Century must incorporate these critical core values.

CORE PRINCIPLES

T he following core principles should inform your beliefs and behavior as you embrace the incredible opportunities and overcome the significant challenges of the 21st Century.

20

AUTHENTICITY

"As I began to love myself, I found that anguish and emotional suffering are only warning signs that I was living my own truth. Today, I know this is authenticity."

—*Charlie Chaplin, English comic actor, filmmaker and composer.*

F acebook and Instagram are not representations of our authentic selves. They are projections that we create to position ourselves in a world that has become increasingly inauthentic.

AUTHENTICITY BEGINS WITH SELF-AWARENESS.

The Greek philosopher Socrates famously asserted, "The unexamined life is not worth living." Gaining self-awareness requires taking inventory—knowing what we like and don't like, what we think and don't think, what we feel and don't feel, what constitutes our strengths and our weaknesses. Authenticity begins with understanding, trusting and embracing our motives, emotions, traits, abilities and preferences.

"UNLESS I AM BOTH CAPABLE OF AND WILLING TO REOPEN THE WOUND EVERY TIME I WRITE A SONG, IF I CHOOSE TO NOT LOOK INSIDE MYSELF TO WRITE MUSIC, I'M REALLY NOT WORTH BEING CALLED AN ARTIST AT ALL."

—*Lady Gaga, American singer-songwriter and actress.*

Authenticity requires acting in ways that are consistent with our needs, values and beliefs, even at the risk of criticism or rejection. Being true to yourself may create dissatisfaction in others. We may therefore hide our true feelings or beliefs to fit in.

Authenticity is critical in relationships, which require honesty and openness. People who are authentic are more likely to have effective coping strategies, satisfying relationships, a strong sense of self-worth and increased confidence. Less authentic people are more likely to be defensive, easily overwhelmed, confused or suspicious. They are more likely to use drugs or alcohol as coping mechanisms.

Feelings of inauthenticity can be so uncomfortable that some people will even undergo sex changes in an effort to be more like what they identify as their true self. Finding oneself can be a difficult challenge for young people or for people in midlife who find themselves reevaluating their life choices.

Authenticity requires accepting contradiction and discomfort and acknowledging our faults and limitations.

WE CAN'T BE PERFECT—BUT WE CAN BE REAL.

Know yourself, love yourself and be yourself. You're more than enough.

21

CHOICE

*"Between stimulus and response there is a space. In
that space is our power to choose our response. In our
response lies our growth and our freedom."*

*—Viktor Frankl, Austrian neurologist and
psychiatrist who survived Nazi death camps.*

Everyone has the power of choice. Regardless of what position you are in
now, what conditions you were raised under or what may have happened
to you, you have the power to choose how to respond and to choose what you
will do next.

Dealing with life's challenges can be extremely difficult. But how you decide
to deal with what you encounter will always be a matter of choice. Never lose
sight of that fact.

**YOU WILL ALWAYS HAVE THE POWER OF CHOICE, EVEN IF
IT IS LIMITED TO CHOOSING HOW TO REACT TO EVENTS OR
CIRCUMSTANCES THAT YOU DID NOT CHOOSE.**

A great deal happens in life that is beyond our control. We don't choose
many of the experiences, disabilities or tragedies that may be thrust upon us
but we do have the power to choose how we respond to them.

We all make choices every day and these choices profoundly affect the lives
we lead. Choices have consequences. Good choices generally have positive
consequences and bad choices generally have negative ones. The problem for
some people is that they don't think about the likely consequences of their
choices. And that failure to think ahead can be costly.

The consequences of some choices may be immediate, intended and/or obvious. Other consequences may be less immediate, less obvious and/or unintended. To make informed decisions, you need to try to anticipate and consider all the potential consequences of your choices; and the list of possible consequences is virtually endless. You therefore need to learn, over time, how to make good choices regardless of the circumstances.

YOU NEED TO LEARN TO THINK AHEAD.

You may not be able to anticipate all potential consequences but you can usually anticipate many. The more you can think ahead and consider what could happen, the better off you'll be. Make the effort.

Think about the potential consequences of your actions—before you act. Make good choices. And understand that you have the power to choose, that the quality of your life will depend on the choices you make and that you alone are responsible for your choices.

In thinking about your choices, reflect upon the below insights of Dr. Wayne W. Dyer, Eleanor Roosevelt and Nelson Mandela.

"In my experience working with a variety of people over several decades, far too many individuals choose to be anonymous members of the pack, therefore suffering from the inner remorse that makes them feel like failures, filled with conflict and resentment and wondering what the meaning of life is." —Dr. Wayne W. Dyer, author and speaker.

"In the long run, we shape our lives and we shape ourselves. The process never ends until we die. And the choices we make are ultimately our own responsibility."—Eleanor Roosevelt, former First Lady of the United States.

"May your choices reflect your hopes not your fears."—Nelson Mandela, former President of South Africa.

Make choices that are consistent with the life you want for yourself. Choose carefully.

22

CURIOSITY

"I have no special talents.
I am only passionately curious."

—Albert Einstein, German-born theoretical physicist

C uriosity has always been at the center of human progress and it always will be because it leads to the discovery of uncommon knowledge. Curious people care more about finding the truth than about how they might appear. They're more open to asking questions and sharing ideas. They're willing to ask questions that others lack the courage or the curiosity to ask. As a consequence of their curiosity, they generally end up acquiring more knowledge over the course of their lives. This, in turn, makes it easier for them to draw parallels from other disciplines and to come up with creative solutions others may not see.

The world's greatest thinkers—people like Aristotle, Marie Curie, Sigmund Freud, Leonardo da Vinci, Thomas Edison, Stephen Hawking, Rosalind Franklin and Albert Einstein—all had insatiable curiosity.

Curiosity can be learned and cultivated.

THE FIRST STEP TOWARD DEVELOPING YOUR CURIOSITY IS DEVELOPING A LOVE OF LEARNING.

If you see learning as a burden, you are less likely to be curious. But if you think of learning as something you love, you will want to learn more.

BE OPEN TO LEARN, UNLEARN AND RELEARN.

Make a conscious choice to look more closely at the world around you. Your curiosity will allow you to discover how and why things work, their potential relationships to other circumstances and disciplines and their possible application to other unrelated problems or solutions.

The technological revolution will create massive disruption and you and/ or your company are certain to be impacted. Today's leaders need to remain curious in order to stay ahead of the curve. They'll need to know how to ask questions that will allow them to consider, embrace and create new ideas.

Management thinker Peter Drucker believes that knowing the right questions to ask is critical to strategic thinking. Drucker's "be (intelligently) curious" philosophy will only become even more important as the world increases in complexity. Tomorrow's leaders will need to ask colleagues, competitors and consultants for their opinions, perspectives and approaches, in an effort to find new answers and solutions to problems hidden in other people's experiences and thinking.

Our better schools are beginning to emphasize "the four Cs" which stand for creativity, critical thinking, communication and collaboration. They will also need to emphasize curiosity and encourage students to ask questions.

Neil DeGrasse Tyson, astrophysicist, said;

"THE PEOPLE WHO DON'T ASK QUESTIONS REMAIN CLUELESS THROUGHOUT THEIR LIVES."

Neuroscientists from the University of California at Davis found that "stimulating curiosity ahead of knowledge acquisition can enhance learning success." Other studies show that those who are more curious about a topic tend to learn faster. Teach your children to be curious. Teach them to ask questions and to listen and learn from the questions asked by others.

The act of asking questions helps students see the connections between what they are learning and what they care about. Listening to the questions of classmates teaches them to think divergently. Through this process, they learn to challenge their own assumptions and those of other students, consider what they know and don't know, learn to ask better questions, recognize the importance of asking questions and see how asking questions and being curious facilitates problem solving.

When students produce questions collaboratively, they become co-constructors in their inquiries. This promotes another critical problem-solving skill—collaboration. One student may shed light on an idea or concept through their questions, which then triggers an idea or question from another student, leading to increased learning.

As Picasso once famously quipped, "computers are useless. They can only give you answers." Leaders don't need to have all the answers; we have Google for that. Leaders need to ask the right questions to find answers that are yet to be discovered. And for that, they need to be insatiably curious.

BECOME MORE CURIOUS BY READING MORE, DEVELOPING A LOVE OF LEARNING, BROADENING YOUR EXPERIENCES, BECOMING MORE OPEN, TOLERANT AND FLEXIBLE.

Learn more about things that are outside your area of expertise, meet new people and do things that you normally don't do. Each of these activities will open your mind to new points of view and new possibilities.

Millennial Samurai are insatiably curious.

COLLABORATION

*"...great things in business are never done by one
person; they're done by a team of people."*

—*Steve Jobs, co-founder of Apple, Inc.*

C ollaboration is critical to the success of any endeavor. Working with
people who have different perspectives or areas of expertise can result in
better ideas and outcomes.

Leaders understand the importance of collaboration. Whether you're
designing a car, a building, a manufacturing or distribution process, an
inventory management system or a phone, input from multiple disciplines and
a diverse array of core competencies is a critical part of the design process. Input
from designers, manufacturers, engineers, technologists, material suppliers,
buyers, advertisers and consumers can all have a significant influence on the
design process.

**"TEAMWORK IS THE ABILITY TO WORK TOGETHER TOWARD
A COMMON VISION; THE ABILITY TO DIRECT INDIVIDUAL
ACCOMPLISHMENTS TOWARD ORGANIZATIONAL
OBJECTIVES. IT IS THE FUEL THAT ALLOWS COMMON PEOPLE
TO ATTAIN UNCOMMON RESULTS."**

—*Andrew Carnegie, American industrialist and philanthropist.*

Why is collaboration necessary? According to Benjamin Jones, a strategy professor at the Kellogg School, part of the reason is specialization. According to Jones' research, our individual knowledge base is becoming more and more specialized and the share of what we know as individuals is declining.

Jones points to the Wright Brothers as an example. In 1903, two men designed and flew an airplane. Today, a Boeing 787 has dozens of specialists working on the engines alone. "There's just so much going on in designing, building and flying that plane," Jones says. "There is an incredible range of specialized skills. Over time, this is an ongoing, never-ending phenomenon of increased specialization, which is ever increasing the demand for collaboration."

Jones' research confirms the value of collaboration. According to Jones, "In the 1950s and '60s, in lots of fields, solo beat teams. It's flipped. Now teams always have a higher homerun probability than solo."

Finding the right balance is the key. Today's digital workplaces simplify and facilitate collaboration. A digital workplace is a platform that empowers individuals, teams, clients and partners to share information, communicate their thoughts and collaborate without delay and with minimum effort.

Yet even with the advantages of improved technology, collaborating isn't always easy. Collaboration often involves leveraging the talents of people from different disciplines, different cultures, different age groups, different socio-economic backgrounds and different sexes. Group members typically have varied backgrounds, biases and beliefs. They may have generational, religious, sexual, cultural and/or political differences.

Leaders need to be skilled at motivating, inspiring, facilitating and harnessing the talents of these diverse groups to achieve the extraordinary results that are often only possible through effective collaboration.

Leaders also need to be able to identify and reward those who contribute to collaborative efforts.

Research at Harvard University shows that in most cases, twenty to thirty-five percent of value-added collaborations come from only three to five percent of employees. As people become known for being both capable and willing to help, they are typically drawn into projects and roles of increasing importance.

A 2017 study led by Ning Li of the University of Iowa shows that a single "extra miler"—an employee who frequently contributes beyond the scope of his or her role—can drive team performance more than all the other members combined.

Steve Kerr, former GE chief learning officer says, "Leaders are hoping for A: collaboration while rewarding B: individual achievement. They must instead learn how to spot and reward people who do both."

Millennial Samurai are skilled at contributing to and leading collaborative efforts.

24

ADAPTATION

"It is not the strongest of the species, nor the most intelligent, that survives. It is the one that is most adaptable to change."

—*Charles Darwin, English naturalist, geologist and biologist.*

Our ability to adapt and thrive in a variety of environments is one of the most defining characteristics of our species.

"THE MEASURE OF INTELLIGENCE IS THE ABILITY TO CHANGE."

—*Albert Einstein, German-born theoretical physicist.*

Life can be difficult to navigate especially in a rapidly changing environment. Our ability to adapt has always been an essential survival tool. And this ability will only prove more essential during the technological revolution, which will usher in a tsunami of social, political and technological change.

Nothing in our experience can adequately prepare us for what the world will be like thirty years from now. The changes that will be created by artificial intelligence, genomics, blockchain technology, 3-D printing, cloud computing, robotics and the internet of things are likely to exceed our wildest imagination. Industries will change, employment will change, governments will change. Social, religious and political institutions that have existed for centuries will experience radical and unprecedented change. The need for adaptation will therefore be critical. Lifelong learning and reskilling will be essential to keep pace with changing technology.

How we adapt to changing circumstances has a major influence on our health and well-being. Unhealthy adaptations include paranoia, passive aggression, projection and fantasy. Healthy adaptations include humor, anticipation (planning for change) and sublimation (channeling aggression into exercise or sports). Embrace change as a positive. Allow it to help you grow as an individual. Use it to help you to develop mentally and physically.

DON'T FEAR CHANGE—CELEBRATE IT.

Instead of thinking about how things can go wrong, think about how things can go right. Accept some uncertainty as a normal part of life. Don't expect to know everything or assume that everything will be perfect. Accept each ending with a sense of gratitude and each beginning with a sense of excitement.

Create strategies for tackling new problems and meeting new challenges. Be alert to opportunities and open to new experiences. If you experience self-doubt, think about all the things that you have accomplished in the past. Reflect upon your qualities and competencies until you feel assured.

When resilient people face ambiguity and anxiety, they use the experience to grow stronger.

RESILIENT PEOPLE EMBRACE CHANGE AND EXCEL AT ADAPTATION.

They identify opportunities in adverse environments and believe in their ability to succeed in the face of uncertainty. They have a clear vision of what they want to accomplish and they use this vision to guide them through uncertainty. They employ creativity to generate ideas and approaches for responding to change. They draw on others for support, guidance and assistance and act in the face of uncertainty, taking calculated risks rather than seeking the false comfort of complacency.

Depending on the situation, one of these traits may be more important than another. One situation may require you to be flexible while another may require you to think of a wide range of options. Still another might require you to stay focused on your objective.

Each of these characteristics can be developed through practice, mindfulness, meditation and self-affirmation. Every change creates opportunity and every successful adaptation makes you stronger.

Millennial Samurai are always prepared to change and adapt.

25

INTENSITY

"To produce at your peak level, you need to work for extended periods with full concentration on a single task, free from distraction."

—*Cal Newport, Georgetown professor and author of Deep Work.*

According to Newport, the type of work that optimizes your performance is "deep work." He defines deep work as "professional activities performed in a state of distraction-free concentration that push your cognitive capabilities to their limit, [which then] create new value, improve your skill and are hard to duplicate."

Newport says, "If you're not comfortable going deep for extended periods of time, it'll be difficult to get your performance to the peak levels of quality and quantity increasingly necessary to thrive professionally."

In an article written for *Inc.,* Jessica Stillman discusses Newport's findings and profiles the intense work ethic of Bill Gates. In early 1975, Bill Gates, a Harvard sophomore, typed line after line of code that would become the software behind Microsoft. Gates, his business partner Paul Allen and a Harvard math student named Monte Davidoff spent two weeks in the school's Aiken lab. Gates was relentless.

In a piece in *Business Insider,* author Walter Isaacson is quoted as writing the following in a 2013 issue of the *Harvard Gazette,* "In the wee hours of the morning, Gates would sometimes fall asleep at the terminal. He'd be in the middle of a line of code when he'd gradually tilt forward until his nose touched the keyboard." Paul Allen said, "After dozing an hour or two, he'd open his eyes, squint at the screen, blink twice and resume precisely where he'd left off—a prodigious feat of concentration."

"OBSTACLES DON'T HAVE TO STOP YOU. IF YOU RUN INTO A WALL, DON'T TURN AROUND AND GIVE UP. FIGURE OUT HOW TO CLIMB IT, GO THROUGH IT, OR WORK AROUND IT."

—Michael Jordan, six-time NBA Champion and five-time MVP.

Professional athletes, musicians and entertainers exhibit the same kind of intensity. Michael Jordan was known to have practiced for hours after completing his team's already grueling practice schedule. Venus and Serena Williams were up hitting tennis balls at 6 a.m. from the time they were seven and eight years old.

Yahoo CEO Marissa Mayer routinely pulled all-nighters and worked 130-hour weeks while at Google. Ryan Seacrest hosts *American Idol*, appears seven days a week on E!, hosts a daily radio show from 5 to 10 a.m., appears on the *Today* show, runs a television production company and in 2012, his company received a three hundred million dollar commitment in private equity funding to acquire even more businesses.

Apple CEO Tim Cook begins emailing employees at 4:30 a.m. He's the first in the office and the last to leave. When starting his first company, Mark Cuban routinely stayed up until 2 a.m., reading about new software and went seven years without a vacation. While launching Amazon, Jeff Bezos worked twelve-hour days, seven days a week and stayed up until 3 a.m. to get books shipped.

IN VIRTUALLY EVERY EXAMPLE OF EXTREME SUCCESS, ONE COMMON DENOMINATOR EMERGES—INTENSITY.

It is a relentless and uncompromising drive to succeed, a willingness to do whatever it takes and a level of commitment that goes above and beyond the norms of expected performance.

26

ADULTHOOD

*This should be obvious, but it bears mentioning,
especially for those who may be in any way unclear on
the subject: in most states, the law recognizes you as
an adult when you reach eighteen years old.*

This creates a variety of legal rights and responsibilities. You now have the right to vote, to enter into contracts and to marry.

These are just some of your legal rights, all of which create corresponding responsibilities.

YOU NEED TO UNDERSTAND THE SIGNIFICANCE OF YOUR NEW RIGHTS AND RESPONSIBILITIES.

The right to vote creates the need to stay informed. The right to contract creates the legal responsibility to honor your contracts. The right to marry creates moral, ethical and legal responsibilities to others.

Before you were eighteen, your parents were legally responsible for your welfare. Once you turn eighteen, you're responsible for yourself. That's a big change. Understand the significance of that change and embrace it.

Think about the choices you're making. What are you posting on social media? How are you interacting with others? Who are your friends? What are you doing to improve your mind and enhance your skill set? What are your goals? What are you doing to earn money—and how are you spending what you do earn? What are you saving for emergencies, or to make a down payment on a car or a home? Are you going to school? Are you using the free educational resources available on the internet? Are you learning about the online resources that can help you to start your own business? Are you reading, exercising and/or volunteering? What are you doing to expand your network of contacts or to build a support system? Are you even thinking about these issues—or are you making excuses for not doing so?

TRAIN YOURSELF TO THINK AHEAD AND TRY TO ANTICIPATE THE CONSEQUENCES OF YOUR CHOICES.

Be prepared to accept responsibility for those choices. And understand that taking action and failing to take action, are both choices—each with its own consequences.

It's time to start planning, designing and living your one and only life.

27

GOING THE EXTRA MILE

If you are going to do something,
do it well or don't do it at all.

Performing poorly will ultimately cost you your job, your customers and possibly your business.

Conversely, performing well will improve the performance of the business and thereby provide increased job security for you and your co-workers. It may also lead to increased personal and professional opportunities. Exceptional performance shows commitment. It demonstrates leadership potential and normally leads to advancement and additional career opportunities.

In *The Habit of Going the Extra Mile*, author Napoleon Hill describes going the extra mile as;

"THE RENDERING OF MORE AND BETTER SERVICE THAN ANYONE EXPECTS AND GIVING THAT SERVICE WITH A POSITIVE ATTITUDE."

He explains the many benefits of this approach. One chief benefit is the fact that it enables you to profit by the law of contrast because the majority of people do not practice the habit.

Hill goes on to point out that going the extra mile provides the only logical reason for asking for increased compensation. He explains that if an employee performs no more service than what he is being paid to do, then he is receiving all the pay he is entitled to.

Instead of asking for a raise, ask your employer how you can do more for the company. By demonstrating a high level of commitment, you are more likely to attract increased responsibilities and a raise.

The Habit of Going the Extra Mile is a twelve-page essay written by a man some call the architect of the philosophy of success. Hill spent most of his life studying and writing about the most successful entrepreneurs in American history. His most famous work, *Think and Grow Rich* (1937), is one of the best-selling books of all time with over seventy million copies sold. All his works are well worth reading.

True commitment, regardless of the endeavor, is absolutely essential not only to the business you work for but to your personal success as well. Commitment can be declared by words but evidence of commitment can only be found in your actions.

"AS I GROW OLDER, I PAY LESS ATTENTION TO WHAT MEN SAY. I JUST WATCH WHAT THEY DO."

—*Andrew Carnegie, American industrialist and philanthropist.*

Whatever you choose to do, do it well. Be committed.

Millennial Samurai go the extra mile.

28

CONSUMERISM

*"We go through life spending money that we haven't
earned to buy things that we don't need, to impress
people that we don't care about."*

—*Will Rogers, American actor, humorist and social commentator.*

W hy? Because we have been programmed, by the millions of advertising and marketing messages we receive over our lifetimes, to believe that consumerism is our path to happiness.

Advertising and marketing are effective. That's why companies spend billions of dollars on them. Advertisements are designed to penetrate our psyches. They influence our thoughts, feelings and behaviors.

What we have all been programmed to believe is simply not true.

**THE IDEA THAT CONSUMERISM LEADS TO HAPPINESS IS
A LIE THAT IS PARTICULARLY DIFFICULT TO RECOGNIZE
WHEN WE'RE YOUNG BECAUSE THAT'S WHEN OUR
RESPONSIBILITIES ARE AT THEIR LOWEST POINT.**

We don't have to worry about supporting ourselves, raising a family, paying for our children's education, rising healthcare costs, or retirement. All these things seem like distant obligations when we're young. They seemingly don't apply to us. During this period of relative irresponsibility, we derive the most joy from our toys—but this doesn't last.

I love my iPhone, I enjoy a great bottle of wine, I still buy clothes I don't need and I get a certain sense of joy from most of the things I purchase. However, at some point, further consumption becomes pointless. More importantly, it can harm us. How many suits does a man need? How many pairs of shoes does a woman need? How big does anyone's house need to be?

As we get older, we begin to realize that we can't take our toys with us. We begin to understand that our gadgets won't pay the rent. They won't put food on the table. They won't help us provide for those we love. They won't allow us to retire and maintain our dignity and independence. They won't allow us to travel and see the world. Only when we begin to focus on our broader, more long-term needs, do we begin to recognize how truly unimportant our material possessions really are.

"THE GREATEST VICTORY IN LIFE IS TO RISE ABOVE THE MATERIAL THINGS THAT WE ONCE VALUED MOST."

—Muhammad Ali, American professional boxer.

Mark Cuban, serial entrepreneur and owner of the Dallas Mavericks, was asked what advice he would give to a twenty-year-old. His answer was, "Don't use credit cards. Stay away from credit."

Beware of the perils of consumerism. Possessions can't bring you long-term happiness.

29

BALANCE / HARMONY

*Try to manage your time in a way that allows
you to explore and embrace your competing
wants, needs and desires.*

W hether you want or need to work or play, focus on your health or family, travel, study, sleep, read or write, enjoy time with your friends, listen to a podcast, go to a concert, or just disengage, try to strike a balance that creates harmony in your life.

That is not to say that you should divide your day to achieve balance. Some days may require a greater emphasis on work. Another day may require that you focus more on family or your relationships. Still another day might be dedicated to rest or relaxation.

Balance is not something that is measured in hours or dayparts. Instead, it's a general principle that you should incorporate into your entire life.

SEEK BALANCE THROUGHOUT YOUR LIFE.

This concept is even more important for those who are intensely driven to succeed. The pursuit of professional and financial success requires intensity and commitment. And intense commitment to your work can take a toll on your personal life. It can adversely affect both your personal and professional relationships.

The world is full of people who paid a very high price for their professional and financial success. For many, it has resulted in failed or dysfunctional relationships, the loss of a loved one—even suicide. Don't allow that to happen to you. Relationships are absolutely essential to a happy, successful and meaningful life. And relationships require nurturing and maintenance.

LIFE IS ABOUT MUCH MORE THAN PROFESSIONAL AND FINANCIAL SUCCESS.

Love, family and friendships are worth far more than the fleeting affirmation of strangers and the needless collection of material possessions.

All work and no play will catch up with you, as will all play and no work. Life requires balance. Wants, needs and desires need to be harmonized and prioritized. A balanced life allows you to get the most out of your one and only life.

Ralph Waldo Emerson, American essayist, lecturer, philosopher and poet, said, "To laugh often and much; to win the respect of intelligent people and the affection of children; to earn the appreciation of honest critics and to endure the betrayal of false friends; to appreciate beauty; to find the best in others; to leave the world a bit better whether by a healthy child, a garden patch, or a redeemed social condition; to know that even one life has breathed easier because you have lived. This is to have succeeded."

30

HEALTH

"Physical fitness is not only one of the most important keys to a healthy body, it is the basis of dynamic and creative intellectual activity."

—*John F. Kennedy, 35th President of the United States.*

Your health is essential to leading a happy, successful and meaningful life. Increase your energy level and it will increase your attention, focus, decision making ability and overall productivity. Successful people don't skip meals or go without sleep. They view food as fuel, sleep as recovery and breaks as an opportunity to think and regain focus.

WHEN WE'RE YOUNG, WE HAVE MORE ENERGY. WE SOMETIMES FEEL INVINCIBLE.

This can cause us to take greater risks with our health. Bungie jumping, cliff diving and hang-gliding are all examples of the kind of risk-taking that may seem more acceptable when we're young.

We're also likely to be more sexually active and engage in excessive drinking and drug use when we're young. Failing to eat properly can result in weight gain and erode your self-esteem, or lead to diabetes, heart attacks and strokes. Smoking can lead to lung disease and cancer. All of these activities create risks that have the potential to adversely impact your health.

You need to cherish and protect your health. Some of the choices that you make when you're young can impact your quality of life for decades. Others can forever change your life.

Pay attention to your health. You only have one body—and it needs to last a lifetime.

- Get sufficient sleep
- Eat healthy
- Avoid sugar
- Exercise
- Take the stairs
- Watch your weight
- Avoid smoking
- Avoid excessive drinking and drug use
- Use precautions when having sex
- Spend time in nature
- Breathe deeply
- Meditate

My young friend Daniel Bissonette, age 14, has written a wonderful book called *Daniel's Breakfast Burst*. At 14, he already speaks internationally and is quickly becoming an authority on nutrition. Learn more at DanielBissonette. com.

31

MONEY

*"Wealth consists not in having great
possessions, but in having fewer wants."*

—*Epictetus, Greek philosopher.*

L ife is *not* about money. Think of money as a means to an end, not as an end in itself.

Money can't buy you love or happiness and you can't take it with you.

"MONEY NEVER MADE A MAN HAPPY YET, NOR WILL IT. THE MORE A MAN HAS, THE MORE HE WANTS. INSTEAD OF FILLING A VACUUM, IT MAKES ONE."

—*Benjamin Franklin, American scientist, inventor, politician and diplomat.*

When Alexander the Great was dying, he gave three instructions for his burial. The first was that only the best doctors be allowed to carry his coffin. The second was that his treasures and possessions should be spread along the path of his funeral procession to the grave. And the third was that his hands be allowed to swing freely at his sides and be open and exposed for all to see.

Why did the greatest and most powerful man of his time leave these instructions? He wanted the people to see that even the best doctors were powerless to stop death, that riches obtained on Earth stay on Earth and that we are born empty-handed and we die empty-handed.

Money pays the bills. It allows you to avoid hardship and makes life more comfortable. It can provide increased independence and freedom. It can be a blessing or a curse. Respect it but don't worship it.

Studies show that when you spend money on others and on experiences, you become happier. So, give generously and spend your money on experiences rather than on things.

**"HAPPINESS IS NOT IN THE MERE POSSESSION
OF MONEY; IT LIES IN THE JOY OF ACHIEVEMENT,
IN THE THRILL OF CREATIVE EFFORT."**

—*Franklin D. Roosevelt, 32nd President of the United States.*

32

DON'T BE A VICTIM

"Above all, be the heroine of your life, not the victim."

—*Nora Ephron, American journalist, writer and filmmaker.*

We too often blame others for our condition when in truth, regardless of what has happened to us, we still have the power of choice. We have the ability to choose how to react or respond. And we have the ability to decide what to do next.

In making those choices, some of us choose to be victims. We choose to blame life, someone else, or circumstance. This is a coping mechanism. It is a form of maladaptation.

To deal with the circumstances we encounter, we adapt.

BLAMING OTHERS, ACTING OUT, PASSIVE AGGRESSION, HYPOCHONDRIA, PROJECTION AND FANTASY ARE ALL UNHEALTHY MALADAPTATIONS.

Healthy adaptations include anticipation (looking ahead and planning for future disappointment or discomfort) and sublimation (finding outlets for potentially harmful feelings like channeling our aggression into sports or our fantasies into writing).

Through our historical neglect of the less fortunate and through programs that have failed to address the root causes of failure in our inner-cities, society has allowed a sense of hopelessness and a victim mentality to flourish. And society is now becoming the victim of its own benign neglect.

"Where aspirations outstrip opportunities, law-abiding society becomes the victim. Attitudes of contempt toward the law are forged in this crucible and form the inner core of the beliefs of organized adult crime."—Robert F. Kennedy, former United States Senator (D) NY and former United States Attorney General.

You have the power to choose between healthy and unhealthy adaptations. Choose healthy adaptations.

You also have the power to reexamine how society responds to those in need—and demand change. Don't repeat society's past failures. Understand that empowering others is in your own self-interest. It may prevent you from becoming the victim of someone with a victim mentality.

Millennial Samurai are not victims.

33

LIVE

*"Our goal should be to live life in radical amazement.
Get up in the morning and look at the world
in a way that takes nothing for granted.
Everything is phenomenal, everything is
incredible. Never treat life casually."*

—*Abraham Joshua Heschel, Polish-born American rabbi and theologian.*

O prah Winfrey, American media owner, talk show host, actress and producer, said, "Breathe. Let go. And remind yourself that this very moment is the only one you know you have for sure."

YOU HAVE ONE AND ONLY ONE LIFE. THIS ISN'T A REHEARSAL. YOU DON'T GET A SECOND CHANCE.

At some point, even if you live a long life, you're going to be too old to do many of the things you want to do, so do them while you still can.

Life is about much more than work. You get to design your one and only life. The choices are yours. Travel, experience nature, love, laugh and live each day mindfully. Smell the roses and dance in the rain. Savor every moment.

Life is short—it can end at any time. Don't take even a moment of your life for granted. Life is extraordinary—enjoy the ride.

34

SPEND TIME ALONE

*"I think it's very healthy to spend time alone.
You need to know how to be alone and not
be defined by another person."*

—Oscar Wilde, Irish poet and playwright.

ALONE TIME CAN BE A BLESSING.

It allows you to focus without distraction. It allows you to read, listen to music or a podcast, watch television, or a film, or simply organize your surroundings or manage your affairs. It allows you to catch up on work or rest.

Solitude also affords an opportunity for self reflection and can enhance decision-making. It can provide a relief from social pressures. It can inspire creativity and spiritual growth. And it can offer opportunities for improved focus without interference or distraction.

Value your time alone and make the most of it.

35

HAPPINESS

Happiness begins with choosing to be happy.

A landmark Harvard University study, led by George Vaillant, followed the lives of 268 Harvard sophomores for seventy-two years. It identified seven major factors that contribute to our health and happiness. They are: employing mature adaptations, education, a stable marriage, not smoking, not abusing alcohol, exercise and a healthy weight.

Other studies suggest that happiness comes from a variety of sources including, but not limited to; genetics, money, work, optimism, giving, exercise, laughter, music, relationships, mindfulness, spirituality and religious practice. Together with choice, all the above factors play a role. We all have the ability to control and influence our level of happiness in many ways.

Adaptation—how you deal with life's challenges—is extremely important. You need to be realistic and adjust your needs, expectations and wishes to reality.

Relationships are critical. They comfort and sustain us. They provide our support structure. Love is impossible in isolation and true happiness is incomplete without love.

Exercise, laughter and enjoying life's simple pleasures—like listening to music and taking time to be with good friends—are essential. Meditation, mindfulness and gratitude can bring you happiness by enhancing your appreciation of each day. Compassion can bring you happiness from what you do for others.

To be happy, you must first look within yourself and make conscious choices. You need to be mindful of all of the above. Ultimately, to be happy, you first need to choose to be happy.

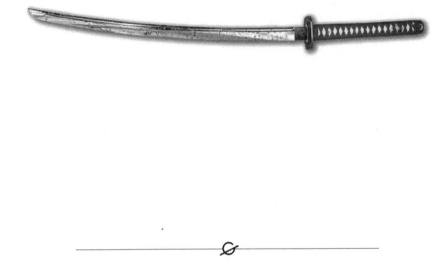

YOUR SWORD

36

YOUR BRAIN IS A DOUBLE-EDGED SWORD

Your brain has two sharp edges—one that can help you and one that can harm you.

Understanding how your brain works, will allow you to gain a greater understanding not only of your own thoughts, but of the thoughts of others.

The following chapters allow you to see the world more clearly, think critically, guard against misinformation and assist you in your search for the truth.

Our brains experience the world and collect information through our five senses—our senses of sight, sound, touch, taste and smell. This sensory information is what creates our thoughts, emotions, perspectives and personalities. Our brains also process information and sensations at different levels of consciousness.

OUR CONSCIOUS MIND PLAYS A CRITICAL ROLE IN SHAPING HOW WE EXPERIENCE AND RESPOND TO THE WORLD, BUT OUR UNCONSCIOUS MIND ALSO EXERTS A HUGE INFLUENCE ON OUR LIVES.

Our brains receive approximately eleven million bits of information per second. Yet our conscious brain can only process fifteen to fifty bits of information per second. The vast majority of sensory information enters through our unconscious brain outside of our conscious awareness.

We believe that when we make decisions, we understand the principal factors that influenced those decisions. Very often, nothing could be further from the truth. Our most basic assumptions about ourselves and society are often based on information that we may not even be aware of consciously.

Our brains do not simply experience the taste of wine or food—they create it. And that creation of taste is influenced by a multitude of factors including the product's marketing, price, label, bottle or brand, our surroundings, music and the people we're with.

Memories are not only the sum of what we have done but also the sum of what we have thought, what we have been told and what we believe. Researchers have shown that it is possible to implant false memories through conscious and unconscious suggestion. These false memories feel no different from memories that are based on reality.

Often our memories are incomplete. We can't remember every detail. In these instances, our unconscious brains may fill in the missing pieces. Our memories then become a combination of what we actually remember and what our brains create to fill in the missing gaps.

The unconscious brain makes the brain extremely susceptible to suggestion—a double-edged sword.

Labeling children as gifted has been proven to be a powerful self-fulfilling prophecy. And branding a child as a poor learner has been shown to have the same self-fulfilling effect.

Music, colors and textures have been shown to influence purchasing decisions in a manner that is outside of our conscious awareness.

Even chemicals can influence our thoughts and actions. Oxytocin, which is released during sexual intimacy, hugs and casual touching, can lead to feelings of emotional closeness even in the absence of a conscious intellectual connection between the parties. It also promotes trust. In one study, in which subjects played an investment game, investors who inhaled an oxytocin nasal spray were much more likely to show trust in their partners by investing more money with them.

Social media and "fake news" provide opportunities for manipulation on a scale never before possible. We have yet to fully understand or appreciate the true nature of this risk.

THE VERY NATURE OF OUR BRAIN MEANS THAT WE ARE HIGHLY SUSCEPTIBLE TO MANIPULATION, MISDIRECTION AND CONTROL.

Advertisers, corporations, politicians and governments all know this and you need to know it as well. This point cannot be overstated. You need to recognize and guard against your inherent, physiological vulnerability to misinformation and manipulation. You do this through increased awareness, inquiry and attention.

You need to be aware of both your brain's immense power **and** significant vulnerability. You need to see your brain as a double-edged sword, both to maximize your potential and avoid harm.

37

THE AGE OF REASON

*The age of reason traditionally refers
to the age at which children become
more capable of rational thought.*

It is generally regarded as the age at which children have internalized a conscience and have a greater capacity to control their impulses. It's the time when a child starts to truly understand the difference between right and wrong and to realize that other people have feelings that might not match their own. For a child, this is thought to occur at or around the age of seven.

Here, I want to alert you to a different "age of reason" which occurs at or around the age of twenty-five. The prefrontal cortex of your brain (the critical area that controls logical reasoning) doesn't fully develop (physiologically) until you're twenty-five. Knowing this information should give you pause—when you're younger than twenty-five. Given this physiological limitation, it may make sense to postpone many of your life-altering decisions until after you're twenty-five.

Parents, if you're reading this, realize that an inability to communicate effectively with your child before they're twenty-five may, in part, be due to this physiological limitation. So, rather than giving up on a child who you're having trouble communicating with, say at eighteen or twenty-one, you might want to cut them some slack and wait for the logical reasoning portion of their brain to fully develop. The difference between a twenty-one-year-old and a twenty-five-year-old can be profound—especially when it comes to what we normally think of as "maturity" which is essentially increased rational behavior.

Always be aware of both your strengths and your limitations. This is a physiological limitation and it should not be ignored.

PERSPECTIVE

Have you ever wondered how two
incredibly intelligent people can see
the same issue very differently?

This used to puzzle me. I would see two brilliant people look at the same issue, the same facts, the same information and arrive at opposite conclusions. It happens every day. And they can't both be right.

WE ALL SEE LIFE THROUGH OUR UNIQUE PRISMS.

Our personal experiences shape the way we see the world. Since everyone's life experience is unique, everyone's prisms are different. This explains why your view of reality may be at odds with someone else's view. One reality, seen through very different prisms, resulting in divergent conclusions.

We share this world with approximately 7.5 billion people and counting. They all have varied backgrounds and personal experiences. They all have unique prisms. They all see things differently. Understanding and having a tolerance for multiple perspectives is therefore critical.

Be open to changing and modifying your perspective. Watch, read and listen to multiple points of view, especially those that you disagree with. Be open, flexible, curious and adaptive. Understand the limitations of your own perspective and the opportunities offered by the perspectives of others.

PERCEPTION

*Just because we see something a
particular way does not make it reality.*

E very moment of our lives, our brains are turning sensory data into what
we believe is reality. Yet there is no provable link between "this is what I
see" and "this is what is real." Your brain determines your perception.

Different brains perceive things differently. Humans, in general, have five
senses that operate within a limited band of reception. For example, we can't
hear frequencies that bats and dogs can hear. Eagles can see clearly eight times
as far as humans can, allowing them to spot a rabbit at a distance of two miles.
They can also see a wider range of colors than we can, as well as UV light.
African elephants can distinguish odor molecules that humans and other
primates can't come close to discerning.

**CONSTRAINED BY OUR PERCEPTUAL TOOLS, WE HAVE
NO WAY TO MEASURE REALITY OUTSIDE OF OUR LIMITED
PERCEPTION.**

Stephen Hawking belonged to the camp of physicists who believe that
reality exists as a material fact but he conceded, as did Einstein, that science
doesn't claim to know what reality is. Even believing in a fixed reality is an
assumption—perhaps the greatest assumption of all time. Einstein called it
"my religion" to denote that this was an article of faith for him. He could not
prove that reality exists as a fixed state or material fact.

Reality may not exist at all as a material fact. What we mistake for reality may simply be a product of our perception. There may be no such thing as provable reality. There may only be your version of it, which is essentially your perception.

Every day, scientists are making new discoveries that are forcing them to disregard that which they previously thought was true. The philosopher Thomas Nagel, who has studied how different species view the world, speculates that our current notions of evolution "will come to seem laughable in a generation or two."

Our perception is not only limited by our senses but by our perspectives and biases as well.

According to the Talmud;

"WE SEE THE WORLD NOT AS IT IS, BUT AS WE ARE."

We often confuse perception with reality. We mistake how we understand things for the way they really are. Our thoughts and feelings seem real to us so we conclude that they must be true. They must be reality.

What if even our most deeply held beliefs were not true? What if what we think is reality is not reality at all? We often don't realize how our perceptions cloud reality. It is extremely important to be aware of the effect that perception has on our beliefs and how this influences our conclusions, decisions, behaviors and actions.

Perception is an extremely powerful and important concept. Our reality is shaped by our perception.

OUR PERSPECTIVES, EXPECTATIONS AND BIASES SHAPE OUR PERCEPTION.

By controlling our expectations, considering multiple perspectives and by being aware of our biases, we can control our perception and see reality more clearly.

Leading a happy, successful and meaningful life requires that we not allow our biases, perspectives, expectations or perceptions to blind us. You need to try to see reality as clearly and objectively as possible, which means that you always need to consider multiple perspectives.

40

TRIBALISM

*Humans have always lived in groups. It comes more
naturally to us than any other way of life.*

F or the overwhelming majority of our time on this planet, the tribe was the
only form of human society. Tribalism is part of our evolutionary DNA.

America has devolved into two tribes, each of which finds the views of the
other tribe unacceptable and often incomprehensible. In each tribe, members
often place their loyalty to the tribe above their loyalty to the country.
Members of both tribes see current events through a prism that advances not
the country's interests but their own and those of their tribe.

One tribe is more ethnically diverse. They live on the coasts and in major
cities. They're skeptical, if not contemptuous, of religion and capitalism and
they're increasingly global in their perspectives.

The other tribe is significantly more white, is spread out across the country,
embraces traditional religious values and capitalism and sees the world from a
nationalist, "America first" perspective.

Each tribe dominates a major political party and both are moving further
apart. Since 2004, the most populous urban counties have moved toward
Democrats while rural counties have shifted toward Republicans.

Race, religion and geography now define our political parties and our
tribes. Our political culture has become one in which the two parties see
themselves not as participating in a process of moving the country forward,
but one where the goal is to defeat the other party by securing a majority.

Scientists call any group that people feel a part of an "in-group" and any group that excludes them an "out-group." We think differently about those in our "in-group" than we do about those in an "out-group." We also behave differently toward members of each group. We do this unconsciously, whether or not we intend to discriminate between the groups.

THE GROUPS THAT WE BELONG TO INFLUENCE THE WAY WE SEE OUR OWN PLACE IN THE WORLD. THEY ALSO INFLUENCE HOW WE VIEW OTHERS.

We all belong to many groups. The same person may think of themself as a woman, a business owner, a mother, or a Mexican, depending on what is most relevant at the time. Our self-identification is shifting and situational.

Advertisers are keenly aware of this dynamic. That's why companies like Apple spend hundreds of millions on advertising campaigns that attempt to position the Apple "in-group" as smart, sexy and successful.

Once we think of ourselves as belonging to a certain group (a member of an exclusive country club, a member of management, a teacher, a Democrat or a Republican), the views of others in the group begin to influence our thinking and the way we see the world. Psychologists refer to these views as "group norms."

Our "in-groups" are, by definition, groups whose members we perceive as having a commonality of interest with us. This shared identity causes us to see our fate as being tied to the fate of our "in-group."

WE SEE THE GROUP'S SUCCESSES AND FAILURES AS TIED TO OUR OWN.

One of the consequences of tribalism is that you don't actually have to think very much. All you need to know on any given subject is which side you're on. You pick up signals from everyone around you. You eventually narrow your acquaintances to those who will reinforce your worldview.

Research suggests that we have a natural tendency to prefer those in our "in-group." Studies show that common group membership will even be more important to us than personal attributes. We may choose to be friends with someone who we dislike simply because they are a group member, while rejecting someone else we like more because they are not a group member.

We may evaluate the work of an "in-group" member more favorably than the work of an "out-group" member, even while we believe we are being objective. We treat our "in-groups" and our "out-groups" differently, whether or not we consciously intend to do so or recognize that we are doing so.

In a new study of the voting habits of professors, Democrats outnumber Republicans twelve to one and the imbalance is growing. Among professors under the age of thirty-six, the ratio is almost twenty-three to one. Conservative dissent therefore becomes tribal blasphemy. Free speech becomes "hate speech" as many of the academic elite regard opposing views as threats to their existence.

Democrats looked the other way as President Obama ramped up deportations. Republicans were obsessed with the national debt when President Obama was in office, but the minute President Trump came to power, they supported a tax package that could add trillions of dollars to the nation's debt.

Remarkably, research has shown that it is not even necessary that you share any characteristics with your fellow "in-group" members, or even for you to have met the other group members.

SIMPLY KNOWING THAT YOU BELONG TO THE GROUP TRIGGERS YOUR "IN-GROUP" LOYALTY AND AFFINITY.

We will identify with a group based on the most insignificant of distinctions and we will see group members differently even if group membership is unrelated to any relevant or meaningful characteristics. Researchers have proven this. Even when group divisions are meaningless, people unambiguously choose to discriminate in favor of their "in-group."

When people find it advantageous to work together, the dynamic changes. The more people find it advantageous to work together the less they will discriminate against each other. We see this in times of crisis, during natural disasters, during wars and during times of human tragedy. This is when the best of our human nature is revealed. Divisions become irrelevant and we come to each other's aid regardless of who we are.

UNDERSTANDING TRIBALISM IS IMPORTANT BECAUSE IT HELPS TO EXPLAIN NOT ONLY OUR OWN BEHAVIOR BUT THE BEHAVIOR OF OTHERS.

Understanding these influences can help you to identify them and address them more effectively. Valuing your unique identity—distinct from any group—being immune from labels, thinking for yourself and considering all views are the antidotes to tribalism.

Dissent from your own group is difficult. Appreciating the views of those in other tribes is even harder. It takes effort, imagination and openness. It may even require the occasional embrace of blasphemy. It may also require forgiveness and magnanimity.

THE SOLUTIONS TO OUR PROBLEMS AS A SOCIETY DO NOT RESIDE IN EITHER TRIBE. THEY RESIDE IN BOTH TRIBES AND IN THE SPACE THAT LIES BETWEEN THE TRIBES.

It is imperative that you understand this.

Dissent from our tribe runs against our evolutionary grain. It's counterintuitive and emotionally difficult. It is much more difficult and dangerous than affirming the shared views of our tribe, yet it is precisely what's required for our shared prosperity and mutual survival. It is absolutely essential for a Millennial Samurai whose reverence for their sword—and the truth—requires independent thought.

41

GROUPTHINK

*During psychologist Henri Tajfel's experiments
in the 1970s, he discovered a phenomenon
called "social identity theory."*

He found that people will not just show allegiance to groups based on what many might regard as meaningful criteria, they will show allegiance to groups based on meaningless, arbitrary and unimportant criteria like shared hair color or being randomly assigned to a group by an experimenter.

Groups are created and led by individuals. And leaders often emerge from within the groups. In the 1990s, psychologist Michael Hogg found that group members often fail to choose the best and the brightest as their leaders. Instead, they will choose individuals that the group members can identify with. This can sometimes be the most average person in the group.

By defining their group in exclusive terms ("White Nationalists" or "Black Panthers"), leaders can reinforce the group's social identity and build power.

THIS IS WHY RACISM AND NATIONALISM ARE OFTEN EFFECTIVE POLITICAL STRATEGIES. THEY ARE USED TO REINFORCE GROUP IDENTITIES.

Experts used to think that groups make more rational and conservative decisions than individuals. The idea was that group decisions would reflect the consensus of the group (the average position of all the group's members), thereby diluting extremist views. In 1961, James Stoner released a groundbreaking study that has since been replicated hundreds of times with different groups. These studies show that groups actually make more polarized decisions than individuals do.

GROUP DECISIONS OFTEN ACCENTUATE THE EXTREME BIASES HELD BY GROUP MEMBERS.

In the early 1970s, Yale University psychologist Irving Janis found that certain conditions can lead to a particularly extreme form of polarization called "groupthink" during which an illusion of consensus takes over. Factors that lead to groupthink include members being close-knit and like-minded, a group leader who makes his or her position known and the group being shut off from other influences and opinions.

If you pay attention, you will see this happening all around you. Universities that have predominantly conservative or liberal faculty members, which discourage or limit speakers with alternative views on campus, create a fertile environment for groupthink. Political parties that promote certain views and are less receptive to alternative perspectives promote groupthink. Companies whose ownership or leadership openly supports certain beliefs also promote groupthink.

Groupthink is dangerous because it can lead to bad decisions and even the widespread adoption and normalization of extremist views.

Millennial Samurai think for themselves.

COGNITIVE DISSONANCE

*Inconsistency between our thoughts
and our actions causes mental discomfort
(cognitive dissonance).*

The human brain resolves that conflict by changing our attitudes to match our behaviors. For example, if you voted for Donald Trump and you heard him say "you can grab them by the pussy," you might excuse the comment as locker room banter.

Conversely, if you voted for Hillary Clinton, you might excuse her destruction of thirty-three thousand emails as unintentional or insignificant.

WE ALL ADJUST OUR THOUGHTS TO CONFORM TO OUR PREVIOUS ACTIONS IN ORDER TO AVOID THE MENTAL DISCOMFORT CAUSED BY COGNITIVE DISSONANCE.

This is how our brains function. Unfortunately, it serves to harden our positions. It doesn't help us find the truth.

To find the truth, we need to be aware of our brain's inherent limitations, be open to all information and realize that our perceptions, clouded by our biases, often differ from reality. We need to challenge our own biases and assumptions.

To see the truth, we must be aware of this inherent, physiological limitation on our reasoning. We must always question our assumptions and constantly guard against our biases. We must protect ourselves from the potentially harmful effects of cognitive dissonance and recognize how it can impede our search for the truth.

MOTIVATED REASONING

Motivated reasoning helps us to believe in our
own competence and goodness, to feel in control,
and to see ourselves in a positive light.

I t shapes the way we interpret information and see our environment. It helps us to justify and validate our preferred beliefs. The way we view and assess information is highly correlated to our vested interests and to our sense of self.

MOTIVATED REASONING HAPPENS OUTSIDE OF OUR CONSCIOUS AWARENESS.

Therefore, people's claims of being objective or unbiased may be entirely sincere even as they make decisions that are, in reality, self-serving.

For example, physicians may believe that they are immune from monetary influence yet studies confirm that accepting industry hospitality and gifts has a significant influence on patient care decisions. Investment managers' estimates of the probability of certain events have been shown to have a significant correlation to their personal interest in those events.

Our computations and calculations are implicitly colored by who we are, what we believe and what we want. In fact, the motivated reasoning we engage in when we have a personal interest in something proceeds along a different neural pathway within the brain than our objective and disinterested analysis. When information that is consistent with our existing beliefs and desires enters the brain, it is immediately welcomed. When information that challenges our existing beliefs and desires, enters our brain, it is subjected to a gauntlet of challenges.

WE POKE HOLES IN INFORMATION WE DON'T WANT TO BELIEVE AND FIND WAYS TO ACCEPT INFORMATION WE LIKE.

The net effect on communication is to amplify rather than reduce disagreement.

When people want to believe a scientific conclusion, they'll accept a vague news report of a random experiment as convincing evidence. And when they don't want to accept something—like global warming exists—the fact that ninety-seven percent of scientists and the National Academy of Sciences support the conclusion will not be enough to convince them.

THROUGH MOTIVATED REASONING, EACH SIDE FINDS WAYS TO JUSTIFY ITS FAVORED CONCLUSION AND DISCREDIT THE OTHER WHILE MAINTAINING A BELIEF IN THEIR OWN OBJECTIVITY.

And since motivated reasoning operates outside of our conscious awareness, those on each side of an issue may genuinely believe that their view is the only rational conclusion. It rarely is.

What we need to learn from this is that those who disagree with us are not necessarily stupid or dishonest in their refusal to acknowledge the validity of our arguments. More importantly, we need to recognize that our own reasoning is very often less than objective. We need to be aware that both sides of any discussion may be assessing information in a biased manner while being unaware of doing so.

THE HUMAN BRAIN IS DESIGNED TO BE BOTH A CONSCIOUS SEEKER OF OBJECTIVE TRUTH AND AN UNCONSCIOUS ADVOCATE FOR WHAT WE WANT TO BELIEVE.

Together these approaches form our worldview. This is the inherent nature of your double-edged sword.

44

MANIPULATION

"Misinformation can be sticky, spreading and replicating like a virus."

—*Sander van der Linden, social psychologist at the University of Cambridge.*

V an der Linden's team of researchers assembled more than two-thousand United States residents across the country from various ages, genders, political leanings and education levels. The researchers presented the group with a number of scientifically sound climate change facts in the form of statements, such as "Ninety-seven percent of climate scientists have concluded that human-caused global warming is happening." They also presented the group with misinformation taken from an Oregon petition that was known to be fraudulent, which stated that "thirty-one thousand American scientists state that there is no evidence that human-released CO2 causes climate change." Those who were shown only the accurate information, described the scientific consensus as "very high." Those who were shown only the false information reported the scientific consensus as "very low." However, when shown both statements one after the other, the statements effectively cancelled each other out, putting people back to a state of indecision. "It's uncomfortable to think that misinformation is so potent in our society," said van der Linden.

THE IMPORTANCE OF THE STUDY, IS THAT CONFLICTING MESSAGES CAN BE AND ARE USED TO CONFUSE US.

Criminal psychologist Julia Shaw, the author of The Memory Illusion, specializes in the science of memory. "I am a memory hacker," Shaw says.

"I use the science of memory to make you think you did things that never happened."

It turns out; planting a false memory is very easy to do. Shaw says, "A memory is a network of brain cells." That network is constantly being updated. This allows humans to learn new things and to problem-solve. But as a result, Shaw says, this network "can be manipulated." Shaw also states;

"IN THE LAB, I CONVINCE PEOPLE THROUGH MEMORY HACKING THAT THEY COMMITTED CRIMES THAT NEVER HAPPENED, I DO IT TO SHOW THAT THE INTERROGATION PROCESS CAN REALLY DISTORT MEMORIES IN CONSISTENT WAYS."

Each time you tell a story, you change the memory. You may change the details based on things you heard from someone else, creating new and possibly inaccurate or misleading connections," she says. To implant a false memory, "you try to get someone to confuse their imagination with their memory…Get them to repeatedly picture it happening," she says.

She'll layer in detail—the person's age, hometown, the name of their childhood best friend—and get them to repeatedly imagine the crime happening over and over again, even if they never did it. Over time, "it gets harder to decipher imagination versus a memory coming back," Shaw says. "By the end, it's easy to think this actually happened."

Medical procedures may also be used to manipulate memories. Optogenetics (a technique that uses light to switch various parts of the brain on and off) has been used to erase the fear associated with bad memories in rats. Optogenetic techniques currently require cutting a hole in the rats' skulls. This has not yet been done in humans but these techniques suggest what could be possible. Video now presents additional and alarmingly significant opportunities for manipulation.

Researchers at the University of Washington have developed an algorithm to take audio of someone talking and turn that into a realistic lip-synced video of someone speaking those words.

In creating a video of President Obama, the researchers used what's called a recurrent neural network to synthesize the mouth shape from the audio. (This kind of system, modeled on the human brain, can take in huge piles of data and find patterns. Recurrent neural networks are also used for facial recognition and speech recognition.) They then trained their system using millions of existing video frames of Obama speaking. Finally, they smoothed out the footage using compositing techniques applied to actual footage of Obama's head and torso.

"We're not learning just how to give a talking face to Siri; we're learning how to capture human personas," says Supasorn Suwajanakorn, a co-author of the research. Samsung, Google, Facebook and Intel all contributed funding for this research.

Imagine a lip-synced video of a world leader saying something that is entirely false, something that could create panic, riots or even war.

All of this highlights the potential threats posed by the malleability of the human brain—our double-edged swords. To guard against these potential threats we must first be aware of them. We must then remain ever alert and vigilant against the potential for manipulation.

45

MILGRAM'S OBEDIENCE STUDY

*Everyone should know about this
landmark study by Stanley Milgram. It confirms one
of our greatest human vulnerabilities.*

M ilgram was inspired by the holocaust. He wanted to understand how ordinary people could take part in extraordinary cruelty—something we all need to understand.

Volunteers in his experiments took part in what they thought was a study of memory, giving electric shocks to a partner whenever he forgot things. In reality, the partner was an actor and no shocks were really being given. The partner screamed and protested as the volunteer delivered what he thought were increasingly intense shocks.

**MILGRAM WANTED TO KNOW IF ORDINARY PEOPLE
WOULD DELIVER SHOCKS OF A LETHAL VOLTAGE
TO AN INNOCENT MAN.**

He had a scientist in a grey coat stand in the corner of the room and assure the volunteers with phrases like "the experiment requires that you continue."

**SIXTY-FIVE PERCENT OF THE VOLUNTEERS DELIVERED
WHAT THEY BELIEVED WERE LETHAL SHOCKS.**

His series of eighteen studies found that the remoteness of the victim, the authority of the person giving the orders and the presence of others in the same situation who obeyed all increased the likelihood of someone complying with orders to kill. Knowing this information is important, because it alerts you to the power of and the potential for manipulation.

46

DELUSION AND ENTITLEMENT

Delusional beliefs and a sense of entitlement
are two incredibly destructive forces.

Either one can prevent you from ever becoming successful or realizing your dreams. Many people have a delusional sense of entitlement. Rather than accepting personal responsibility, they think that someone else is responsible for them or they think that rules don't apply to them. We see this sense of entitlement everywhere: people who cut in line, people who take more than their fair share, people who run red lights, those who expect or demand accommodation or assistance and those who fail to show gratitude for the help they do receive. All these people suffer from a delusional sense of entitlement.

We are seeing more and more examples today of youth walking into stores and restaurants and simply stealing merchandise, or ordering and consuming food and not paying. We see the same sense of entitlement and delusion in those who operate under the false assumption that intelligence somehow guarantees success. Intelligence alone does not guarantee success. Intelligence plus hard work, plus core values, generally equals success. But even then, there is no guarantee.

We see a similar sense of entitlement in those who believe that they deserve the respect of others, including but not limited to their parents, teachers, employers and even the police. Some expect and demand respect even though they offer little respect in return. Respect is not something that can be demanded—it must be earned. The idea that we are somehow entitled to the respect of others, regardless of our own actions, is a false assumption. We are not. Civility is something people often exchange freely in a civilized society. Respect, on the other hand, is something you must earn. We earn the respect of others through our own positive actions.

These irrational and destructive mindsets are not reserved to Millennials. They are exhibited by and adversely affect people of all ages.

IF YOU SUFFER FROM DELUSIONAL BELIEFS OR A SENSE OF ENTITLEMENT AND IF YOU DON'T RESOLVE TO GET PAST THESE MALADIES, YOU WILL, WITHOUT QUESTION, INCREASE YOUR LIKELIHOOD OF FAILURE.

Accept personal responsibility for your actions and understand, very clearly, that no one owes you anything.

For those interested in engaging with me and learning more, here's an opportunity. Watch one or more of the following videos and comment on them at MillennialSamurai.com/entitlement.

From those commenting, I will select up to five people to participate in Facebook Live broadcasts that will also be featured on YouTube.com and MillennialSamurai.com, in which we will together explore this topic.

Please provide your email when commenting so that we can reach you.

- Video # 1. https://www.youtube.com/watch?v=U2uG8Fc8ZuA
- Video # 2. https://www.youtube.com/watch?v=-9omkdPGNmo
- Video # 3. https://www.youtube.com/watch?v=Ff6M8mtQx-k
- Video # 4. https://www.youtube.com/watch?v=Y5zx1xzzi7k
- Video # 5. https://www.youtube.com/watch?v=n4obCt-l7Z4
- Video # 6. https://www.youtube.com/watch?v=C-3XbycyQrk
- Video # 7. https://www.youtube.com/watch?v=zkCGzJ20-OU
- Video # 8. https://www.youtube.com/watch?v=psFx_UiXtCk
- Video # 9. https://www.youtube.com/watch?v=w4XOi5DDM68
- Video # 10. https://www.youtube.com/watch?v=thRsikyXuSk

To participate, answer the following questions for any or all of the above videos. The above videos and the below questions can also be found at MillennialSamurai.com/entitlement.

First, identify the video you watched. Then answer the following questions:

1. Who was in the right and who was in the wrong in the video you selected and why?

2. Why do you think that the person who was in the wrong behaved the way they did?

3. What do you think are the major causes of an entitled mindset?

4. What, if anything, do you think people can do to rid themselves of an entitled mindset?

5. What would you do, as a parent, to deal with a child who exhibited an entitled mindset?

47

THE
DUNNING-KRUGER EFFECT

"If a nation expects to be ignorant and free,
in a state of civilization, it expects what
never was and never will be."

—*Thomas Jefferson, 3ʳᵈ President of the United States.*

I n America today, we are both free and, far too often, incredibly ignorant. That can't last.

David Dunning and Justin Kruger, two Cornell psychologists, coined the term; the "Dunning-Kruger Effect."

IT IS A COGNITIVE BIAS THAT CAUSES SOME PEOPLE WHO ARE INCOMPETENT AT SOMETHING TO BE UNABLE TO RECOGNIZE THEIR OWN INCOMPETENCE.

Some incompetent people not only fail to recognize their incompetence, they overestimate their competence.

Professor Dunning states, "The knowledge and intelligence that are required to be good at a task are often the same qualities needed to recognize that one is not good at that task and if one lacks such knowledge and intelligence, one remains ignorant that one is not good at that task."

One study of high-tech firms discovered that thirty-two to forty-two percent of software engineers rated their skills as being in the top five percent of their companies. A nationwide survey found that twenty-one percent of

Americans believe that it's "very likely" or "fairly likely" that they'll become millionaires within the next ten years. In a classic study of faculty at the University of Nebraska, sixty-eight percent rated themselves in the top twenty-five percent for teaching ability and more than ninety percent rated themselves above average. These self-ratings are mathematically impossible.

A little knowledge is a dangerous thing. Those with a little knowledge think they know it all. With increasing experience, people begin to realize how little they do know and how modest their skills really are. Those at the level of genius recognize their talent, although they tend to lack the supreme confidence of the ignoramus.

Dunning has said, "The presence of the Dunning-Kruger effect, as it's come to be called, is that one should pause to worry about one's own certainty, not the certainty of others."

THERE IS A HIGH STATISTICAL PROBABILITY THAT YOU OVERESTIMATE YOUR KNOWLEDGE AND ABILITY.

The lower your intellect and ability, the more likely this is and the less likely you are to recognize it.

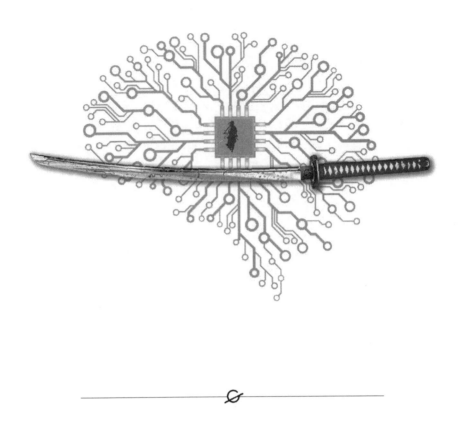

SHARPENING YOUR SWORD

LIFELONG LEARNING

Learning is an investment in yourself.

THINK OF YOUR BRAIN AS YOUR SWORD AND THINK OF LEARNING AS SHARPENING THAT SWORD.

You will carry that sword throughout your life wherever you go. The sharper your sword is the more prepared and formidable you will be regardless of the situation you may encounter.

Increase your intelligence through using your five senses. Learn by watching, reading, listening, touching, tasting and smelling. Learn through experience, practice and repetition. Awaken your senses through mindfulness, meditation, concentration and reflection.

LEARNING IS A LIFELONG PROCESS.

Even single subjects like law, medicine, art and wine take a lifetime to learn. The more we learn, the more we realize how little we know. The ancient Greek philosopher, Socrates, said;

"THE MAN WHO THINKS HE KNOWS EVERYTHING KNOWS NOTHING AT ALL."

A Millennial Samurai never stops learning; they never stop sharpening their sword. The opportunity to learn is a gift. Treasure that opportunity. Develop a love of learning. Learn everything you can. Devour information and experience life's wonders gratefully and mindfully. Never stop sharpening your sword.

NEUROPLASTICITY

*Neuroplasticity is the ability of the brain
to form new connections and pathways
and change how its circuits are wired.*

Neuroplasticity is a term used to describe the brain's ability to reorganize itself by forming new neural connections throughout your life. For many decades, it was thought that the brain was a nonrenewable organ—that we are born with a fixed amount of brain cells and they slowly die as we age, regardless of what we do. This theory is now widely discredited.

We now know that the human brain has the ability to form new connections and pathways and change how its circuits are wired. Different brain pathways form and fall dormant, are created and discarded, according to our experiences.

When we learn something new, we create new connections between our neurons. We rewire our brains to adapt to new circumstances. This happens on a daily basis. And we can encourage and stimulate this process.

The relation between neuroplasticity and learning is easy to understand.

**WHEN WE LEARN, WE FORM NEW PATHWAYS IN THE BRAIN.
EACH NEW LESSON HAS THE POTENTIAL TO
CONNECT NEW NEURONS AND CHANGE OUR
BRAIN'S WIRING AND OPERATION.**

In a famous example, research showed that the part of the brain involved in navigation is larger in London cab drivers who spend their adult lives finding their way around the city. Other significant examples would be learning a new language or a musical instrument, both of which profoundly rewire the connections in our brains. A person with a growth mindset believes that he or she can get smarter, better, or more skilled at something through sustained effort—which is exactly what neuroplasticity tells us.

Have you ever driven to your house on auto-pilot, without thinking about where you're going? That's neuroplasticity in its simplest form. Over time; your brain has learned how to get home without continuous conscious thought. Just as it has learned how to breathe without continuous conscious thought.

Neuroplasticity can also help you manage and treat anxiety and depression. It is well established that chronic stress can result in anxiety and depression. Studies have also found that chronic stress inhibits neuroplasticity and adversely impacts certain regions of the brain. One of the formal diagnostic criteria for depression, according to the American Psychiatric Association (APA), is a "diminished ability to think or concentrate."

Yoga, meditation and exercise, for example, have been shown to reduce stress. By reducing stress, these activities can actually restore function to areas of the brain that have been impaired by stress.

FOCUSED ATTENTION AND CHALLENGE ARE BOTH CRITICAL TO PROMOTING NEUROPLASTICITY.

Travel and exposure to unique experiences and environments, learning a new language or musical instrument, reading, expanding your vocabulary, creating art, dancing, sleeping, intermittent fasting, mindfulness and meditation can all promote neuron growth, form new neural connections and improve overall cognitive function. Essentially, focused attention on new and novel experiences and developing new skills all promote neuroplasticity and sharpen your Millennial Samurai sword.

50

MINDFULNESS

"We are capable of mindfulness. We are capable of
changing our thoughts and changing our brains."

—*Jill Bolte Taylor, American neuroanatomist, author and speaker.*

M indfulness is a state of active, open attention to the present moment. When you're mindful, you observe your thoughts and feelings more consciously. Instead of letting your life pass you by, mindfulness means living in the moment and awakening to all types of experiences.

MINDFULNESS IS THE ESSENCE OF ENGAGEMENT.

When we are living in the present, in the moment, we are less likely to plague ourselves with fears about the future or regrets about the past. By paying attention to what's happening around us instead of operating on autopilot, we can reduce stress, unlock creativity and improve our performance. We also become more alert to opportunities.

Henry Miller, American writer, said;

"THE MOMENT ONE GIVES CLOSE ATTENTION TO
ANYTHING, EVEN A BLADE OF GRASS, IT BECOMES
A MYSTERIOUS, AWESOME, INDESCRIBABLY
MAGNIFICENT WORLD IN ITSELF."

Mindfulness comes from Buddhism and is key to meditation in that tradition. Be mindful of your daily life—the people, the places, the reactions of your senses and the beauty that surrounds you. Take time to smell the flowers and the grass. Look up at the sky and marvel at the passing clouds. Lie in the sun and feel the warmth of its rays. Feel the wind, the snow and the rain. When you eat something, smell it, touch it and savor it. Look into the eyes of the people you meet. Shake their hands. Listen to what they say. Connect with them. Make an effort to remember their names.

Be present in the moment. We all rely very heavily on our unconscious thoughts; we have to, as our unconscious thoughts are required to process the eleven million bits of information that impact all of our brains every second.

We rely on our unconscious minds to handle our sensory perception, our memory recall and most of our routine, everyday decisions. Some scientists estimate that we are conscious of less than five percent of our cognitive function. The other ninety-five percent happens outside of our conscious awareness. That being said, we not only have the ability to control our conscious thoughts, through mindfulness we have the ability to influence many of our unconscious thoughts and impulses as well.

Successful people operate on a different level than most people. They focus more intently.

THOSE WHO PERFORM AT THE HIGHEST LEVELS ARE THE MOST FOCUSED AND THE MOST MINDFUL.

They develop and improve their minds and their ability to perform at a higher level. They read—some voraciously. They practice—some relentlessly. They exercise control over their conscious thoughts. And through their positive thoughts and activities, they are able influence and impact the development and nature of their unconscious thoughts and impulses. In sum, they mindfully use and develop their conscious and unconscious brains.

Think about the joy and excitement that children experience when they taste their first strawberry, see a mirror for the first time, meet their first puppy, look up and feel the rain or snow on their face, or see the white clouds drifting across a bright blue sky. That excitement comes from being naturally mindful. We are all surrounded by life's natural wonders. The gravity of these incredible experiences hasn't changed. What has changed, with age, is our appreciation of them.

In her book *The Little Book of Mindfulness*, Patrizia Collard says, "By reconnecting with these simple moments in life, by truly living moment by moment, it is possible to rediscover a sense of peace and enjoyment. We may, at least sometimes, once again feel truly enchanted by life."

WHEN WE START TO FOCUS ON POSITIVE THOUGHTS, WE LET GO OF OUR FEARS AND ANXIETIES.

We become more joyful and less stressed. We perform at a higher level. Even focusing on things that are painful can be beneficial by preventing us from staying in a bad relationship or helping us to understand and overcome our depression or anger.

Collard talks about how mindfulness can facilitate acceptance that leads to healing. She offers the example of Buddha telling the story of the two arrows to his visitors: life often shoots an arrow at you and wounds you. However, by not accepting what has happened, by worrying about it, by saying it was unfair and wondering how long the pain will last, we tend to shoot a second arrow into the open wound and increase and prolong the pain.

PAIN IS OFTEN A GIVEN BUT SUFFERING IS OPTIONAL.

People who are struggling with weight problems can use mindfulness to control their weight. Imagine eating a strawberry very slowly while contemplating and appreciating everything about it: the smell, the texture, how it looks, the taste. By practicing mindfulness while eating, we can cultivate an appreciation for the food we have and develop a sense of well-being that eliminates our emotional cravings.

IN SUM, THERE IS SCIENTIFIC EVIDENCE THAT WE HAVE THE ABILITY TO CONTROL OUR THOUGHTS. WE DO THIS BY EXPERIENCING LIFE MORE FULLY, MORE CONSCIOUSLY AND MORE MINDFULLY AS IT UNFOLDS.

It is important that you understand this critical concept. You have the ability to control your thoughts and you need to use that ability. Learning to control your thoughts is an ongoing process that requires focus and effort. You won't gain control over your thoughts immediately and your level of control will never be total or absolute but with effort, focus and mindfulness, greater control over your thoughts is absolutely possible.

By controlling your thoughts, you will develop the courage to overcome your fears and begin to recognize your immense human potential. Begin by accepting personal responsibility for changing your condition. Learn how to pivot and adapt to changing circumstances. Recognize the need to push forward and persevere to overcome the challenges you face. Think about all your choices more carefully and make the right choices. Focus and commit to doing that which is required to achieve your objectives. All this begins and ends with your thoughts.

You have the ability to develop and improve both your conscious and unconscious mind through reading, experience and practice and you have the ability to gain greater control over your thoughts through focus, meditation, positive affirmation, visualization and mindfulness.

51

MEDITATION

"Eighty percent of world-class performers meditate."

—Tim Ferriss, American entrepreneur, author and speaker.

R esearch suggests that meditation may be associated with structural changes in areas of the brain that are important for sensory, cognitive and emotional processing and can have a positive impact on age-related declines in brain structure. Other physical and mental health benefits associated with meditation include decreased pain, better immune function, less anxiety and depression, a heightened sense of well-being and greater happiness and emotional self-control.

A 2011 study by Dr. Elizabeth Hoge, a psychiatrist at the Center for Anxiety and Traumatic Stress Disorders, at Massachusetts General Hospital and an assistant professor of psychiatry, at Harvard Medical School, found that mindfulness meditation helps ease anxiety symptoms in people with generalized anxiety disorder, a condition marked by hard-to-control worries, poor sleep and irritability.

According to Dr. Hoge, if you have unproductive worries, you can train yourself to experience those thoughts completely differently. "You might think 'I'm late, I might lose my job if I don't get there on time and it will be a disaster!' Mindfulness teaches you to recognize, 'Oh, there's that thought again. I've been here before. But it's just that—a thought and not a part of my core self,'" says Dr. Hoge.

To see if mindfulness meditation can help you, try one of the guided recordings by Dr. Ronald Siegel, an assistant clinical professor of psychology at Harvard Medical School. They are available for free at www.mindfulness-solution.com. Apps like Headspace and Calm are also available to help you get started. Start with small sessions of just two or three minutes. Do it every day for twenty-one days to develop the habit. Once you see how it makes you feel you'll want to do more.

52

LEARN A FOREIGN LANGUAGE

Speaking two or more languages enhances
cognitive development and function.

The brains of bilingual people operate differently than single-language speakers and these differences offer multiple benefits.

Numerous studies suggest that students who learn a foreign language perform better on standardized tests.

ACCORDING TO A 2012 STUDY FROM THE UNIVERSITY OF CHICAGO, BILINGUALS TEND TO MAKE BETTER, MORE RATIONAL DECISIONS.

According to a 2011 study from Pennsylvania State University, being multilingual improves the ability to multitask. A 2015 study from Spain's University of Pompeu Fabra found that multilingual people are better at observing their surroundings. They are more adept at focusing on relevant information and more skilled at spotting misleading information.

Research shows that learning a foreign language provides a variety of important benefits including, but not limited to, the following:

- It enhances brain function
- It improves reading, comprehension and vocabulary
- It expands negotiating and problem-solving abilities
- It improves the ability to multitask
- It improves memory

- It enhances critical thinking
- It improves decision-making
- It builds self-confidence
- It increases employment, networking and relationship opportunities
- It broadens perspectives by enabling a greater understanding and appreciation of alternative cultures
- It delays Alzheimer's and dementia

The earlier you can learn a foreign language the better — but you are never too old to begin.

53

LEARN TO PLAY
A MUSICAL INSTRUMENT

*Playing a musical instrument engages
and strengthens practically every area of
the brain—more than virtually any other activity.*

According to Robert Zatorre, a McGill University neuroscientist;

"LISTENING TO AND PRODUCING MUSIC IS THE FOOD OF NEUROSCIENCE."

Zatorre says, "It involves a tantalizing mix of practically every human cognitive function including attention, memory, pattern detection, motor coordination, hand-eye coordination and sensory-motor integration. It involves pairing behavior with information derived from the five senses." Playing an instrument requires integrating information from multiple senses like vision, hearing and touch.

Albert Einstein, German-born theoretical physicist, once said, "Life without playing music is inconceivable for me. I live my daydreams in music. I see my life in terms of music. I get most joy in life out of music."

STUDIES HAVE SHOWN THAT MUSICAL TRAINING CHANGES BRAIN STRUCTURE AND FUNCTION.

Brain scans have been able to identify the differences in brain structure between musicians and non-musicians. Studies also show that the areas involving movement, hearing and visuospatial abilities appear to be larger in musicians.

A 2014 study from Boston Children's Hospital found a correlation between musical training and improved executive function in both children and adults. Executive functions are high-level cognitive processes that enable people to quickly process and retain information, regulate their behaviors, make good choices, solve problems, plan and adjust to changing mental demands. Additional research shows that musical training can enhance verbal memory, spatial reasoning and literacy skills. Multiple studies of cancer patients have found that listening to and playing music reduced anxiety and depression.

Musicians also exhibit greater sensitivity to the nuances of emotion in speech. This ability to detect emotion is a fundamental skill that facilitates social and professional interactions.

Cognitive scientist Douglas Hofstadter once compared Johann Sebastian Bach's musical abilities to "playing sixty simultaneous blindfolded games of chess and winning all of them."

Some argue that the most developed brains of all time may have belonged to musicians.

PRACTICE AND REPETITION

*The brain contains billions of neurons. Each neuron
links to so many others that the entire network has
trillions of connections, making the brain the most
complicated known object in the universe.*

These connections are constantly rewiring themselves every second. Your
brain is physically different from one moment to the next. The brain that
you had before reading this book is different from the brain you have now.
Motor memory allows us to learn and master new skills. The brain recruits and
forms neural networks, employing our eyes, ears, arms, legs, fingers, or mouth
to facilitate the motions required for certain skills. After the basic motions are
mastered, the brain recruits additional neurons to refine the motions.

**IF YOU LOOK AT ALL THE GREATEST ATHLETES, MUSICIANS
OR PERFORMERS, THEY WILL ALL HAVE ONE THING IN
COMMON—RELENTLESS PRACTICE AND REPETITION.**

It is this practice and repetition that forms and builds the neural pathways
that make their extraordinary performance possible.

In his bestselling book *Outliers*, Malcolm Gladwell describes what he calls
"the story of success." One of his observations is that it takes ten thousand
hours to master something. We develop this mastery through practice and
repetition.

Tiger Woods, Stephen Curry, Cristiano Ronaldo, LeBron James, Michael
Phelps, Tom Brady, Michael Jackson, Elvis Presley and Beyoncé all have/had
an intense commitment to their craft. They practice relentlessly and in doing
so, create and refine the neural networks that allow them to become masters
of their chosen professions.

If you want to master anything in life, it will require a passionate
commitment to years of practice. Practice makes perfect.

CREATIVITY

After surveying over fifteen hundred CEOs,
IBM found that the most critical skill required
to be a successful CEO is creativity.

In 2015, Red Bull (the energy drink company) completed the first phase of "Hacking Creativity," the largest meta-analysis of the subject ever undertaken. After reviewing more than thirty thousand scientific studies and conducting hundreds of interviews with experts, researchers concluded that creativity is the most important skill for success.

Creativity requires thinking outside the box and challenging your assumptions. It's about doing something others haven't done and discovering or developing a new path to improvement. IBM's 2010 Global CEO study concluded, "CEOs and their teams need to lead with bold creativity, connect with customers in imaginative ways and design their operations for speed and flexibility to position their organizations for 21st Century success."

Uber is the world's largest car service but it owns no cars. Alibaba is one of the world's most valuable retailers but it holds no inventory. Airbnb is the world's largest provider of accommodations but it owns no real estate. In each instance, these companies' creators found ingenious new ways to rethink and redesign old business models.

Studies by Clayton M. Christensen, Professor of Business Administration at the Harvard Business School, indicate that your ability to generate innovative ideas is not merely a function of the mind; it is also a function of the following five key behaviors that optimize your brain for discovery:

- **Associating:** drawing connections between questions, problems or ideas from unrelated fields.

- **Questioning:** posing queries that challenge common wisdom.

- **Observing:** scrutinizing the behavior of customers, suppliers and competitors to identify new ways of doing things.

- **Networking:** meeting people with different ideas and perspectives.

- **Experimenting:** constructing interactive experiences and provoking unorthodox responses to see what insights emerge.

The idea that geniuses such as Shakespeare, Rembrandt and Mozart were naturally gifted is a myth. Numerous studies from around the world have concluded that excellence is determined by:

- opportunities

- encouragement

- training

- motivation

- and most of all, practice

TO BE MORE CREATIVE, YOU NEED TO TRAIN YOUR BRAIN TO THINK MORE CREATIVELY. YOU DO THAT BY PRACTICING BEING CREATIVE.

In 2009, psychologists at the University of North Carolina found that even four days of meditation significantly improved both creativity and cognitive flexibility.

The protocols below were developed at Google. Over a six-week period, with sixty minutes a day of required practice, the subjects in the Google study experienced substantial increases in creative flow and heightened performance. These are the protocols:

- **Enforce rigorous sleep habits:** Sleep in a dark, cold and quiet room.

- **Prioritize the first hour after waking:** How we start our day is critical. Take time to hydrate, reflect, move, stretch and fuel.

- **Make the most of your first ninety minutes of work:** Eliminate distraction. Push calls and meetings to the afternoon and focus only on your most important tasks, not your inbox.

- **Allow for recovery:** Get up and move for five to ten minutes after every hour spent working. This will allow you to stay in peak productivity longer.

- **Practice active recovery:** Work out and meditate. Build time into your calendar to soak in an Epsom salt bath or take a sauna before bed. Get outside and move. Studies have shown that hiking in nature or even walking on a treadmill boosts creativity and memory.

- **Plan experiences and adventures:** Book a float tank session. Go on a weekend silent meditation retreat. Train for and compete in something that challenges you. Travel or go to a concert or a festival. Anything that gets you out of your routine pays big dividends over time.

- **Create quiet time for yourself:** Recent studies show that taking time for silence restores the nervous system, helps sustain energy and conditions our minds to be more adaptive and responsive to complex environments. Silence is associated with the development of new cells in the hippocampus, the key region of the brain associated with learning and memory.

Google found a two-hundred percent boost in creativity, a 490 percent boost in learning and a five-hundred percent boost in productivity from following the above protocols.

Changing your channel of consciousness (changing your environment, experience, or state of mind) boosts creativity. There are now decades of research conducted by hundreds of scientists on thousands of participants showing that changing the channel of consciousness, no matter the method used, can unlock the creativity you've been searching for.

LEARN TO CODE

*"Everybody in this country should learn
how to program a computer because it
teaches you how to think."*

—*Steve Jobs, co-founder of Apple Inc.*

C oding isn't nearly as difficult as you may think. It's not easy either or everyone would be doing it. But if you have an aptitude for math or science, computer technology may be the perfect field for you. You can learn to create and execute your own programs on your laptop or smartphone in a matter of weeks. You can also spend a lifetime learning more and perfecting your craft.

Coding can provide you with an amazing and rewarding career. An experienced software developer can earn over one hundred thousand dollars a year. More importantly, when combined with creative and original thought, it can open up entirely new worlds.

If you are interested in learning to code, many free options are available online. You can take free online introductory computer science courses from Harvard (Course CS50 at www.edx.org) or Stanford (Course CS101 at www.cousera.com). These are the same courses that some of the greatest minds in the country have taken and they are available to you for free.

READ

Reading improves your vocabulary, increases your knowledge, builds self-confidence, broadens your perspective and reduces stress.

B oth Bill Gates, founder of Microsoft and Warren Buffett, Chairman and CEO of Berkshire Hathaway, make a point to read every day. Gates says, "I've been reading about a book a week on average since I was a kid. Even when my schedule is out of control, I carve out a lot of time for reading." Every evening before bed, Gates reads for one hour. By making time every day, he reads fifty books each year.

Warren Buffett credits much of his success to reading. He says he starts every morning by reading several newspapers. Buffett estimates that he spends as much as eighty percent of his day reading.

BOOKS WORTH READING

B elow are just a few of the many books worth reading.

- *Brave New World* by Aldous Huxley
- *The Adventures of Huckleberry Finn* by Mark Twain
- *How to Win Friends and Influence People* by Dale Carnegie
- *The Art of Happiness* by the Dalai Lama
- *Homo Deus: A Brief History of Tomorrow* by Yuval Noah Harari
- *The Art of War* by Sun Tzu
- *Mindset: The New Psychology of Success* by Carol Dweck
- *The Road to Character* by David Brooks
- *21 Lessons for the 21st Century* by Yuval Noah Harari
- *The Better Angels of Our Nature* by Steven Pinker
- *Merchants of Doubt* by Erik M. Conway and Naomi Oreskes
- *The Intelligent Investor* by Benjamin Graham
- *Lord of the Flies* by William Golding
- *Autobiography of a Yogi* by Paramahansa Yogananda
- *Zero to One: Notes on Startups, or How to Build the Future* by Peter Thiel
- *The Stories of John Cheever* by John Cheever
- *The Remains of the Day* by Kazuo Ishiguro
- *The New Jim Crow* by Michelle Alexander
- *A Wrinkle in Time* by Madeleine L'Engle
- *Structures: Or Why Things Don't Fall Down* by J.E. Gordon
- *The Foundation Trilogy* by Isaac Asimov
- *Traction* by Gino Wickman

- *Think and Grow Rich* by Napoleon Hill
- *Mastering Influence* by Tony Robbins
- *The Richest Man in Babylon* by George S. Clason
- *Stem Cell Therapy: A Rising Tide* by Neil Riordan
- *The Hitchhiker's Guide to the Galaxy* by Douglas Adams
- *The Obstacle is the Way* by Ryan Holiday
- *Meditations* by Marcus Aurelius translation by Gregory Hays
- *Enlightenment Now* by Steve Pinker
- *Sapiens* by Yuval Noah Harari
- *Benjamin Franklin: An American Life* by Walter Isaacson
- *Einstein: His Life and Universe* by Walter Isaacson
- *Our Mathematical Universe* by Max Tegmarks
- *Brief Answers to the Big Questions* by Stephen Hawking
- *The Book* by Alan Watts
- *Why Buddhism is True* by Robert Wright
- *Polishing the Mirror* by Ram Das
- *How to Change Your Mind* by Michael Pollan
- *The Doors of Perception* by Aldous Huxley
- *Mindful Games* by Susan Greenland
- *Critical Thinking Skills Workbook* by Steven West
- *Upheaval: Turning Points for Nations in Crisis* by Jared Diamond
- *If I Could Tell You Just One Thing* by Richard Reed
- *The Manual: A Philosopher's Guide to Life* by Epictetus
- *Architects of Intelligence* by Martin Ford
- *The Demon Haunted World* by Carl Sagan
- *Good To Great* by Jim Collins
- *The Black Swan* by Nassim Nicholas Taleb

KHAN ACADEMY

Khan Academy (www.khanacademy.org)
is a nonprofit online resource with the mission
of providing a free world-class education for
anyone, anywhere.

Khan Academy offers courses that cover all levels of math and science, economics and finance, arts and humanities, computer programming and even test preparation for admission to colleges and graduate programs. It's an incredible online educational resource and it's free!

EVEN IF YOU DIDN'T DO WELL ENOUGH IN HIGH SCHOOL TO GET INTO COLLEGE, YOU CAN LEARN EVERYTHING YOU NEED TO KNOW TO GET INTO COLLEGE AT KHAN ACADEMY.

You can learn how to use a computer or even program one. Khan Academy can help you prepare for and take your college entrance exams. For some students, Khan's tutoring is all they need to succeed in high school or college.

This free online school is a resource for learning that could move your life in a whole new direction. Take advantage of it.

THE SOCRATIC METHOD

Use questions to encourage dialogue and reveal insights.

Socrates was a Greek philosopher, a father of Western philosophy and one of the greatest minds to have ever lived. The Socratic Method (the use of questions to encourage dialogue and insight) remains a commonly used method of teaching today.

The quotes below represent a small fraction of the wisdom Socrates left us and these insights still have profound meaning today.

If you are interested in connecting, go to MillennialSamurai.com/Socrates and answer one or more of the questions below. From those commenting, I will select up to five people to participate in a Facebook Live broadcast that will also be featured on YouTube and MillennialSamurai.com. **Please provide your email address when commenting so that we can contact you.**

Choose one of the quotes below and answer the following: what did Socrates mean when he said this and why is the quote still significant to humanity today?

Identify the quote you are commenting on before commenting.

"True wisdom comes to each of us when we realize how little we understand about life, ourselves and the world around us."

"Let him who would move the world first move himself."

"The mind is everything; what you think you become."

"The secret of happiness is not found in seeking more but in developing the capacity to enjoy less."

"Beware the barrenness of a busy life."

I look forward to reading your answers and connecting with some of the best and the brightest among you.

RELATIONSHIPS

RELATIONSHIPS

"The meeting of two personalities is like the contact of two chemical substances: if there is any reaction, both are transformed."

—*Carl Jung, Swiss psychiatrist and psychoanalyst.*

Relationships are critical to life. Nothing is more important. Your relationships with your spouse, parents, children, siblings and friends will have a more profound impact on your quality of life than virtually anything else. Value your relationships with those you love above all else.

Relationships create and require an ongoing personal connection. Texting is not connecting. Talking and listening while being mindful is connecting. Touching is connecting. Looking in each other's eyes and smiling is connecting.

Relationships require forming and maintaining connections. Being in a meaningful relationship requires talking about things that matter and listening attentively. It requires an investment of quality time while being present. Relationships are formed and maintained by interacting with others on a more personal and meaningful level.

Nurture and treasure your relationships. Experience life more fully and profoundly through your connections to others.

LOVE

"Love is the center of human life."

—14ᵗʰ *Dalai Lama of Tibet.*

L ove is impossible in isolation. It flourishes, reaching its highest potential in relationships.

LOVE IS THE ESSENCE OF LIFE.

Don't compare yourself to others. We're all unique. We all have faults and weaknesses. Recognize your limitations and work on improving them but don't dwell on them. Focus on your strengths. Be kinder to yourself. You're amazing. Know that and believe it. Your potential is virtually unlimited. Celebrate that potential by loving others and by loving yourself.

SAY "I LOVE YOU" OFTEN AND MINDFULLY.

Be fully present in the moment. While those that we love may know how we feel—it never hurts to remind them. Telling someone that you love them will brighten the day for both of you. We assume that the people we love will be with us tomorrow. That assumption will one day prove false. When you lose someone you love it will be too late to say I love you. At that moment, the true importance of this advice will reveal itself. Don't wait. Tell those you love how you feel. Do it now.

LIFELONG RELATIONSHIPS

*Your friends and your family
are your support system - treasure them.*

You need to develop, nurture and maintain your relationships. You do that by investing time and energy in those relationships. Develop your support system by networking with people from all walks of life—people from different countries, people with different educational backgrounds and experiences, people whose age, race, religion and/or sexual orientation may be different from your own.

Every positive relationship adds value to your life. Some may offer skills that you don't have or experience that you have yet to acquire. Others may offer insights and perspectives that you haven't considered. Still others may lead to new introductions that allow you to further expand your support system or achieve your objectives.

Nurture your relationships by cultivating a genuine interest in other people. Try to make meaningful lifelong connections. Maintain your relationships by being reciprocal and by adding value to those relationships.

We are born with very few people in our lives—our parents, siblings, grandparents, aunts, uncles, cousins and family friends. Most of the other relationships in our lives we must create, nurture and develop. All the relationships that we want to flourish and maintain require an investment of our time and attention.

FRIENDS

*"Be courteous to all but intimate with few
and let those few be well tried before you give
them your confidence."*

—George Washington, 1ˢᵗ President of the United States.

Friends represent a unique class of relationship. They are not our family yet we let them into our inner circle. They have significant access to us and often learn intimate details about us. We trust them.

Getting to know new people is an important part of life, but you need to surround yourself with the right people—people who add value, meaning and/or purpose to your life rather than detract from it. You might really enjoy hanging out with a particular group on weekends, but what do you really know about them?

Friends come from all walks of life. They grow up in different places and different homes; they have different parents, different educations and different experiences. They are born with different mental and physical characteristics and limitations.

Clinical psychologist Martha Stout, former Harvard Medical School professor and author of *The Sociopath Next Door*, tells us that one in twenty-five Americans are sociopaths who simply do not feel shame, guilt, or remorse. Not all sociopaths are violent criminals; they may be your boss, your ex-boyfriend, or your ex-girlfriend. They may even be your best friend. Sociopaths are often charismatic. They use flattery, lies and deception to lure you into their web of deceit. They prey upon your good nature and generosity for their own selfish purposes.

THE PEOPLE YOU SELECT AS FRIENDS AND THOSE YOU CHOOSE TO ASSOCIATE WITH CAN HAVE A PROFOUND IMPACT ON YOUR LIFE AND SAFETY.

Be careful. Look for warning signs. Stay away from people that you have concerns about. If you sense danger, trust your instincts.

TRUE FRIENDS ARE A TREASURE.

When you have good friends, life can be a lot easier. Friendships bring you laughter, joy, tears, advice, companionship and compassion. True friends are there for you through good times and bad times. But many so-called friendships are not healthy; in fact, many people are bad friends.

If you have a bad friend, then the best thing to do is to end the relationship.

BAD FRIENDS CAN BE MENTALLY AND EMOTIONALLY DRAINING. THEY CAN HOLD YOU BACK OR WORSE.

You don't need to confront people you want to disassociate with; just back away. Start to limit your contact with them until you no longer have any contact.

Again, if you sense any risk at all, trust your instincts. Tell your parents or an authority figure about these people. Choose your friends wisely and be a good friend in return.

THE GOLDEN RULE

A rule without equal.

The Golden Rule, "Do unto others as you would have others do unto you," has been adopted by every major world religion. It provides a standard of behavior which, if followed, would allow all people of all faiths, backgrounds and descriptions to live in harmony.

**IT IS A CARDINAL RULE THAT SHOULD GUIDE
ALL YOUR INTERACTIONS WITH OTHERS.**

Some argue that the Golden Rule is imperfect because it assumes that everyone wants to be treated as you do. The Golden Rule is a general moral principle, not a hard and fast rule. We all want and deserve to be recognized and treated as individuals, each with our own unique identities, opinions, beliefs, feelings and needs. Once we recognize that reality, the Golden Rule promotes harmony, inclusion, acceptance and mutual respect.

CRITICISM

"Criticism may not be agreeable but it is necessary. It fulfills the same function as pain in the human body; it calls attention to the development of an unhealthy state of things."

—*Winston Churchill, former British Prime Minister.*

NEVER BE AFRAID OF CRITICISM. EMBRACE IT. IT'S A GIFT. LEARN FROM IT.

When offering feedback, you want the recipient to listen. You don't want them to be defensive. So, begin offering constructive criticism by asking permission to provide feedback. When someone knows beforehand that they are about to receive constructive feedback rather than pure criticism, it will put their mind at ease.

Start with explaining your intention. Why are you offering this feedback and how can you help? Choose a location that's confidential. Don't provide criticism in front of others who don't need to be present.

PRAISE IN PUBLIC. CRITICIZE IN PRIVATE.

Be respectful of the person's dignity and choose your words carefully. Try not to put the receiver on the defensive.

FEEDBACK THAT IS MOST LIKELY TO BE WELL RECEIVED AND ACTED UPON IS FEEDBACK THAT COMES FROM SOMEONE YOU TRUST.

Someone you believe is looking out for your interests—like a coach. If someone doesn't trust you, they won't care what you think about their performance and they won't change their performance to please you.

Provide constructive feedback by pointing out the problem and asking for reasons why the problem arose. Then, ask the people involved if they have ideas for a better approach or more effective solutions. Avoid imposing a solution. Instead, draw out ideas from the people involved in the problem by asking the right questions.

One of the guidelines for giving constructive criticism is that it should be focused on a particular situation and not a general behavior.

Never be afraid to ask others for their constructive criticism. Accept it and offer it graciously. Offer it to others only when your intention is to help them and make that intention clear.

When receiving criticism, don't be defensive. Look at the criticism as an opportunity to learn and grow. See it as a gift rather than a setback. Use it to improve yourself and to become even more formidable.

APOLOGIZE

*"Mistakes are always forgivable
if one has the courage to admit them."*

—*Bruce Lee, actor, director and martial artist.*

P eople who say "never apologize" or "apologies are a sign of weakness" are wrong. The opposite is true. Never be afraid to apologize. Only the weak see an apology as a sign of weakness. Strong people recognize it as a sign of maturity, responsibility and strength.

AN APOLOGY COSTS NOTHING, YET ITS VALUE CAN BE IMMENSE.

Don't confuse excuses with apologies. People who say "never make excuses" are right. Your friends don't require them and your enemies won't believe them. Apologies are very different. Accepting responsibility for your mistakes is rarely, if ever, wrong.

Saying I'm sorry is one of the easiest and most effective things you can do to improve a relationship. An apology can transform an adversary into a friend. It can save or nurture a relationship. Taking responsibility for your mistakes is essential. It's not optional; it's required.

An apology is the very least you can do to accept responsibility for your mistakes. Apologizing demonstrates and builds character. It creates and restores trust.

68

INTELLIGENCE

*"An intellectual is someone
whose mind watches itself."*

—Albert Camus, French philosopher, author and journalist.

Smart people sometimes assume that their intelligence will ensure their success. Relying on their significant intellect they fail to invest the time and effort required to develop other important skills, like the skills required to nurture and maintain relationships, the courage required to take action, or the commitment required to overcome obstacles. Life teaches us that we need more than intelligence to succeed.

LEVERAGE YOUR INTELLIGENCE TO BROADEN YOUR SKILLS.

You will need to use your strengths to overcome your weaknesses. You will need to learn the required skills that don't come naturally to you.

If you're intelligent, use your intelligence to become more courageous and committed. And if you're already courageous and committed, use those strengths to expand your knowledge and improve your intelligence.

Smart people often find that their self-esteem is tied to being smart. This can decrease their resilience and lead to avoidance.

WHEN YOUR SELF-ESTEEM IS TIED TO YOUR INTELLIGENCE, IT CAN BE DIFFICULT TO BE IN SITUATIONS THAT REVEAL YOUR WEAKNESSES.

Working with people who are more intelligent, receiving critical feedback, or taking a risk and failing might challenge your sense of self-worth or feel threatening. You may even avoid those situations, which can ultimately hold you back. It is therefore important that you understand the benefits of working with people who are, in some respects, smarter than you are as well as those who are, in some respects, less skilled or less smart. Embrace opportunities to work with others even if you believe that you can learn nothing from them. At minimum, you will learn how to collaborate more effectively.

If you're smart, curious and have a love of learning, you might find that you're more easily bored with things or tasks that you find mundane or unchallenging. Often, tolerating short periods of boredom can enhance your chances of success. Devoting time to an activity that's monotonous, but lucrative, might be one example. Compensate for that by making sure you have other outlets for learning and creativity in your life.

Thinking is always appropriate. But overthinking can be counterproductive. Sometimes we learn by doing rather than through thought or research.

Don't rely exclusively on your intelligence.

EXPAND YOUR RANGE OF SKILLS TO BECOME MORE COMPETENT, ADAPTIVE, FLEXIBLE AND WELL-ROUNDED.

Here are some ways to expand your skill sets and become more balanced and effective:

- **Be adventurous.** Instead of saying no when asked to join others on social outings, say yes.

- **Be curious.** Devour popular culture. Examine the work of artists, musicians, actors and playwrights.

- **Be observant.** Travel and take photos of what you see. Meet new people and engage in conversations with them.

- **Be inquisitive.** Ask questions and listen carefully.

- **Be still.** Relax. Take time for thought and reflection. Find time to seek refuge from the hustle, the stress and the noise.

- **Be happy.** Find time for fun, laughter and amusement.

69

COMMUNICATION

*"The single biggest problem in communication is the
illusion that it has taken place."*

—*George Bernard Shaw, Irish playwright, critic and political activist.*

We all communicate verbally and nonverbally. However, not all of us communicate effectively.

PEOPLE WHO COMMUNICATE EFFECTIVELY FIND THAT THEIR COMMUNICATION SKILLS OFTEN LEAD TO SUCCESS.

Those who do not communicate effectively often find that their poor communication skills can lead to misunderstandings and failure.

Effective communication is about more than just exchanging information. It's also about understanding the emotions behind the information. Effective communication utilizes a set of skills that includes nonverbal communication, active listening, the ability to control your own stress and the capacity to recognize and understand your emotions and those of the person you're communicating with.

LISTENING IS ONE OF THE MOST CRITICAL COMPONENTS OF EFFECTIVE COMMUNICATION.

How do you become an effective listener? Focus on the speaker. What are their body language and other nonverbal cues saying? What are yours saying? If you're not paying attention because you're reading emails or checking text messages, you're not listening effectively. Stay focused. Avoid interrupting. Avoid being judgmental. You don't have to agree with the speaker but you do need to listen carefully to what he or she is saying.

Listening carefully doesn't indicate agreement. It indicates understanding. The speaker needs to see that you understand what they are saying. Otherwise, the speaker will keep trying to make you understand.

DEMONSTRATING THAT YOU UNDERSTAND THE OTHER PERSON'S MESSAGE ALLOWS THEM TO STOP TALKING AND TO LISTEN TO YOUR MESSAGE.

This is an essential element of effective communication. If you are not a good listener, you simply cannot be an effective communicator.

Many people are incapable of listening to what you are saying unless and until they believe that you understand their position. So, listen to their position and, most importantly, let them know that you truly do understand their position. One way to do that is by repeating their position back to them before you tell them your position. Then tell them your position.

According to a study conducted by Albert Mehrabian of the University of California, Los Angeles, fifty-five percent of the emotional messages conveyed in face-to-face communication result from body language. Mehrabian's study found that when an incongruity exists between the spoken word and how you deliver it, seven percent of the message is conveyed through your words, thirty-eight percent is revealed through your vocal quality and fifty-five percent comes through your gestures, expression and posture. How we communicate is inseparable from the feelings we project, consciously or not.

It is therefore essential that we recognize the importance of nonverbal communication and the role of our unconscious mind in understanding, processing and communicating information. It is equally important that we consciously work to improve our ability to observe, identify and interpret the nonverbal and unconscious communication of others.

BE ALERT TO ALL THE NONVERBAL CUES THAT PEOPLE AROUND YOU ARE SENDING.

Don't wait for people to tell you verbally what they want — if they have already told you nonverbally.

When people are under emotional stress, the region of the brain responsible for emotion (the amygdala) releases the chemicals adrenaline and cortisol. These chemicals can impair cognitive performance of the prefrontal cortex and interfere with the brain's ability to process logical information. If someone is angry, depressed or emotionally erratic, their ability to process logical information may actually be physiologically impaired. If you can learn to wait for these emotions (caused by stress) to subside, you can facilitate more effective communication. ·

Be alert to this issue. If the person you are speaking to is upset or emotional, that is one of the worst times to try and talk to them. Getting angry yourself makes effective communication even less likely.

IN ORDER TO INCREASE THE LIKELIHOOD OF EFFECTIVE COMMUNICATION, YOU NEED EMOTIONAL EMPATHY.

You need to recognize and address the emotional needs of others as well as your own. When you are trying to reach someone with a logical argument, understand that you are least likely to do so when either or both of you are upset. In those instances, the best thing to do is to take a break. Go outside, walk, breathe, unwind. Then resume the communication.

70

MEANINGFUL CONVERSATIONS

Small talk doesn't facilitate an emotional connection.

If you want a relationship with someone, create a connection by having conversations that have meaning, purpose and depth. Show genuine interest in others, making it easier for them to engage and connect.

HAVE AN AUTHENTIC INTEREST IN THOSE AROUND YOU.

Put down your smartphone and focus on the people you're with. Focus on what they're saying. Listen and think about what they're saying and why they're saying it, then formulate your response. And when trying to formulate an intelligent response, understand that the most intelligent response may simply be, "I hear what you're saying. Let me think about it and get back to you."

HANDLE CONTROVERSIAL TOPICS AND SENSITIVE SUBJECTS WITH GRACE AND POISE.

Feel free to share your opinions, but make it clear that they're opinions, not facts. Understand that many people who are just as intelligent as you—and others who may be more or less intelligent—may see things very differently than you do. Try to understand why they see things differently.

What is it that they may see that you don't see? What is it about their life experience that is different from your own, that may account for why you see certain issues differently? Think about what insight may be gained from considering their perspective—a perspective that is born out of their unique experiences; a perspective that you may not have. Approach conversations as a learning experience, an opportunity to form and build relationships and a genuine search for truth rather than a competition.

LISTEN

*"We have two ears and one tongue so that
we would listen more and talk less."*

—Diogenes, Greek philosopher.

John Marshall, former Chief Justice of the United States, said;

**"TO LISTEN WELL IS AS POWERFUL A MEANS OF
COMMUNICATION AND INFLUENCE AS TO TALK WELL."**

Active listening shows respect for the other person. It establishes that you are a reasonable person who is entitled to respect in return.

It shows that you are committed to a full, fair and rational dialogue. It makes you someone that others will want to communicate with. It is essential to effective communication.

Speak to teach. Listen to learn. And learn before you teach.

SILENCE

"Better to remain silent and be thought a fool than to
speak out and remove all doubt."

—*Abraham Lincoln, 16ᵗʰ President of the United States.*

S ometimes it is better to listen than to speak.

**SPEAK WHEN YOU HAVE SOMETHING TO SAY, NOT WHEN
YOU FEEL THE NEED TO SAY SOMETHING.**

Some people feel threatened or uneasy with silence. They're constantly talking. It's as if they see silence as a void that needs to be filled. Don't be alarmed by moments of silence and don't feel as if it's somehow your responsibility to fill them. It's not.

It's good to be conversational, but it's also good to be comfortable in the company of others without speaking incessantly.

Noise affects our stress levels. It causes the brain to release cortisol and adrenaline. A 2006 study in the journal *Heart* found that silence can relieve tension in just two minutes.

Lowering sensory input helps us to restore our cognitive resources. Silence lowers our blood pressure and increases blood flow to the brain.

**SOMETIMES, THE BEST PRACTICE IS TO
REMAIN SILENT AND LET OTHERS SPEAK.**

George Washington was chosen to preside over the Constitutional Congress. Since he was arguably more responsible for independence than any man alive, he could have dominated the convention. Instead, he elected to allow his peers to lead the conversation, offering his opinion only when asked. His peers ultimately elected him to lead the nation.

Silence is a tool, a means to contribute through listening—especially when you have nothing that needs to be said.

73

WORDS MATTER

Choose your words carefully.

I n September of 2016, while running against Donald Trump, in America's presidential election, Hillary Clinton had this to say about Trump supporters, "You could put half of Trump supporters in what I call the basket of deplorables. The racist, sexist, homophobic, xenophobic, Islamaphobic, you name it."

Donald Trump kicked off his 2016 campaign for President of the United States (POTUS) with these remarks about Mexico, "They are not our friends, believe me. They're bringing drugs. They're bringing crime. They're rapists. And some, I assume, are good people."

Both of the above comments evidence a poor choice of words.

HOW YOU COMMUNICATE A MESSAGE CAN BE AS IMPORTANT AS THE MESSAGE ITSELF.

The human brain often mimics and mirrors what it sees. These comments from candidates for POTUS, from both parties, set the tone for political discourse in America. And it is a divisive and polarizing tone. We now see the mirroring of these examples on social media. Rather than rational discourse and common courtesy, we see insults and invective.

We have access to amazing social media tools that should be used to promote education and understanding, tools that could allow us to communicate and coordinate our efforts. Instead, these tools are being misused to fuel mindless criticism and needless conflict. This troubling dynamic is relatively new and we have no way of knowing where this may lead, but given the nature of the human brain and the power of social media, the possibilities are ominous.

DO NOT MIRROR THIS BEHAVIOR. RISE ABOVE IT.

Embrace civility. And don't feed the trolls. Don't engage the ignorant and the uncivil with more ignorance and incivility. Either engage them with magnanimity, forgiveness and compassion, or not at all. And if they can't be counseled and they persist in being obnoxious, then separate yourself from them. If necessary, block them. Don't become them.

74

IN BUSINESS - BE BRIEF

Work is very different from school. School is an academic exercise where the goal may be to gain an in-depth understanding of a given subject. Those seeking a degree may spend years studying a topic of interest or their chosen field.

In the workplace, decisions are often made with less information than might be included in a term paper.

TIME IS MONEY, SPEED TO MARKET IS OFTEN AN IMPERATIVE AND THERE ARE FEW IF ANY MINIMUMS ON THE LENGTH OF ANY COMMUNICATION.

In my entire career, I can count on one hand the instances when an email, presentation, or report was too short. As a general rule, workplace communications should be no longer than is necessary for the communication to be complete.

Here are some general guidelines:

- **Emails**—one to five sentences.
- **Presentations**—ten slides and up to twenty minutes.
- **Reports**—one to five pages.

In 1941, Winston Churchill, former British Prime Minister, wrote the following to the First Lord of the Admiralty;

"PRAY STATE THIS DAY, ON ONE SIDE OF A SHEET OF PAPER, HOW THE ROYAL NAVY IS BEING ADAPTED TO MEET THE CONDITIONS OF MODERN WARFARE."

If one page is sufficient to answer that question, ask yourself why you need more to explain your position.

75

NONVERBAL CUES

*A great deal of communication is nonverbal and
unconscious. It is therefore critical that you develop
an ability to pick up on the nonverbal cues and
unconscious communication of others.*

People often use a facial expression, a gesture, or a body posture in either a
conscious or unconscious effort to communicate a message. Some people
pick up on these nonverbal communications. Others don't; they need to be
told what the other person is thinking.

**SOME OF THE MOST SUCCESSFUL PEOPLE DON'T NEED TO BE
TOLD WHAT SOMEONE IS THINKING. THEY ALREADY KNOW.**

Many of the world's most successful poker players fall into this category.
They have a highly-developed ability to observe and read people. They
analyze their body movements, gestures, betting patterns, eye contact, facial
expressions, posture, even their heartrate and breathing patterns. They pick up
on cues—both consciously and unconsciously. I occasionally play poker and I
use my time at the table to employ and further develop these skills.

In *Subliminal: How Your Unconscious Mind Rules Your Behavior*, author
Leonard Mlodinow tells us that "Human behavior is the product of an endless
stream of perceptions, feelings and thoughts at both the conscious and the
unconscious levels."

Conscious thought is what we use when we focus our attention on a task
such as designing a car or solving a math problem. Unconscious thought is

what our mind relies upon to recognize and avoid danger or to perform a variety of routine yet highly complicated tasks.

Mlodinow explains, "The human sensory system sends the brain about eleven million bits of information each second. Our conscious mind can only process fifteen to fifty bits of information per second." Although we don't realize it, our brains make many decisions each second. Most of these decisions are unconscious. According to Mlodinow, "Evolution has provided us with an unconscious mind because our unconscious is what allows us to survive in a world requiring such massive information intake and processing."

One of the most important functions of your unconscious is the processing of data delivered by your eyes. About a third of your brain is devoted to processing vision, interpreting color, detecting edges and motion, perceiving depth and distance and identifying objects and faces. All that unconscious brain activity proceeds outside of your conscious awareness.

Mlodinow tells us, "We look to faces to quickly judge whether someone is happy or sad, content or dissatisfied, friendly or dangerous. And our honest reactions to events are reflected in facial expressions controlled, in large part, by our unconscious minds."

EXPRESSIONS ARE CENTRAL TO HOW WE COMMUNICATE AND ARE DIFFICULT TO SUPPRESS OR FAKE.

In fact, facial expressions are such an important part of how we communicate that there is a specific part of the brain that is used to analyze faces called the "fusiform face area."

We can tell, within seconds, how someone feels by the expression on their face. How a person moves their body; how they position their head, arms, hands and legs; how their eyes, mouth, fingers and toes move; and whether their eye pupils are dilated or contracted; are all unconscious signals. These unconscious signals can reveal an emotion, feeling, attitude, or mood that the person exhibiting these reactions may prefer to conceal.

INVOLUNTARY, NONVERBAL SIGNALS TELL AN ALERT OBSERVER MORE ABOUT OUR STATE OF MIND—INCLUDING OUR ATTITUDES, EMOTIONS, THOUGHTS AND FEELINGS— THAN ANY WORDS WE CAN SAY.

Your unconscious mind will pick up on many of these cues. Evolution has caused our brains to develop this unconscious ability for survival. But if you're observant, if you focus your attention on these areas, your conscious mind can also identify subtle gestures that convey a feeling or transmit a thought.

By paying attention, you can identify gestures and expressions that reveal a person's inner feelings at that moment. Interpreting this nonverbal language can give you a much more accurate understanding of a person's thoughts, feelings and intentions.

In the 1970s, Paul Ekman and Wallace V. Friesen developed the Facial Action Coding System (FACS) to measure, describe and interpret facial behaviors. This instrument is designed to measure even the slightest facial muscle contractions and determine what category or categories each facial action fits into. It can detect what the naked eye can't and is used by law enforcement agencies, film animators and researchers of human behavior.

It is essential that you recognize the importance of nonverbal communication and the role of our unconscious mind in understanding, processing and communicating information. Practice awareness of your own body language and analyze specific cues—such as posture, expressions and gestures—being made by others, whether or not they're speaking. Consciously work to improve your ability to observe, identify and interpret the nonverbal and unconscious communication of others.

76

COMPLIMENT OTHERS

Look for genuine and sincere
opportunities to compliment others.

By taking a moment every day to enrich someone else's life, you enrich your own as well.

THE EASIEST WAY TO MAKE THE WORLD A BETTER PLACE IS TO BE A BETTER PERSON.

We all have a desire to be acknowledged. When someone notices us, it changes the way we think about ourselves. It emboldens us. It can change our entire day—and much more. It can make us more satisfied and grateful—even more creative. This change in mindset can be especially significant in the workplace, where these feelings can make us more engaged and productive.

Compliments are a powerful source of motivation—and they're free. They motivate not only the subject of the compliment—they motivate others as well. People strive to do that which brings recognition and praise. When you compliment one employee, other employees are alerted to the fact that you're watching their performance and that they too can be recognized and rewarded for their superior performance.

Compliments can change the atmosphere in any environment by elevating moods, creating increased positivity, fostering interaction and improving communication. Don't limit your compliments to one person or group. Look for opportunities to compliment others. And always make sure that your compliments are genuine and sincere. An insincere compliment is counter-productive—it will undermine trust.

Compliments are not only good for the recipients—they're good for those who give them as well. When you compliment someone, their reaction has an immediate influence on you. It increases your self-confidence and self-esteem. You feel better about yourself—by making others feel better.

There is only one way to respond to a genuine and sincere compliment—graciously and gratefully.

77

KINDNESS

"Kindness is the language the deaf
can hear and the blind can see."

—*Mark Twain, American writer, humorist and publisher.*

His Holiness, the 14th Dalai Lama of Tibet, said, "It is tremendously important that we try to make something positive of our lives. We were not born for the purpose of causing trouble and harming others. For our life to be of value, we need to foster and nurture such basic good human qualities as warmth, kindness and compassion. If we can do that, our lives will become meaningful, happier and more peaceful; we will make a positive contribution to the world around us."

ACTS OF KINDNESS ENRICH ALL OF US. THEY'RE LIKE DEPOSITS IN THE GLOBAL BANK OF GOODWILL.

When you buy a stranger a cup of coffee, open a door for someone, or surprise someone with your kindness or generosity, you not only enrich your life and theirs; you make the world a better place.

Research conducted by Dr. Michael Tomasello of the Max Planck Institute demonstrated that children begin to help others at an astonishingly early age—even before they're two years old. It's inherent in our nature—and it naturally makes us feel good.

Studies have found that kindness is also contagious. Your acts of kindness often motivate the recipients to pay it forward and be kind to others.

Author and philosopher Aldous Huxley, who wrote *Brave New World* and fifty other books, said, "People often ask me what is the most effective technique for transforming their life. It is a little embarrassing that after years and years of research and experimentation, I have to say that the best answer is—just be a little kinder."

The fact that Huxley and many others, including the 14th Dalai Lama of Tibet, point to kindness as our salvation shouldn't be ignored. It should be examined, understood and embraced. It will undoubtedly be a key element to our growth and mutual survival moving forward.

Always be kind to everyone you meet.

TOUCH

"Touch seems to be as essential as sunlight."

—*Diane Ackerman, American author and poet.*

T ouch is the first sense we acquire and it is a powerful means of communication.

WE FEEL MORE CONNECTED TO
SOMEONE IF THEY TOUCH US.

We have the ability to send and receive emotional signals solely by touching.

According to a study by psychologist Matthew Hertenstein of DePauw University, we can use touch to communicate at least eight distinct emotions— anger, fear, disgust, love, gratitude, sympathy, happiness and sadness—with accuracy rates as high as seventy-eight percent. Scientists used to believe that touching was simply a means of enhancing messages signaled through speech or body language, "but it seems instead that touch is a much more nuanced, sophisticated and precise way to communicate emotions," Hertenstein says.

TOUCHING IS FAR MORE IMPORTANT THAN WE THINK.

Understanding the importance of this critical sense can improve your relationships, support your mental and emotional health and influence your interactions with others.

SMILE

"The expression one wears on one's face
is far more important than the clothes
one wears on one's back."

—*Dale Carnegie, American author and lecturer.*

Smiles are contagious. Humans instinctively mirror other people's emotional expressions on their own faces. This facial mimicry helps us to empathize with other people and share their emotions. Children smile approximately four hundred times per day compared to just twenty times a day for adults. Much of that is the child mimicking the smiles they see.

RESEARCH HAS SHOWN THAT SMILING RELEASES SEROTONIN, A NEUROTRANSMITTER THAT PRODUCES FEELINGS OF HAPPINESS AND WELLBEING.

Research has also shown that we find others more attractive when they are smiling.

A study out of the University of Wisconsin found that "different smiles have different impacts on people's bodies." The researchers discovered that there was sixteen times more of the stress hormone cortisol in the saliva of those test subjects who were exposed to someone with a dominance smile (I'm in control) than there was in the saliva of those who were exposed to a reward smile (Do that again). Our bodies react physiologically to the facial expressions of others.

YOUR FACIAL EXPRESSIONS ARE PHYSIOLOGICALLY AFFECTING OTHERS AND THEIR FACIAL EXPRESSIONS ARE AFFECTING YOU.

Smiling when you first meet someone is important in establishing a positive relationship. It indicates that you're happy to see them and that you're a positive person. People naturally gravitate toward positive people. People are also more inclined to like someone who they believe likes them. A smile is one of your most important assets. Use it as often as possible.

80

NETWORKING

*Seek out people you believe may be able to help you
and try to make new connections.*

N ever overlook people you believe can do nothing for you; you may be surprised. Some of my greatest successes in life can be traced to introductions from people I never would have imagined might play an important role in my life.

Always treat everyone with kindness and respect. A seemingly insignificant stranger may later become someone who changes your life forever.

BY EXPANDING YOUR NETWORK OF CONTACTS, YOU EXPAND YOUR POTENTIAL FOR NEW OPPORTUNITIES.

Networks are not just about who can help you today. Networks can and should last a lifetime.

Technology platforms like LinkedIn and Facebook can be invaluable in developing and maintaining networks. Think about how you are using these platforms and how you are presenting yourself online.

Becoming visible is an important part of networking. Create visibility for yourself by attending events, posting information online, writing a blog, commenting on posts and asking or answering questions. In all instances, make certain that the visibility you create places you in a favorable light. Continue to build, develop and maintain your relationships throughout your life. And never underestimate the importance of any relationship.

Leverage your relationships for job referrals, recommendations and/ or introductions. If you don't have relationships with individuals who can mentor you or give you advice, get involved in your community and work to develop helpful relationships, referrals and recommendations. If you're already employed, join industry groups, attend conferences, volunteer at your children's school, or offer your volunteer services to nonprofits. Try to meet new people.

Set a goal for yourself of trying to meet one new person every day. If this seems too ambitious, try to meet at least one or two new people every week. Look for opportunities at school, at your job, at the grocery store, at the car wash, at the mall—wherever you happen to be. Introduce yourself to new people. Your instincts will tell you when it's the right time.

Start by simply being open to people and to opportunities when they present themselves.

BE FRIENDLY, WARM, RESPECTFUL AND INVITING WHEN YOU MEET NEW PEOPLE.

Say hello to people and make it easy for them to say hello to you. Don't be afraid of rejection. Have courage and confidence.

Don't expect every encounter to be positive or instantly lead to a new friendship. Good things take time and effort. Invest the time. Make the effort. Radiate a warm, positive and authentic personality. Carry a genuine and compassionate confidence rather than a boastful or contrived confidence.

LET YOUR POSITIVE, AUTHENTIC PERSONALITY ACT LIKE A MAGNET OF ATTRACTION.

You never know where a chance encounter may lead. I am always looking for talented people who can add value to the businesses I am involved with or whose talents and skills may present new opportunities. So are many other employers and businesspeople. Great people are hard to find. Be one of them and don't be hard to find. Get out there and get noticed.

81

COMMUNITY

"Our ambitions must be broad enough to include the aspirations and needs of others, for their sakes and for our own."

—Cesar Chavez, American labor leader and civil-rights activist.

The origin of the word "community" comes from the Latin word "communis," which means shared by all. So, community literally means to share among each other. Communities are as varied as their members. Often people belong to multiple communities. Communities can be families, educational institutions, businesses, religious groups, or teams.

Communities are the very essence of how we live and socialize with others.

THEY PROVIDE A SENSE OF IDENTITY AND PURPOSE, A SENSE OF BELONGING.

Disadvantaged or marginalized people often have limited opportunities to develop any personal or professional communities. Their disadvantages (a physical or intellectual disability, a drug dependency, or any other limiting characteristic) reduce their abilities to develop social networks.

Many gang members join gangs not because they want to live that life but because they need the security and sense of belonging that a gang provides.

WE ALL NEED A SENSE OF BELONGING.

It doesn't matter how successful we are; if we have no one to share our successes with, life becomes meaningless.

Relationships are essential to both our happiness and success. Communities are where we make friends, develop personal and business contacts, share experiences and resources, learn, teach, advise and support one another.

Virtually every community has groups and organizations whose mission is to help those within their community. Become part of your community. Gain what others in your community have to offer and give back by showing pride and respect for the community you live in. Regardless of what community you are part of, the people and resources in that community can add value to your life if you allow yourself to be open to them.

Your community represents an incredible asset that can assist you and your family in achieving your goals. Embrace your community and it will embrace you.

VOLUNTEERING

The impact of volunteering extends well beyond the causes you serve. It helps you as much as anyone else.

In a recent study on people who volunteered, researchers found that:

76% felt healthier

96% felt an enriched sense of purpose

90% felt happier

95% felt they were improving their community

Volunteerism is an investment in your community—one that pays personal dividends. Helping others has a profoundly positive impact on your emotional wellbeing and can help you to reach your personal goals.

VOLUNTEERING ALLOWS YOU TO MEET NEW PEOPLE AND DEVELOP NEW RELATIONSHIPS THAT CAN BE LIFE-CHANGING.

It allows you to develop new skills that you can't learn in a classroom. Volunteering can act as a gateway into the workforce, especially if you volunteer in areas that are related to a field of employment that interests you. It can also put you in contact with potential mentors.

Find an area that interests you and volunteer your time. It will be time well spent.

HELP

Never be afraid to ask for help.

There are many good people who genuinely want to help you. They don't want to support you and they don't want to take on an unnecessary or excessive burden, but they are often willing to lend a hand, offer advice, or be there for you in a moment of need.

Be independent. Strive to be self-sufficient. Never abuse the generosity of others. Always be grateful for any assistance you receive. Never assume that you're entitled to receive anything you haven't earned. But never be afraid to ask for help.

The world is changing rapidly and radically. We're at the threshold of a technological revolution that will swell the ranks of the unemployed.

PEOPLE WHO DON'T NEED HELP TODAY WILL NEED HELP TOMORROW.

And that could include you or someone in your family.

We already see it happening all around us—friends who have lost their jobs or can't get jobs; students who graduate with crushing debt and can't find jobs requiring a college degree; people over forty who have lost their jobs and have difficulty securing new jobs because of their age. Times are tough for many. And the changing nature of employment, together with the absence of available resources for retraining and reskilling, will make things tougher for millions more.

So, it's important that you understand that you can and should ask for help. It is even more important that you understand that humanity is profoundly interdependent—we need each other to survive and thrive. Millions more will soon be unemployed—not as a consequence of a poor economy but as a consequence of an automated economy. A poor economy would further increase these numbers.

If we operate on the principle of "survival of the fittest" or "I'm not my brother's keeper," what do you believe will happen to the unemployed? Do you believe that millions more will suffer in silence—as many do in third world countries? I don't. America's poor are far more educated, empowered and entitled than the poor of third world countries. They will not suffer and/ or starve in silence. Many will commit crimes to feed themselves and their families. And this will affect everyone's quality of life.

THE CHANGES THAT ARE COMING WILL NOT ONLY ADVERSELY AFFECT THE DISPLACED AND THE DISENFRANCHISED. THEIR PLIGHT WILL ADVERSELY AFFECT ALL OF US.

Ultimately, we will come to understand that "survival of the fittest" is not in our mutual self-interest. Rather, it is in our mutual self-interest to help our neighbor to not only survive but to thrive. It is only through that recognition that real and sustainable progress will be possible.

Nature provides an interesting example of profound interdependence. The fire ant can't swim. In heavy rains, they lock their legs and form floating rafts to avoid drowning. Alone, they would perish—together they survive. Humans behave the same way in times of crisis. We see this in natural disasters all across the world.

We need to learn that it is essential for us to help others before crisis strikes. Our own quality of life and that of our family, ultimately depends on our helping others.

IN OTHER WORDS, HELPING OTHERS IS NOT ONLY THE RIGHT THING TO DO FOR THOSE IN NEED—IT IS ESSENTIAL TO OUR OWN QUALITY OF LIFE AND OUR OWN SURVIVAL.

84

MENTORS

*"A mentor is someone who allows you
to see the hope inside yourself."*

—*Oprah Winfrey, American media owner, talk show
host, actress and producer.*

I f you are fortunate enough to find yourself in the presence of greatness or
have the opportunity to know or work with an individual whose example
you would like to follow, recognize the importance of that opportunity and
capitalize on it by learning all that you can.

IF YOU WANT A MENTOR, UNDERSTAND THAT MENTORS ARE ATTRACTED TO PEOPLE WHO HAVE TALENT AND SHOW PROMISE.

So, exhibit talent and show promise. Once you identify someone you would
like to have as a mentor, find a way to help that person. Don't ask or expect them
to help you before you have established a firm relationship. If they eventually
do help you with anything, it means they see something in you that they like.
They may see your promise and potential, or they may see how you could be
able to help them in some way.

Show gratitude. Thank them for their time, support and interest. Work
tirelessly to impress them. Earn their support and admiration; deserve it but
don't expect it. If it comes, cherish it.

If a prospective mentor doesn't respond to you, it may mean that you
haven't done enough to impress them or they may need more time to see if you
stay the course. It may mean that they saw something or heard something they

didn't like. More likely, it may simply mean that they're just too busy or not inclined toward mentorship. Whatever the reason, don't blame the individual you admire for not noticing or embracing you. Don't assume you deserve it. You may not. You're certainly not entitled to a mentor.

MENTORS ARE A RARE GIFT THAT IS OCCASIONALLY BESTOWED UPON A SELECT FEW.

If you are fortunate enough to attract one, treasure that person and the incredible opportunity that their guidance represents. Great people all seem to have one thing in common—a reverence for excellence. If you share that reverence and exhibit excellence, you are more likely to attract them.

RESPECT

"I speak to everyone the same way, whether he is a garbage man or the president of the university."

—*Albert Einstein, German-born theoretical physicist.*

P eople often make the mistake of ignoring people they think can do nothing for them—the door man, the receptionist, the secretary who they pass in the hallway, the janitor, or the waitress. Each of these people deserve as much respect as you do and, as odd as it may seem, any one of them could hold the keys to your future.

Someone you meet who may seem insignificant to you could have a relative that works at, or even owns, a firm you want to join. A complete stranger could know someone who needs your services. The guy who takes care of your lawn could have a son or a daughter that you fall madly in love with. You just never know.

SOME OF THE MOST MOMENTOUS TRANSACTIONS ORIGINATE FROM THE MOST UNLIKELY SOURCES.

How you interact with everyone will speak volumes about who you are as a person—and that will not go unnoticed.

In many cases, you will be judged by those who *can* help you by how you treat those that *can't* help you. A CEO of a Fortune 500 company recently said in an interview that he will take people he is interviewing for employment to lunch and arrange in advance to have the waiter screw up their order "just to see how they respond."

Treat everyone you meet with kindness and respect.

AUTHORITY

*The law requires that all of us obey the
lawful orders of a police officer. Absent such
understanding and agreement, this world would
quickly devolve into chaos.*

When you look at the tragic police encounters that plague our country, virtually all of them have one thing in common and it's not race, geography, or economics. In the vast majority of cases, tragic police encounters begin with a breakdown in communication.

When police officers encounter someone who runs, someone who fails to follow their lawful orders, or someone with a defiant or disrespectful attitude, that encounter quickly results in failed communication and inevitably ends in escalation. Generational differences relating to our varied perceptions about the proper role of police and authority are a common theme and a major contributing factor to the increases in police shootings we are all witnessing.

Prior generations could generally be expected to respect authority—rarely did they question or defy authority. That is not the case with Millennials. Far too often, Millennials of all ethnic backgrounds routinely question and defy authority. This is already raising serious issues between Millennials and police.

ACCORDING TO A STUDY PUBLISHED BY THE JOURNAL OF PEDIATRICS, BY THE AGE OF TWENTY-THREE, OVER FORTY PERCENT OF YOUNG ADULT MALES HAVE BEEN ARRESTED AT LEAST ONCE FOR SOMETHING OTHER THAN A MINOR TRAFFIC VIOLATION.

The Huffington Post estimates the number of those arrested by age twenty-three to be as high as fifty percent of African-American males and forty percent of Caucasian males. This high arrest rate is troubling because of the corrosive effects that arrests and incarceration can have on a young person's emotional, mental and social development. These arrest records will follow these individuals and make it far more difficult for them to obtain employment, get housing, loans, or an education.

There are, no doubt, a number of reasons for these increases in arrests. But again, one of the major contributing factors may well be an increase in defiant attitudes and a lack of respect for authority.

Police often exercise discretion in making arrests for minor infractions and police officers are human beings. Some would argue that such discretion is being exercised with racial bias. This is true in some cases. And when it is true, that is entirely unacceptable and it needs to be addressed, whether through increased training, improved hiring, termination and/or prosecution. However, I would argue that a lack of respect for authority has a far greater influence on the exercise of police discretion than race.

COMMON SENSE WOULD SUGGEST THAT POLICE ARE LESS LIKELY TO ARREST SOMEONE WHO IS RESPECTFUL THAN SOMEONE WHO IS DISRESPECTFUL, REGARDLESS OF RACE. IT'S HUMAN NATURE.

My five points of advice are as follows:

- **Respect.** Show respect for the police at all times.
  When interacting with the police, be open, honest and forthright.

- **Visibility.** Do not attempt to hide or conceal anything. Keep your hands out of your pockets and where the police officer can see them. This is critical. Your life may depend on it.

- **Obedience.** Do not make any sudden moves whatsoever. Do exactly as you are told without delay and without objection. If a police officer says don't move—don't move. Period.

- **Courtesy.** Never argue with a police officer. If you have an argument to make, you can make it with the district attorney, your lawyer, or the judge.

- **Restraint.** Do not involve yourself in police matters that do not involve you personally. Do not attempt to make arguments on behalf of someone else or in any way interfere with a police officer who is doing his or her job.

If you follow this advice, you will be far less likely to have any problem with ninety-nine percent of the police officers you encounter. You will be less likely to be arrested and you will come home to your family alive and well. If you choose to disregard this advice, understand that you do so at your peril. This isn't something you should take lightly.

Police are human. They make mistakes. They have stressful jobs and are constantly involved in high-risk encounters filled with uncertainty. They have families at home. They will protect themselves. And they carry guns.

WHEN YOU ARGUE WITH A POLICE OFFICER OR FAIL TO IMMEDIATELY FOLLOW THEIR LAWFUL INSTRUCTIONS, YOU CREATE UNNECESSARY RISKS FOR THEM, FOR YOURSELF AND FOR OTHERS.

You make the situation far more dangerous for everyone.

A civilized society cannot long endure if people are allowed—let alone encouraged—to challenge or interfere with police on the street. If you want to live in a civilized society, then you need to understand, accept and embrace this concept. Failure to follow a lawful order of a police officer, interfering with a police officer and resisting arrest are all crimes punishable by fines and/or imprisonment for good reason. Without these rules, all members of society would be at greater risk.

Do not attempt to substitute your judgment for theirs about what should or should not happen during an encounter with police. Accept and respect their authority. Do not disrespect them. If you feel that you have an argument to make or you feel that your rights have been violated, you are not without recourse. Tell your parents, call a lawyer, or take it up with the judge, but never argue with a cop on the street. Anyone who advises you differently is giving you very bad advice and may be risking your life.

Watch the following videos and comment on them at MillennialSamurai. com/authority.

From those commenting, I will select up to five people to participate in a Facebook Live broadcast that will also be featured on YouTube and MillennialSamurai.com. **Please provide your email address when commenting so that we can contact you.**

- Authority – Taser Coma – Bryce Masters
  https://www.facebook.com/NowThisNews/videos/1080103675413089/

- Authority – 18-year-old and bystander both arrested.
  https://www.facebook.com/NowThisPolitics/videos/1887782687919879/

- Authority – Kevin J. Ferguson
  https://everipedia.org/wiki/lang_en/kevin-j-ferguson-police-officer/#lg=1&slide=1

- Authority - 15-year-old girl and bystander.
  https://www.facebook.com/ABCNews/videos/10154817234088812/

Identify the video that you watched and then answer the following questions for that video:

1. What do you think of the conduct of the individuals being arrested?

2. What do you think of the conduct of the police officers?

3. Do you believe that following the above advice would have prevented any or all of these incidents from escalating? Why?

4. How would you have handled these encounters with police?

5. How would you have responded in these situations if you were the police officer?

PARENTING 101

*"No man should bring children into
the world who is unwilling to persevere
to the end in their nurture and education."*

—Plato, Greek philosopher.

R esearch shows that the architecture of our brain is developed by our early interactions with parents and caregivers. Eighty percent of the connections between the neurons in our brains develop after birth. When babies observe another person, their own neurons respond by firing. These responsive neurons are referred to as "mirror neurons." We learn, in part, through observation. We also learn by mirroring and mimicking the behavior of others.

ENHANCING YOUR BABY'S BRAIN DEVELOPMENT REQUIRES SOCIAL INTERACTION.

Playing with babies, reading to them, talking to them and holding them enhances the learning process.

According to J. Kevin Nugent, PhD, director of the Brazelton Institute at Boston's Children's Hospital, "Nothing is a substitute for relationship-building and the exchange of tactile and verbal interactions with a caregiver. That's what makes the difference in a baby's brain development."

What your baby does with his/her brain is what they are going to be good at. If you read to them, they will develop an increased interest in and an increased aptitude for reading.

BY EXPOSING YOUR CHILD TO MULTIPLE ACTIVITIES AND MULTIPLE STIMULI, YOU WILL INCREASE AND STRENGTHEN THE CONNECTIONS BETWEEN THE NEURONS IN THEIR BRAIN.

According to Nicole Letourneau, author of *What Kind of Parent Am I?* "Toxic stressors such as a mother's depression, exposure to family violence, or a parent's addiction can indirectly reduce a baby's cognitive capacities."

When babies are exposed to stressors, their cortisol levels increase. Too much cortisol can be neurotoxic.

BRAINS OF BABIES RAISED IN STRESSFUL ENVIRONMENTS HAVE BEEN SHOWN TO BE SMALLER AND LESS DEVELOPED.

Enhancing your baby's brain development requires that you provide a safe, secure and stress-free environment. It requires that you introduce and expose them to all that you can.

Ignoring a crying baby can negatively affect their brain development, creating changes in the brain similar to those found in depressed adults. It can increase the release of adrenaline and cortisol, which can suppress the brain's development and the functioning of the immune system. These early changes in the brain can adversely affect a child's intellectual, social and emotional development and can have a profound impact on how they function as adults.

Read to your baby. Make their surroundings playful and colorful. Get on the floor and play with them, kiss them, hug them, sing to them, play music for them.

GIVE THEM LOTS OF LOVE AND ATTENTION.

Introduce them to new and varied textures, colors, sounds, tastes and sensations. Provide them with a safe and secure place to play—one that allows them to explore the environment around them. These are the best things you can do to enhance your child's brain development and prepare them for their future.

The following is an overview of issues to consider during your child's development:

- Touch is the first form of communication. Hug and kiss your child. Hold them and carry them. Touch and play with their hands and feet. Smile and use a comforting tone and welcoming body language when you communicate. Respond to baby talk with conversation; it will assist with the development of your child's language skills. Read to your child as often as possible. Provide your child with a safe, stress-free, comforting and secure environment.

- Give your child your complete and mindful attention whenever possible. Help your child use words to express their emotions. Laugh and play with your child. Read to your child as often as possible. Show them how things work. Introduce them to as many new things as possible. Give them age-appropriate puzzles to solve. Find educational videos that they can watch on YouTube. Take them outside and expose them to nature—including the rain and snow. Spend mornings or afternoons on walks or in the parks. Take them to plays, movies and museums. Try to give them a wealth of experience that costs little or nothing.

- As your child begins to mature, make time to talk to your child in a respectful way that encourages development and maturity. Listen attentively to what your child is saying and repeat it back to them in a more articulate and mature manner. Allow your child to have some input into family decisions. Laugh and engage in activities with your child. Lead by example. Continue to enrich your child's life and development with as many experiences as possible. Encourage them to learn a second language and to play a musical instrument. Introduce them to music and art. Provide them with good behavioral examples.

- As your child moves into their teen years, continue to talk with your child and begin discussing more significant social and political issues. Learn more about their friends. Have their friends over to your home and make them feel welcome. Show respect for their opinions. Listen attentively and mindfully to what they are saying. Respect their privacy and keep their confidences, unless you have a compelling reason not to do so, like substance abuse, mental illness, or criminality. Trusting your teen will encourage them to confide in you. Let them know that they can always confide in you and, when they do, do everything you can to maintain their trust and confidence.

If you can't, as Plato said, "persevere to the end in their nurture and education," then wait until you can before having children. And if you already have children, it's never too late to be a good parent.

88

HOW TO BE A GOOD FATHER

B egin by understanding the responsibility, the importance and the joy of fatherhood. Far too few men understand the importance of this sacred obligation.

43% of U.S. children live in fatherless homes. → **72%** of all Americans believe this is most signicant social problem in the U.S. today.

The statistics on children from fatherless homes, show that:

90% of homeless and runaway children are from fatherless homes.

85% of youths in prison are from fatherless homes.

80% of rapists are from fatherless homes

71% of high school dropouts are from fatherless homes.

63% of youth suicides are from fatherless homes

Your participation in any activity can have consequences and you need to be prepared to accept personal responsibility for those consequences, especially the consequences that can arise from sexual intercourse.

It doesn't matter how or why you became a father. It doesn't matter how you feel about the mother. All that matters is that you are a father—and with that status comes certain responsibilities. You need to understand and accept that reality before you engage in the unprotected sexual activity that creates that responsibility.

I have done and accomplished a great deal in my life, but there is no experience that I treasure more, or am prouder of, than my experience as a father.

MY MOST TREASURED MEMORIES ARE OF TIME SPENT WITH MY DAUGHTER, MY NIECES AND MY NEPHEWS.

It should be noted that you don't need to wait to be a father to experience the joy of fatherhood. There are millions of children who need a father figure in their lives today. If you're interested in helping these children, there are many things you can do. Contact local schools, churches and community organizations to offer assistance. Offer to mentor children whose fathers are absent from their lives. Determine what level of commitment works for you. Once a year. Once a month. Once a week. Offer these young people the same advice, guidance and encouragement that any good father would offer to their own children. Take them to see where you work, to lunch, to a meeting, to a movie. Read to them. Encourage them to read. Read them passages from this book or give them a copy of their own. There are very few things that you can do with your time that would be more important or fulfilling.

RESPECT YOUR ELDERS

Treat your elders as you would want your children
to treat you. Lead by example.

The older citizens of ancient Greece and Rome were highly respected for their wisdom. Councils of elders helped rule these societies. In Greek and Greek-American culture, old age is still honored and celebrated. Respect for elders is central to Greek and Italian families. The same is true of many cultures.

The traditional basis for elder respect in Asian cultures is Confucian teachings. In the teachings of Confucius, respect for parents and elders is a central theme and is seen as an essential foundation for a good society. Essentially, it directs offspring to recognize the care and aid received from their parents and, in return, to pay respect to their parents. Material support for one's parents is not all that is expected; deference to your elders and a genuine reverence for them is also expected.

According to Confucius, the legendary Chinese philosopher, elder respect must also extend beyond the boundary of the family. "At home, a young man should be dutiful toward his parents; going outside, he should be respectful toward other elders and be cautious in deeds and trustworthy in words." (Analects of Confucius).

We all grow old. Whenever you look at an elderly person, understand this: one day, that will be you.

HOW DO YOU WANT TO BE TREATED WHEN YOU'RE OLD?

Mountaineers normally have the most experienced member of the team lead the group and for good reason. They do it because experienced climbers either know the best routes and/or know where to step to avoid hurting or killing themselves. The idea is that the more experienced climber is the expert and younger members of the team—even if they are more physically fit—need to learn from them and respect their knowledge. Not using their knowledge would be foolish.

WHEN YOU HAVE AN AMAZING KNOWLEDGE BANK, WHY WOULDN'T YOU USE IT?

Simply by virtue of their age, your elders have seen more than you have. They may not know what you know—their experiences and their knowledge may be very different from your own—but that does not mean that you can't learn from them. On the contrary, you can learn a great deal from them that will be very relevant to your life.

People who have experienced many years of life have a different perspective from someone who is seeing things for the first time. With this experience comes wisdom that can be handed down.

The history of our lives comes from our elders. Who we are derives from our parents and our ancestors. Disrespecting those who came before us is like disrespecting ourselves.

Your elders know you better than anyone and are therefore in a better position to advise you than most. Learn from them. Treasure them.

ACTION IS MAGIC

ACTION

"Action is the foundational key to all success."

—*Pablo Picasso, Spanish painter, sculptor, printmaker and ceramicist.*

EVERY JOURNEY BEGINS WITH A FIRST STEP.

You can have a great idea. You can even have the right plan. But only action can transform your idea into reality. If you are to achieve your goals, you must act.

The nature of your action will normally, although not always, determine the outcome. Luck, timing and circumstance can and will influence outcomes as well. But it is excellence and consistency of action, more than any other factor, that will most reliably determine outcome.

Reading this book will inform you—but only applying what you learn will advance you.

TAKING ACTION HELPS YOU TO OVERCOME YOUR FEARS.

It changes the way others perceive you—and the way you perceive yourself. It changes your attitude, builds your self-confidence and improves your self-image.

When you take action, it not only affects your life; it impacts the lives of all those around you. Taking action exposes you to new people; it provides you with new experiences and opportunities. It allows you to acquire new skills.

Whatever your goals, dreams or aspirations might be—action is required to achieve them. #ActionIsMagic

DELEGATION

Delegation is a multiplying force.

Delegation allows one person to direct and leverage the efforts and talents of many. It facilitates execution, growth and expansion.

DELEGATION IS ESSENTIAL TO SCALE.

Think about what's stopping you from delegating. Are you a perfectionist, impatient or intolerant? Do you have a need for control? Do you have difficulty working with others? Perhaps you're simply not good at managing people.

It is important that you understand the importance of delegation and create circumstances that allow for it. Either become good at delegating or work with others who are good at it.

Success should not be dependent exclusively on your own efforts. If it is, your success will be limited.

DELEGATION ALLOWS YOU TO LEVERAGE THE IMPACT AND INFLUENCE OF OTHERS.

It allows you to accomplish multiple tasks simultaneously—through using multiple human resources.

Learn to delegate.

GRIT AND
A GROWTH MINDSET

"Grit" is defined by Angela Lee Duckworth,
a distinguished professor of psychology at the
University of Pennsylvania, as "perseverance and
passion for long-term goals."

D r. Duckworth and her colleagues studied grit as a personality trait and observed that individuals high in grit were able to maintain their determination and motivation over long periods despite experiences with failure and adversity; and they concluded that grit is a better predictor of success than intellect or talent.

Her team went to West Point Academy and tried to predict which cadets would stay in military training and which would drop out. They went to the National Spelling Bee and tried to predict which students would advance farthest in the competition. They went to high-risk schools and tried to predict which teachers would be there at the end of the school year and which teachers would have the best outcomes in their classes. They looked at sales people in private companies and tried to predict who would keep their jobs and who would make the most money.

In all these different environments, one characteristic emerged as the most reliable predictor of success. It wasn't social intelligence. It wasn't appearance. It wasn't physical strength or health. And it wasn't IQ. It was grit.

Grit has nothing to do with intelligence or talent. It's passion and perseverance for long-term goals. Passion and perseverance require stamina.

Grit requires sticking with your future day in and day out—not just for the week, not just for the month, but for years and years—and working really hard to make that future a reality. Grit is living life like it's a marathon, not a sprint.

Albert Einstein, German-born theoretical physicist, said, "It's not that I'm so smart, it's just that I stay with problems longer."

Dr. Duckworth asked thousands of highschool students to take grit questionnaires and then waited more than a year to see who would graduate. She found that grittier kids were far more likely to graduate.

Dr. Duckworth doesn't know where grit comes from. However, she believes that grit can be developed by having a "growth mindset," a concept developed by Dr. Carol Dweck, the Lewis and Virginia Eaton Professor of Psychology at Stanford University.

A GROWTH MINDSET IS A BELIEF THAT THE ABILITY TO LEARN IS NOT FIXED, THAT IT CAN CHANGE WITH YOUR EFFORT.

Neuroscientists now know that this is in fact possible. (See, Neuroplasticity)

Dr. Dweck has shown that when kids read and learn about the brain and how it changes and grows in response to challenge, they're much more likely to persevere when they fail because they don't believe that failure is a permanent condition.

Success requires a growth mindset and grit.

TOUCH THINGS ONCE

We often read an email and then leave it in our inbox. We may flag it—to deal with it later. When someone tells us to send them a text or an email, more often than not, we don't do it immediately. We wait. We procrastinate. We create to-do-lists.

Successful people try to "touch things once." They don't wait or procrastinate; they deal with the issue right then and there. This practice is far more efficient. It avoids forgetting and the need to reread or revisit the item a second or third time.

Try to touch things only once.

WHEN SOMEONE ASKS YOU TO DO SOMETHING, DO IT IMMEDIATELY WHENEVER POSSIBLE.

If I ask you to send me your contact information, don't make a note on your to-do-list to send it to me later; just text or email it to me immediately. By getting into this habit, you will save time and you will complete the task while eliminating the risk of forgetting or failing to complete the task.
Avoid to-do-lists. Many of the items on to-do-lists never get done.

PUT EVERYTHING ON YOUR CALENDAR AND THEN WORK AND LIVE FROM THAT CALENDAR.

Schedule your entire day into segments and try to group like items (family and friends) into blocks. This will help to keep you organized and help you to avoid forgetting important tasks.

PRIORITIZE

"Do the hard jobs first.
The easy jobs will take care of themselves."

—Dale Carnegie, American writer and lecturer.

When deciding what action to take, we often focus on the smaller (easier to complete) items first. This is generally a mistake.

FOCUS ON COMPLETING THE MOST IMPORTANT AND/OR TIME-SENSITIVE ITEMS FIRST.

Check the items off your calendar as you complete each one of them. Completing insignificant items while ignoring or delaying the completion of more important and/or time-sensitive items is a failure to prioritize properly.

SPEED

Speed has always been an asset. In ancient times, it may have allowed you to run from a wild animal or warn your village of an impending attack.

TODAY, IT MAY ALLOW YOU TO BUILD, GROW OR SAVE YOUR BUSINESS.

Time is money, yet few employees seem to grasp this concept intuitively. We see the absence of a sense of urgency in virtually every workplace. How often have you been on a lunch break concerned that you have limited time? You go to a "quick service" restaurant to save time. Unfortunately, the service is anything but quick. As you're standing in a long line, waiting to order, you notice that the cashier is moving with glacial speed. Even worse, there are two registers but the manager is socializing with one of the other workers rather than opening the second register. No one working at this "quick service" restaurant is quick and you're not getting the service you need.

It happens all too often in stores, at the bank, in movie theaters—everywhere.

PEOPLE LACK A SENSE OF URGENCY.

They're often slow. Sometimes irritatingly slow. There is no excuse for it. It results from inadequate training on the part of management and a lack of commitment on the part of employees.

YOU HAVE TO TRAIN YOUR EMPLOYEES WHY SPEED MATTERS.

The absence of a sense of urgency is bad for business. Companies lose customers because of it and people lose jobs when companies lose customers. People want and have a right to expect service from a service business. If they are not getting that service within a reasonable amount of time, they will leave and take their business elsewhere.

SLOW EMPLOYEES COST THEIR EMPLOYERS MORE IN TIME AND MONEY WHILE PROVIDING LESS VALUE THAN FAST EMPLOYEES.

They accomplish less and they irritate customers. This can result in lost business, fewer jobs and even store closures. Not only can it cost you your job—it can cost everyone you work with their jobs if the business fails.

Don't waste your time and don't waste other people's time.

TRAIN YOURSELF TO MOVE QUICKLY WITHOUT MAKING MISTAKES.

Make moving quickly a priority. Work on improving your speed the same way you would work on improving any other skill—practice.

If you have employees—share this information with them. Copy this page and the next chapter on "Time" and hand the copies to every employee. It will help your business be more profitable; and help your employees guarantee their own job security. Better yet, get them their own copy of *Millennial Samurai*. The more informed and empowered your employees are—the more they can help to grow your business.

96

TIME

"Time is really the only capital that any human being has and the only thing he can't afford to lose."

—Thomas A. Edison, American inventor and businessman.

TIME IS THE MOST IMPORTANT ASSET YOU WILL EVER HAVE. IT IS THE MOST PRECIOUS RESOURCE THAT ANYONE WILL EVER HAVE.

With time, anything is possible. Eventually, advances in technology and learning will allow us to extend life—perhaps indefinitely (*see,* Longevity Escape Velocity).

The more time you have, the greater your ability to access and leverage opportunities—some that we can't even yet imagine. Respect your time and the time of others.

In our busy culture, it's easy to lose sight of the benefits of "free time"— time to relax and unwind. Not every moment of your day can or should be managed. Doing things that you enjoy is not wasted time. Enjoy your time off. And be mindful of those moments—in order to get the most out of your time devoted to them.

When someone gives you their time, understand that they are giving you a gift. Cherish that gift and show gratitude when receiving it.

"A man who dares to waste one hour of life has not discovered the value of life."—Charles Darwin, English naturalist, geologist and biologist.

Procrastination, which should be avoided, is essentially a misuse of time.

Instagram founder Kevin Systrom, who believes that we can overcome our tendency to procrastinate by bargaining with ourselves, says, "If you don't want to do something, make a deal with yourself to do at least five minutes of it. After five minutes, you'll end up doing the whole thing."

We postpone tasks that we don't feel good about doing. But once engaged in doing them, we're more likely to develop positive feelings about getting them done—which leads to task completion.

Punctuality is a recognition of the value of time.

BEING PUNCTUAL SHOWS THAT YOU RESPECT THE TIME OF OTHERS.

Being late suggests a lack of respect for the time of others. Being late can also have adverse consequences. It can result in cancelled meetings, withdrawals of offers and missed opportunities.

People are generally late for one of two reasons: either they miscalculated the amount of time required to be punctual or they failed to make being on time a priority. Avoid both of these mistakes. Always make being on time a priority. Always allow yourself more than sufficient time to be punctual. Use your time wisely and always try to be on time.

THE 80/20 RULE

The Pareto Principle, also known as The "80/20 Rule," is a very simple yet important concept. It's named after the Italian economist Vilfredo Pareto who discovered that eighty percent of the land in Italy was owned by twenty percent of the people.

What's important about the principle is that it occurs extremely frequently. Here are some examples:

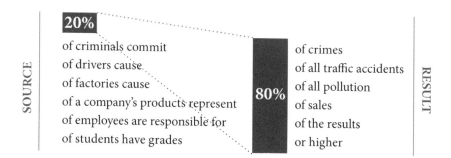

SOURCE	**20%**		**80%**	RESULT
	of criminals commit		of crimes	
	of drivers cause		of all traffic accidents	
	of factories cause		of all pollution	
	of a company's products represent		of sales	
	of employees are responsible for		of the results	
	of students have grades		or higher	

IF YOU LOOK, YOU'LL FIND THAT ABOUT EIGHTY PERCENT OF YOUR BUSINESS COMES FROM APPROXIMATELY TWENTY PERCENT OF YOUR CUSTOMERS.

Even more importantly, if you look closely at that twenty percent, it may be that the top twenty percent of that twenty percent (or the top four percent overall) may represent sixty-four percent of your sales (calculated as eighty percent times eighty percent).

Twenty percent of your time likely accounts for eighty percent of your results.

Focus on ways to leverage this information in order to grow your business and use your most precious resource—your time—most effectively.

DECLUTTER

A study at Princeton University found that
clutter decreases our ability to focus.

C lutter causes us to pay attention to our stuff rather than our goals. This leads to distraction and delayed response time.

DECLUTTERING CAN REDUCE STRESS AND ANXIETY AND INCREASE OUR ABILITY TO FOCUS ON THE TASKS AT HAND.

Researchers at UCLA's Center on Everyday Lives and Families (CELF) found that cluttered homes create stress. Minimalists restrict themselves to only those items that are essential to their lives. They strive to be free from attachment to material possessions and find joy from their experiences and relationships rather than their possessions.

The benefits of decluttering can be profound. It can not only lower your stress and anxiety, it can shift your focus from the unimportant (material possessions) to the important (relationships and experiences).

Start by getting rid of unnecessary stuff like old toiletries, duplicate cooking utensils, extra coffee mugs, old spices that you never use, expired food in the pantry, worn out sheets and bedding, clothes that you haven't worn in the past year, old toys, magazines and instruction manuals. Then decide how streamlined you want to get.

Check out this post on Medium, from my friend Jeff Jonas;

"OVER A FORTY-FIVE DAY PERIOD, I GOT RID OF ALMOST EVERYTHING I OWNED. I'M NOW A NOMADIC CEO, RUNNING MY COMPANY FROM WHEREVER I NEED OR WANT TO BE."

What he's done is amazing.

Jeff was chief scientist of the IBM Entity Analytics group and an IBM Distinguished Engineer. He's also a serial entrepreneur. He's a brilliant scientist, businessman and legendary triathlete who has now gone completely nomadic. He's an inspiration who is living his life to its full potential and he's doing it as a minimalist. How cool is that?

BE ORGANIZED AND PREPARED

"It takes as much energy to wish as it does to plan."

—*Eleanor Roosevelt, former First Lady of the United States.*

KEEP TRACK OF YOUR ESSENTIAL TOOLS. YOUR WALLET, PURSE, KEYS AND CELL PHONE ARE ESSENTIAL TOOLS AND YOU SHOULD KNOW WHERE THEY ARE AT ALL TIMES.

Our phones are our primary means of communication and will soon replace our wallets and our keys. These items carry a unique significance because of their special utility. They're not the equivalent of your sunglasses or your low-fat mocha. Recognize their essential utility—and treat them accordingly.

One of my professors at the University of San Diego School of Law told us "Always remember the three Ps—preparation, preparation and preparation." I always did; and I always tried to be more prepared than anyone I ever interacted with—whether in a business deal or in a court room.

Roger Fisher was a professor at Harvard Law School for more than four decades, a pioneer in the field of international law and negotiation and the co-founder of the Harvard Negotiation Project. When I participated in the Harvard Negotiation Project in 1995 and 1996, one of the many important things he taught us was this:

"YOU CAN SPEND ONE HOUR PREPARING FOR A NEGOTIATION AND NINE HOURS NEGOTIATING. OR YOU CAN SPEND NINE HOURS PREPARING AND ONE HOUR NEGOTIATING."

Organization and preparation are both keys to success. As the Boy Scouts of America say, "Be Prepared."

100

COOL APPS

The best apps add value to your life. Some can save you time and money. Here are some you may want to consider:

- **Signal**—Allows you to place calls and send texts with end-to-end encryption over Wi-Fi or your data connection. You can also make your chat history disappear.

- **Mobile Passport**—You can use this app to scan your passport and create a QR code you can present to United States Customs. It's a government-approved backup that anyone who travels internationally should have.

- **Wolfram Alpha**—This app crawls thousands of domains and uses its complex algorithm to compute data and answer your questions—all in seconds. It answers things Siri and Google don't.

- **FoneTrac**—This app allows you to check in with your contacts or send a panic alert with the touch of a button.

- **Bear**—This is a note-taking app. It has a variety of tools offering lots of flexibility including easy export.

- **Haven**—This is a cool surveillance app. Install this app on a cheap Android phone and leave it in your hotel room. It acts as a digital spy. It uses the phone's camera, mic and other sensors to detect motion and sound. It then sends photos and audio of any activity to the phone you have with you.

- **Google Translate**—This app allows you to point your phone camera at a street sign or a menu and obtain an instant translation.

- **Overcast**—This app allows you to listen to podcasts with a smart speed feature that omits pauses so you can save time.

- **Waking Up: Guided Meditation**—This guided meditation app, by Sam Harris, leads you through simple, easy to follow meditation exercises.

- **RoboKiller**—This app allows you to block 90% of spam calls.

- **Skiplagged**—This app searches a little-known area of bookings called "Hidden City" flights. Essentially, these are flights that can be booked more inexpensively than normal flights because they occur as layovers to other destinations.

- **PicsArt Animator**—This is a creative app that lets you make short, shareable videos, animations, and GIFs with the ability to record voiceovers on your mobile device.

- **Citymapper**—If you live in or are travelling to one of the cities that Citymapper covers (New York, San Francisco, Toronto, Seoul, Tokyo, São Paulo, Moscow, etc.), it'll give you the fastest, most comprehensive list of options for public transportation.

- **Otter Voice Notes**—This creates "smart notes." It records live conversations, transcribes them and can even differentiate between voices for more organization and accuracy.

- **10-Minute Mail**—Set up a temporary email address to receive discount code emails and the address will self-destruct after 10 minutes.

- **FaxZero**—If you need to send a fax, use this site to upload documents straight from your computer and send them within the United States and Canada for free.

- **WhatTheFont**—Find the name of the font used in a particular image.

- **Scr.im**—Converts your email address into a short, custom URL you can share on public sites without getting picked up by spam bots and email harvesters.

- **Think Dirty**—This lets you scan a household item, beauty or cleaning product and the app rates it on a scale of 1 to 10 as being harmless or very toxic.

- **Gabsee**—This lets you create a real-life 3D avatar of yourself reading the paper, partying, working out, or having a drink.

101

MORNING AND EVENING ROUTINES

"We are what we repeatedly do. Excellence, then, is not an act, but a habit."

—*Aristotle, Greek philosopher.*

In the words of Hal Elrod, author of *The Miracle Morning*, "Focused, productive, successful mornings generate focused, productive, successful days—which inevitably create a successful life—in the same way that unfocused, unproductive and mediocre mornings generate unfocused, unproductive and mediocre days and ultimately a mediocre quality of life."

United States Navy Admiral William H. McRaven believes that making your bed every morning helps you start your day with a sense of accomplishment that will drive your performance throughout the day. He's right.

Consider starting your day by making your bed, followed by this 30 to 60 minute routine:

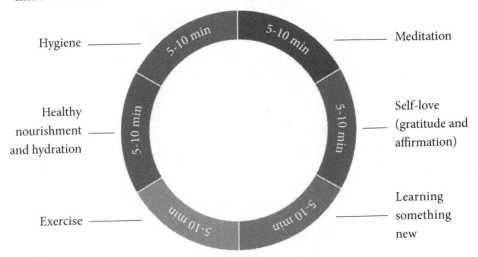

THIS MORNING RITUAL WILL JUMPSTART YOUR DAY.

Before going to bed, plan and calendar your priorities for the next day. For example; on Sunday night, decide what you need and intend to accomplish on Monday and put each item in your calendar for Monday. Do this every night. Wake up every day knowing your priorities for the day.

USE THE FIRST PART OF YOUR DAY TO
WORK ON YOUR TOP PRIORITIES.

Determine what will have the greatest impact on reaching your goals. Do that first. Know in advance what you intend to work on first, second and third, after you wake up and complete your morning routine.

Before going to bed, try to forgive anyone that has offended you and seek forgiveness from anyone that you may have offended. This is especially important if they happen to be sleeping next to you. This will allow you to begin the next day unencumbered by conflict and with the full support of those you love.

Try to get a good night's sleep. You can do that by sleeping in a cool and dark room; ideally, one that is free of phones and computers. If your pets prevent you from getting a good night's sleep, have them sleep in their own bed or in another room.

Beginning each day with a morning ritual, which has been planned the night before, allows you to start your day with focus and intention. This increased focus and intention will profoundly affect your day and if that's happening every day, it can't help but affect your life.

You want your morning and evening routines to become habits. Habits are formed in 21 days. So, you need to continue the practice for 21 consecutive days.

Here's how you stick with it:

1 Establish the goal of consistently doing your morning and evening routines for 21 days. Know why you're doing this and keep that purpose in mind for the full 21 days.

2 Think about your goal every morning and every night. Think about how this will help your physical and emotional health, your career and your finances. Think about how the habit of a morning and evening ritual can change your life.

3 Think about the benefits associated with the habit—greater productivity, more success, less stress and increased happiness.

4 Visualize yourself being successful with your morning and evening routines.

5 Record your performance on your calendar so you can visually see your progress.

Develop your own morning and evening routines. The links provided at the back of the book, in the Resources section under Morning and Evening Routines, will help you decide what works best for you.

You have to decide what works for you. Apple's Tim Cook begins his day at 3:45 a.m. Virgin's Sir Richard Branson starts his day around 5 a.m. Jeff Bezos of Amazon, on the other hand, insists on a full night's sleep and spends his mornings more leisurely. He doesn't get fully engaged in his work until 10 a.m.

How you start and end your day is important. Do it with thought, intention and purpose.

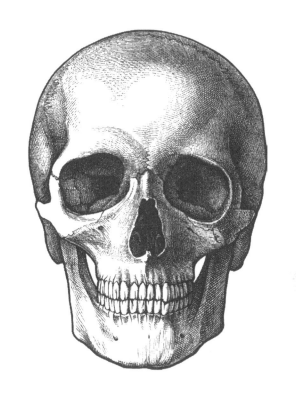

FEAR AND FAILURE

UNDERSTANDING FEAR

*"We all have self-doubt. You don't deny it, but you
also don't capitulate to it. You embrace it."*

—*Kobe Bryant, American basketball player.*

Our fears can paralyze us. We become preoccupied with failing. We become hypersensitive to the opinions of others. For many of us, fears come from our childhood. Fears can be caused by ignorance and the unknown. And failure to confront our fears can allow them to increase. As your fears increase, your self-confidence and self-respect diminish.

THE ACT OF GATHERING INFORMATION AND DOING RESEARCH CAN CAUSE US TO BECOME LESS FEARFUL.

When you confront your fears, your self-confidence and self-respect grow. By objectively analyzing your fears, you can begin the process of eliminating them.

You overcome your fears by taking action that is inconsistent with your fears and consistent with courage. You do this one step at a time. It begins with taking action—a first step. Action is magic.

BABY STEPS BECOME POWERFUL STRIDES.

With each step forward, our fears diminish and our confidence grows. Over time, this practice reduces our fears resulting in confidence and courage.

Understand that your fears are simply thoughts. And you have the ability to control your thoughts. By examining your fears calmly and objectively, you will begin to see that you have the ability to overcome them. You do that by gathering information and by taking small and gradual steps that are inconsistent with those fears and consistent with courage.

OVERCOMING FEAR

*"It's very important to take risks. I think that research is
very important, but in the end you have to work from your
instinct and feeling and take those risks and be fearless."*

—Anna Wintour, journalist, and editor of Vogue.

The Navy SEAL Special Warfare Command puts recruits through a special training program to change and condition the way their brains react to fear. The Navy understands that mistakes in the field normally result from fear and panic. Therefore, they have developed training exercises that are specifically designed to reduce or eliminate fear and panic.

Our brain's amygdala is the command center for our emotions, including fear. The amygdala is the first region of the brain to react to fear. The prefrontal cortex is the brain's center for conscious, rational thought. It analyzes and reacts to fear impulses immediately after the amygdala does.

Navy SEAL training exposes recruits to constant and extreme high-risk situations, conditioning their minds and bodies (through this constant exposure) to suppress and control their fears. Through repeated exposure to risk, recruits are taught to suppress and override the responses of the amygdala by using their prefrontal cortex to control their fears, allowing recruits to respond more calmly, more quickly and more rationally.

Navy SEALs are put in a ten-foot-deep pool as part of Navy SEAL training. They are given a mask and oxygen tanks, weighed down with weights and told to remain underwater for forty-five minutes. Once at the bottom of the pool, two instructors begin to harass and wrestle with the recruit underwater. They rip away their mask and breathing apparatus. This continues for the full forty-five minutes. During this period, the amygdala generates a fight-or-flight response, sending danger signals to the recruit's brain and telling them to get out of the water.

To help recruits deal with these primal fears, the Navy's Mental Toughness Program contains four parts:

PART 1
GOAL SETTING

Goal setting conditions the prefrontal cortex to anticipate fear, providing organization that helps the brain to avoid chaos. By setting the goal of remaining underwater, the recruits essentially preprogram the prefrontal cortex to anticipate and override the fear signals from the amygdala.

PART 2
MENTAL REHEARSAL/ VISUALIZATION

Continuous mental rehearsal and visualization makes the actual event more anticipated and less frightening, again reducing the likelihood of chaos and fear.

PART 3
SELF-TALK

The Navy teaches SEAL recruits to focus on positive thoughts to help override the amygdala's automatic responses. Self-talk constantly reinforces positive thoughts and blocks negative thoughts. Examples of self-talk might be: "I can do this," "This is only a test," or "I need to pass this test."

PART 4
AROUSAL CONTROL

The training on arousal control focuses on breathing, using deep inhales and long exhales to remain calm under pressure.

The combination of all four approaches provides a tested and proven method to reduce fear. Why is this important for you to know? We all face fear—the fear of going on a job interview, starting a new job or starting a new business. Using the above techniques can allow you to overcome your fears and meet life's challenges more calmly and more effectively.

104

FAILURE

*"Only those who dare to fail greatly
can ever hope to achieve greatly."*

—Robert F. Kennedy, former United States Senator (D) NY,
and former United States Attorney General.

From an early age, we are taught to fear failure. The truth is that failure is often a natural consequence of action and innovation. You need to work tirelessly, persist, pivot and persevere; but never fear failure.

"Failure can be the greatest thing in our lives." —Steve Jobs, co-founder of Apple, Inc.

You need to see each failure as a learning experience, analyze your failures, learn from them and make appropriate adjustments. Many of the most successful people in history have had to overcome multiple failures.

Michael Jordan was cut from his high school team.

Walt Disney was told he lacked imagination and was fired from the newspaper where he worked.

Thomas Edison is said to have failed ten thousand times before inventing the light bulb.

Oprah Winfrey was told that she was unfit for TV.

All these people have at least three things in common: they had the courage to reach for success, they failed and they persevered until they achieved success.

FAILURE IS AN INTEGRAL PART OF THE LEARNING PROCESS.

It gives us valuable feedback on what we need to work on next. If you're not failing, you're not trying, you're not reaching and you're not growing.

In everything you do, every time you have the courage to try something new, you will either succeed or you will fail. In each case, you will learn from the experience. Both add value to your life but failure is by far the better teacher.

It doesn't matter how many times you fail. What matters is your dedication and commitment to success. See each failure as an opportunity to learn, make adjustments and keep trying. Failure is an important part of your foundational strength—strength that you can build upon.

Failure shows us our capacity for resilience, our power to overcome obstacles and our ability to endure. It evidences our core strength and that strength should be used as a source of pride and inspiration. The more we fail and persevere, the stronger we become.

"THAT WHICH DOES NOT KILL US MAKES US STRONGER."

—Fredrick Wilhelm Nietzsche, German philosopher.

Use your failure to your advantage. Build upon the strength and the lessons that it provides.

105

MISTAKES

*"A person who never made a mistake
never tried anything new."*

—*Albert Einstein, German-born theoretical physicist.*

We all make mistakes. We lack the ability to be error-free but we can try to do what is right and it is by constantly trying that we build, over time, both our characters and our reputations.

HAVING GREAT CHARACTER DOES NOT REQUIRE
THAT YOU NEVER MAKE MISTAKES.

If it did, no one could be said to have great character. Instead, it requires that you work hard to avoid mistakes and make good choices.

Each person that you deal with will judge you based upon his or her own personal standards. Some may require less of you. Others may require more. Your character and your reputation will constantly be assessed by others based on your words and your deeds. Your mistakes will be evaluated based upon their nature and your intent. Innocent and trivial mistakes may offer some insight into your character but are unlikely to significantly impact your reputation unless they are ongoing. More significant mistakes or errors in judgment, especially those that are intentional, can say a great deal about your character and can have a profoundly negative impact on your reputation.

In the final analysis, you can't control what others think so you shouldn't allow yourself to be defined by the standards of others. Be defined by your own values, your own standards and your own sense of character.

HAVE HIGH STANDARDS AND DEMAND MORE OF YOURSELF.

We all make mistakes. People with great character simply make fewer of them. Their mistakes are also normally unintentional and less significant. Given that you are bound to make certain mistakes in your life, it is important that you know what to do when that happens.

HAVING GREAT CHARACTER REQUIRES THAT YOU ADMIT YOUR MISTAKES.

It requires that you do whatever is necessary to correct your mistakes. It requires that you accept responsibility for your mistakes and graciously accept the consequences of your mistakes. To do otherwise only compounds your mistakes and evidences a serious lack of character.

Part of accepting responsibility for our mistakes includes apologizing to those you have hurt or disrespected. Be honest and humble. Admit when you're wrong, acknowledge your mistakes and always be willing to apologize.

Most people are, by nature, very forgiving. We believe in second chances. We want to forgive. But in doing so, we expect those who have made mistakes to admit their mistakes and to accept responsibility for their mistakes.

NEVER ALLOW YOUR POOR HANDLING OF YOUR MISTAKES TO SAY MORE ABOUT YOUR CHARACTER THAN THE MISTAKES THEMSELVES.

Instead, use your mistakes as opportunities to show the true substance of your character by immediately owning and accepting responsibility for them.

These are critically important concepts. Successful people understand and embrace these core values. Moreover, most of them expect that the people they work with and associate with, both personally and professionally, embrace these same core values.

Regardless of your social or economic condition or circumstances, when you practice these core values, others will respect and admire you. You will build lasting and important personal and professional relationships. Conversely, failure to adopt and practice these core values will undermine and/or preclude such relationships and lead to failure and despair.

A person's reputation is his or her most valuable asset. It can take a lifetime to build and only a single poor choice to destroy. Build your reputation by practicing these core values and guard and protect your reputation zealously. Nothing you possess will ever be more important.

106

STRESS

"I don't worry about stress. I create it."

—James N. Mattis, former United States Secretary of Defense.

S tress not only has wide-ranging effects on emotions, mood and behavior; it affects systems, organs and tissues all over the body. It activates the nervous system's fight-or-flight response, which releases adrenaline and cortisol. These hormones make the heart beat faster, raise blood pressure, change the digestive process and boost glucose levels in the blood stream.

Stress triggers tension headaches and migraines. It can bring on panic attacks. It can lead to heart attacks. Stress can kill.

WHEN PEOPLE USE SUBSTANCES AS A COPING MECHANISM FOR STRESS, EVENTUALLY THEIR STIMULI-RESPONSE PATTERN (I.E. STRESS = DRINK OR DRUG) BECOMES HARDWIRED INTO THEIR BRAINS AND THEIR LIFE.

Therefore, it is important to recognize and guard against these maladaptive patterns of behavior.

Some professions and activities can produce more stress than others. Law.com surveyed two hundred lawyers about substance abuse and mental health problems in large law firms and asked them to speculate about the causes. When asked to rank five possible causes for substance abuse and mental health problems in firms, the overwhelming majority of respondents (seventy-nine percent) cited stress and workload as the primary culprit.

According to the 2016 American Bar Association/Hazelden Betty Ford study on substance use and mental health disorders in the legal profession, the self-reported lifetime prevalence of depression among attorneys (forty-seven percent) is roughly two and a half times higher than in the general population (seventeen to twenty percent). This is due to the chronic stress in the profession as well as the lack of healthy coping skills to deal with stress.

According to the survey, the factor viewed as the next most likely cause of substance abuse and mental health problems in the legal profession is a reluctance to acknowledge or discuss the issue; followed by a lack of support for personal well-being, social and cultural influences and toxicity within the profession.

If depression in the legal profession is twice that of the general population, what is the prevalence of substance abuse, depression and mental illness among other high-stress professions like law enforcement, finance or politics, which have some of the same or similar influences?

Be alert to the relationship between stress, substance abuse and mental illness and seek treatment immediately if a problem develops.

FIND OPPORTUNITY
IN ADVERSITY

"The Chinese use two brush strokes to write the word
'crisis.' One brush stroke stands for danger; the other
for opportunity. In a crisis, be aware of the danger—
but recognize the opportunity."

—*John F. Kennedy, 35th President of the United States.*

We all encounter difficulties in life. Often these difficulties create or reveal opportunities. It may simply be the opportunity to learn from a mistake. It may be much more.

LOOK FOR THE UNIQUE OPPORTUNITIES
THAT ADVERSITY OFTEN CREATES.

Think of the gang member turned rapper, author, or consultant; the alcoholic turned counselor or motivational speaker; the scientist or entrepreneur whose early failures reveal the path to success; the entrepreneur whose failure in one area leads to success in another.

Always look for opportunities to grow and prosper in adversity. Learn to see problems as opportunities. When life gives you lemons, make lemonade.

NEVER QUIT

"You can never quit. Winners never quit and quitters never win."

—Ted Turner, founder of CNN.

Candidates in Navy SEAL training can quit at any time. Those who quit are required to go to the center of the training compound and ring a brass bell three times. On the first day of training, an instructor will tell the recruits that his goal is to push them to ring that bell but he'll also tell them, "If you quit, you will regret it for the rest of your life. Quitting never makes anything easier."

Airbnb went for four years, unable to secure more than a minimum of funding until it ultimately received over $100 million in funding. In 1997, when Steve Jobs returned to Apple, a share of Apple stock would barely buy you a cup of coffee. Thomas Edison is said to have failed 10,000 times before inventing the light bulb.

Edison famously said;

"I NEVER QUIT UNTIL I GET WHAT I WANT."

It was only after Abraham Lincoln had lost two runs for a senatorial seat that he ran for President of the United States—and won.

JUST BECAUSE YOU STOP DOING SOMETHING DOESN'T MEAN YOU'RE QUITTING.

Sometimes it takes vision and courage to know when something is not right—and to stop and walk away. Letting go doesn't mean you're giving up.

And stopping isn't always quitting; sometimes, it's a conscious choice that allows you to move in another, more promising, direction. Sometimes, it's the right choice. In our win-or-lose society, we reject quitting and celebrate perseverance. But life is more nuanced than that.

Isaac Newton failed miserably at being a farmer before he ultimately found a career in science. He wasn't good at farming but he was a genius at science.

If you're trying and failing, it may be that you're not trying hard enough or it may be that you just haven't tried the right thing yet.

DON'T GIVE UP ON YOURSELF OR YOUR GOALS JUST BECAUSE YOU'VE FAILED IN ONE AREA, OR EVEN SEVERAL AREAS.

Every time you try and fail, you learn something new. You learn more about yourself, about life and about your own strengths and weaknesses. You gain valuable insight and experience that can help you to succeed next time.

So keep trying. Try something different and don't let past failures keep you from your future success.

109

NEGATIVITY

"The world is full of a lot of fear and negativity,
and a lot of judgment. I think people need to start
shifting into joy and happiness."

—*Ellen DeGeneres, American comedian, television*
host, actress, writer and producer.

Humans have a tendency to be more negative than positive. It's evolutionary; it helps us to avoid danger and react more quickly to crisis. Our brains also function in a way that can reinforce negative thoughts. Our brains recognize patterns. As neuroscientists say, "neurons that fire together wire together." Having a negative thought makes it more likely that you will have another negative thought. Spending more time with negative people has the same effect as spending more time thinking negative thoughts.

In some instances, to avoid this evolutionary instinct requires conscious effort. Consciously try to limit your negative thoughts—not by ignoring them but by deemphasizing them and by trying to think more positive thoughts. Do your best to avoid negative people. I know; that's easier said than done. You may have family members or co-workers that are generally negative. If so, either try to help them by being positive when you're around them or minimize your interactions with them.

When we witness behavior, our brains mimic it. We share excitement at concerts and sadness at funerals. This process is called mirroring or empathy.

Negative thoughts trigger the release of the stress hormone cortisol. Elevated levels of cortisol have been shown to weaken your immune system, raise your blood pressure and increase your risk of heart disease, obesity and diabetes.

STUDIES HAVE ALSO SHOWN THAT PROLONGED EXPOSURE TO STRESS CAN ACTUALLY IMPAIR BRAIN DEVELOPMENT.

Gratitude can work in the opposite way. Having a positive thought makes it easier for you to have more positive thoughts. Spending more time with positive people will make you more positive.

TRY TO SURROUND YOURSELF WITH POSITIVE PEOPLE.

Find things that make you feel good—a warm bath, a child's smile, being outdoors, music, a massage, an embrace, the smell of lilacs—anything that makes you feel good. These things will help turn off the part of your brain that is wired for negativity and rewire your brain for positivity.

Notice your thoughts. Separate yourself from negative thoughts. When faced with bad news, imagine that your friend is the one who received the bad news. How would you advise them? Examine the news objectively rather than emotionally.

THINK OF YOUR NEGATIVE THOUGHTS AS JUST THAT— THOUGHTS. NOTHING MORE.

Don't try to avoid or suppress them. Acknowledge them and address them as you would any other transitory packet of sensory information. You might think, "Oh, there's that negative thought again. It's telling me to worry about being late for work." Instead of worrying, focus on getting to work, apologizing for being late and getting up earlier next time.

Take a deep breath. Controlled breathing can lower stress. Set reasonable goals. Turn problems into challenges or opportunities. Make positivity and gratitude a way of life. Wake up every morning thinking about who and what you are grateful for and how you can replace negativity with gratitude. Doing this as a ritual every morning will literally rewire your brain. It will make you more positive, happy and productive.

DRAMA QUEENS

Drama is a distraction and a waste of time.

Avoid drama queens—people who thrive on drama and chaos. They are emotional vampires and their narcissism and/or insecurity drives an insatiable need for attention. They don't advance others; they impede them.

There is only one place for drama—the theater. In all other areas of your life, avoid it.

FORGIVE

*"As I walked out the door toward the gate
that would lead to my freedom, I knew if
I didn't leave my bitterness and hatred
behind, I'd still be in prison."*

—*Nelson Mandela, revolutionary and former President of South Africa.*

Holding a grudge and harboring grievances is detrimental to your physical and mental well-being. It does nothing to move your life forward. It limits you by shifting your focus from the present (where it should be) to the past.

"IT IS ONE OF THE GREATEST GIFTS YOU CAN GIVE YOURSELF; TO FORGIVE. FORGIVE EVERYBODY."

—*Maya Angelou, American poet.*

Learn how to forgive and move on with your life. Focus on what matters today, not yesterday.

DON'T WORRY

"If something is wrong, fix it if you can. But train yourself not to worry: worry never fixes anything."

—*Ernest Hemingway, American writer.*

When worrying becomes excessive, it can lead to feelings of anxiety. It can adversely affect your health, your appetite and your sleep. It can affect your job performance and your relationships. It can create changes in lifestyle habits such as overeating, smoking, or using alcohol and drugs.

IF SOMETHING IS FIXABLE, FIX IT. IF IT IS NOT FIXABLE, ADAPT. IN EITHER CASE, WORRY NOT.

Sometimes we become so preoccupied with negative thoughts that we can suffer severe anxiety or even panic attacks. It can happen to anyone. Panic is most likely to occur when you feel that you have lost control. So stay in control.

Think of negative thoughts as nothing more than transitory packets of sensory information. Treat them as passing clouds on an otherwise sunny day.

Remain calm; nothing is as bad as it seems. Remember that all storms pass and worrying solves nothing. Relax, breathe deeply and let the storm pass.

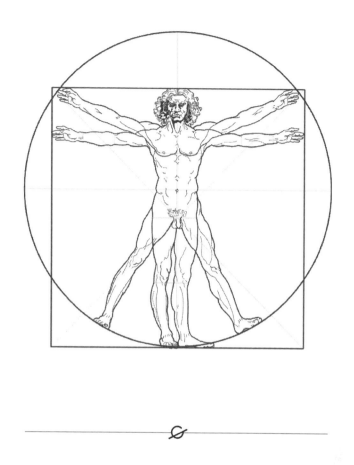

YOUR ONE AND ONLY LIFE

DISCOVER YOUR PURPOSE IN LIFE

"Not all those who wander are lost."

—J.R.R. Tolkien, English writer and poet.

G ive yourself time to discover your purpose in life. Your choices are as varied as the human personality.

Changes in access to capital, technology, media, manufacturing, publishing and distribution have created unprecedented opportunities for creativity, independence, mobility and prosperity.

Focus on your strengths and your passions.

TRY TO DO SOMETHING THAT INSPIRES YOUR DEDICATION AND COMMITMENT, SOMETHING THAT MAXIMIZES YOUR INNATE GIFTS AND BRINGS YOU HAPPINESS.

Try to do something that is meaningful to you. Consider doing something extraordinary. Think about issues that concern you, issues you care about, then think about how you can play a role in bringing about the change required to help resolve those issues.

Be thoughtful while you discover your own essential nature. Design your life as you would design a temple—one carefully laid and thoughtfully considered brick at a time.

IKIGAI

*In Japanese, ikigai is written by combining the symbol
for "life" with the symbol for "to be worthwhile."*

D an Buettner, author of *Blue Zones: Lessons on Living Longer from the
People Who've Lived the Longest,* suggests making three lists: your values,
things you like to do and things you are good at. The cross section of the three
lists is your ikigai. Western writers sometimes add a forth element—what you
can get paid for doing.

According to those born on Okinawa, the island with the most centenarians
in the world, our ikigai is the reason we get up in the morning.

**THEY BELIEVE THAT ONCE YOU DISCOVER YOUR IKIGAI,
PURSUING IT AND NURTURING IT EVERY DAY WILL
BRING MEANING TO YOUR LIFE.**

"Older people are celebrated in Japan; they feel obligated to pass on their
wisdom to younger generations," Buettner says. This gives them a purpose in
life, in service to their communities.

"Japanese workers are driven by being useful to others, being thanked
and being esteemed by their colleagues," says Toshimitsu Sowa, CEO of HR
consulting firm Jinzai Kenkyusho.

Research by Wharton management professor Adam Grant suggests that
"doing work that affects the well-being of others" and to "see or meet the
people affected by their work" is what motivates many employees.

In one experiment, cold callers at the University of Michigan who spent
time with a recipient of the scholarship they were trying to raise money for

brought in 171 percent more money when compared with those who were merely working the phone. The simple act of meeting the student beneficiary provided meaning to the fundraisers and boosted their performance.

Ikigai is the feeling that your work makes a difference in people's lives.

115

PHILOTIMO

*The word philotimo comes from the
Greek root words "filos," meaning friend
and "timi," meaning honor.*

Vassilios P. Vertoudakis, a lecturer in ancient Greek philology at the National and Kapodistrian University of Athens, told the BBC, "Philotimo describes virtues that include honor, dignity, pride and the ideal actions and behaviors, hospitality and warmth received by another."

Philotimo, at its core, is about goodness, selflessness, giving without wanting anything in return and the force that drives individuals to think about the people and the world around them. It is an all-encompassing concept that gives meaning to life and stretches well beyond ourselves.

The Greeks have always believed that your behaviors are not only a reflection of yourself but also a reflection of your family, your community and your country. Plutarch, the ancient Greek biographer, said, "Lovers are the greatest fighters because they avoid by all means to appear to their beloved ones as cowards or as anything inferior and unworthy of their expectations." This is philotimo at work.

When one takes pride in what they do simply because they have chosen to do it; when they help others simply because they need help; when they try to do the right thing because they believe that they have a duty to do so, expecting nothing in return; this is philotimo. Today, people rarely do things for others without expecting something in return. The virtue of personal sacrifice has become increasingly rare.

Philotimo is a concept that strengthens the bonds between people. It is a concept that has united the Greek community for thousands of years in a way that no law or government ever could. "Greek communities were imbued with philotimo, which was triggered not by law and logic but intense emotion and some degree of intimacy," Vertoudakis told the BBC.

For Greeks, philotimo is much more than a virtuous way of life. It means love of honor, love of family and community, a sense of belonging, a sense of obligation, doing the right thing, dignity and respect. Yet even mentioning all these nuances still falls short of capturing the essence of philotimo.

President Barack Obama, referred to philotimo as;

"THE QUINTESSENTIAL SENSE OF RIGHT AND WRONG AND THE DUTY TO DO WHAT'S RIGHT."

No one has been able to provide a complete definition of philotimo—a word that many believe has no precise definition. But the Greeks don't need one; they know it when they see it.

Integrating philotimo into your life, however broadly you define it, can only strengthen you. A life guided by the principles of philotimo is a life of purpose, contribution and meaning—a life worth living.

DHARMA

*Much more than finding work you love, it means finding
work that will be supported by your innate gifts.*

D harma is a central concept shared by many religions on the Indian
subcontinent including Hinduism, Buddhism, Jainism and Sikhism; as
well as in the Indo-Iranian faith of Zoroastrianism.

In Hinduism, your calling or the thing you were meant to do that is closest
to your essential nature is called your dharma. In Buddhism, dharma is ideal
truth.

It means adopting behaviors that are in accordance with the order that
makes life and the universe possible.

You only have one life and you alone have the power to design it. If possible,
try to discover something you love and try to do it well. Try to do something
that inspires your dedication and commitment.

**TRY TO DO SOMETHING THAT MAXIMIZES YOUR
INNATE GIFTS AND BRINGS YOU HAPPINESS.**

Try to do something that is meaningful to you.

If you are truly passionate about your work, it will never seem like work. You
will wake up every morning excited to meet the challenges and opportunities
your work presents. When you do something that you love, it doesn't feel like
work. It becomes something you actually crave.

Most people work for a living. Some take any job that will pay the bills and
believe they have no other choice. For some people, that may be true. Some

people may have more limited choices than others. But if you're reading this book, that's probably not true for you.

Individuals who have the capacity and desire to read a book on self-improvement have the potential to find work that they love, work that they are passionate about and work that allows them to lead happy, successful and meaningful lives.

You have many choices. Be thoughtful while you discover your own essential nature, your own truth. Choose wisely.

STRENGTHS AND WEAKNESSES

*Self-examination and reflection are important
because we all need to take inventory of ourselves to
determine our strengths and weaknesses.*

This is an important concept that many people fail to understand or fully appreciate. From childhood, we are placed in an education system that rewards conformity. We are given standardized tests and graded on a standardized curve. We seldom explore, let alone value or leverage, a child's unique gifts. It's like taking a fish and a bird and expecting them both to thrive in the same environment. We need an education system that values and leverages a child's unique strengths while mitigating their weaknesses.

KNOWING, UNDERSTANDING AND LEVERAGING YOUR UNIQUE STRENGTHS WHILE MITIGATING YOUR WEAKNESSES IS A KEY TO SUCCESS.

Once you understand your strengths, you can seek out opportunities that allow you to leverage those strengths. Understanding your weaknesses will allow you to mitigate those weaknesses by focusing on areas in need of improvement.

People are unique. We all have distinct strengths and weaknesses. Know and understand yours and use them to your maximum advantage.

DESIGNING YOUR FUTURE

*The first step in designing your future
is self-examination.*

In considering your employment and career options, you first need to ask what's important to you. Is it gaining wealth, status, position, or power? Is it acquiring recognition or fame? Is it to please, satisfy, or impress someone other than yourself—perhaps your family, a spouse or a love interest, classmates, colleagues or friends; or the views of society in general? Is it having more time for your family, the flexibility to work from home, the ability to get time off for travel? Is it having a real passion for your work, doing something you love, a desire to learn, or a desire to help others?

BEGIN YOUR ANALYSIS BY EXAMINING AND UNDERSTANDING YOUR MOTIVATIONS AND ESTABLISHING YOUR PRIORITIES.

The next thing to consider is what are the critical tasks or key responsibilities of a given job or career that you are considering. What skills will be required to excel at those tasks and successfully discharge those responsibilities?

Next, ask yourself what specific skills you have that will allow you to succeed in performing the tasks that will likely be expected of you. What are your strengths (existing skills that will help you excel in a position) and what are your weaknesses (required skills that you lack)?

If you lack the skills required to succeed in a specific job or profession, then pursuing that job or profession at this time is probably a poor choice. There is no point in pursuing a job, trade, or career when you lack the basic skills required to succeed. A better decision would be to take a step back and acquire, at minimum, the core skills required to succeed before attempting to secure such a position or simply choose a job, trade, or career that is more aligned with your existing skillset.

You don't need to have perfected the skills required for a given position before seeking out that position. Your skills can and will develop on the job. But you should, at minimum, have a strong aptitude and preferably above average competency, with regard to the skillset required for the position, prior to seeking the position.

Below is a list of skills that are commonly required in order to excel at various jobs and professions. Rank yourself, on a scale of one to ten (with one as the lowest and ten as the highest), on each of the below skills. Then identify the skills that you believe will be required to excel at a given position. Do some research to confirm your assumptions concerning what skills are likely to be required of a given position.

WHEN YOU FIND A MATCH BETWEEN YOUR SKILLSET AND THE SKILLS REQUIRED OF A GIVEN POSITION, YOU WILL HAVE IDENTIFIED A JOB, TRADE, OR CAREER, WHERE YOU ARE LIKELY TO FIND SUCCESS.

This is important because you are far more likely to be happy in a job or profession where you can and will excel than in one where you lack the basic skillset required to excel.

Proficiency in one or more of the below skills is typically required of most jobs and professions. The exact skillset required will depend on the position.

How would you rank yourself on the following skills?

☐ Leadership	☐ Financial	☐ Social
☐ Judgement	☐ Accounting	☐ Marketing
☐ Organizational	☐ Mathematical	☐ Creative
☐ Management	☐ Observational	☐ Graphic
☐ Strategic	☐ Listening	☐ Design
☐ Motivational	☐ Negotiating	☐ Computer
☐ Relationship	☐ Dispute-resolution	☐ Sales
☐ Communication	☐ Analytical	☐ Physical ability
☐ Teaching	☐ Writing	☐ Language
☐ Coaching	☐ Public speaking	☐ Technology
☐ Delegation	☐ Social media	☐ Technical
☐ Supervision	☐ Networking	☐ Typing

After assessing your skillset, consider the skills required of various positions and then decide where you are most likely to find success. Then consider how those positions might meet your overall goals, priorities and objectives. This should allow you to narrow down the choices that are most likely to lead to a happy, successful and meaningful life.

Finally, consider other intangible issues such as how you feel about the people you would be working with, how you and your family feel about the city you would be working in and what level of compensation and benefits come with the position. Are you motivated and excited about the position? Do you have a real passion for the work, the mission of the company and the overall opportunity? Based on these considerations, you should be able to make a good, well-informed decision.

THE MAPP CAREER TEST

The MAPP career test is a comprehensive online career test. More than seven million people in nearly every country in the world have taken the MAPP test since its inception in 1995.

The fifteen-minute MAPP test is comprised of seventy-one different triads. You simply choose which one you would most prefer and least prefer, with one left blank. Since there are so many different combinations of answers, there are literally more than a trillion different possible test results—more than there are people in the world.

More than thirty-five hundred affinity partners—including career counselors, outplacement firms and school psychologists—use the MAPP test to gain insights and counsel their current and prospective students and clients.

After completing the test, you can see your results immediately. A MAPP package, which is available at various price points, can help you find your ideal career. Your personal test results are scored against nine hundred jobs and you can see what jobs are the best fit, along with the education needed, career outlook and real job openings.

HOW ARE YOU PERCEIVED?

*Everything you do or say affects
the way you are perceived.*

How you dress, your grooming, your posture, your hygiene, your breath, your eye contact, your demeanor, your attitude, your handshake, your table manners, how you speak, your phone manners, the format of your resume, the way you phrase a letter, your presence on social media and your views on social and political issues—all affect the impression you make on others.

Think about how you may be perceived by others and about how you want to be perceived. Then work with patience, humility and dedication toward meriting the perception that you want and believe you deserve.

Social media is an amazing tool for reaching new audiences and building influence. However, it can also be a liability. Social media can strengthen or weaken a reputation.

THINK TWICE BEFORE POSTING ANYTHING.
USE COMMON SENSE AND GOOD JUDGEMENT.

Read over that tweet or post a second time to make sure it's something you want to post.

If you have any doubts about something you're about to post, give yourself time to think it over and consider if it's still a good idea. Don't rush to post. Post slowly and deliberately.

Platforms like Facebook, Instagram, Twitter and LinkedIn have democratized media. They have given the individual the potential for significant influence. Facebook has over two billion users. Cristiano Ronaldo, a Portuguese footballer, is the most followed individual on Instagram with more than 160 million followers. These statistics are mind boggling.

These platforms have the potential to change governments. They already have, by swiftly spreading revolutions in what came to be known as the Arab Spring.

SOCIAL PLATFORMS REPRESENT THE FIRST WAVE OF THE TECHNOLOGICAL REVOLUTION AND YOU HAVE THE POWER TO USE THEM.

What will you use them for? To post nonsense or trash, to advance your objectives, to help others, or to change society for the better? How you answer that question will influence how you are perceived—and rightly so.

People have different views. Don't be afraid to express yours. Be thoughtful in doing so, have good intentions and be respectful. Speak the truth and others who share your views and beliefs and find value in what you have to share, will follow.

YOUR OPPORTUNITIES
ARE UNLIMITED

OPPORTUNITY

Opportunity comes to all of us in one form or another.
Unfortunately, we don't always recognize it,
we aren't always ready for it and we don't
always take advantage of it.

Opportunity is rarely patient. It doesn't normally announce itself and it sometimes comes disguised as misfortune. We often find opportunity in the most unlikely places. It can come from the most unlikely sources and appear when you least expect it.

YOU NEED TO LOOK FOR OPPORTUNITY AND RECOGNIZE IT WHEN IT DOES APPEAR. AND YOU NEED TO BE PREPARED TO SEIZE IT AND MAKE THE MOST OF IT WHEN IT DOES COME.

The 21st Century is the first century in human history that allows individuals to leverage their connections to other individuals via the internet. This generation has the ability to create careers and businesses that have never existed before.

YOUR OPPORTUNITIES ARE ENDLESS.

Make the most of those opportunities by being prepared for them, by looking for them, by recognizing them when they appear and by embracing them.

Certain traits and behaviors attract opportunity. Openness, authenticity, flexibility, tolerance, adaptability, extroversion, integrity, courage, commitment, creativity, gratitude, collaboration and compassion—all attract opportunity.

Other traits and behaviors reduce opportunity. Negativity, inauthenticity, inflexibility, rigidity, introversion, dishonesty, fear, ingratitude, selfishness, self-centeredness and greed all reduce opportunity.

THE VALUE OF WORK

*"Far and away the best prize that life has to offer
is the chance to work hard at work worth doing."*

—*Theodore Roosevelt, 26th President of the United States.*

The work that you choose to do over the course of your life will profoundly impact your quality of life. Work is essential because it provides us with money which influences our ability to access virtually all essential goods and services.

Work impacts our physical, social and mental well-being, facilitates social integration and influences virtually all our relationships. It gives us purpose, self-respect and the chance to make a contribution to our family and society.

Conversely, unemployment, a lack of work, or work that we find unfulfilling robs us of these opportunities which can lead to frustration and despair.

In a society that equates personal success with wealth and status, loss of work and low-paying work relegate individuals to the margins of society. This can have a devastating effect on an individual's self-image and self-esteem.

When considering what work to do, try to be thoughtful and selective.

**WHENEVER POSSIBLE, LOOK FOR JOBS THAT KEEP YOU
MOTIVATED, ENGAGED AND COMMITTED.**

This is the kind of work at which you are more likely to excel. Look for jobs or careers that you enjoy, that leverage your innate talents and that allow you to realize your goals and aspirations.

THE BEST POSSIBLE WORK IS WORK THAT YOU LOVE.

Look for jobs, careers and/or business that allow you to make a meaningful contribution to yourself, your family, your employer, your co-workers, your partners and society as a whole. This alone will allow you to lead a more meaningful life.

Whenever possible, try to find work that you love, work that is consistent with your values and work that allows you to generate the income you desire.

123

CROWDFUNDING

In the past, you had to know someone
with money to have access to investor capital.
Today, that's no longer true. This represents a sea
change in personal empowerment.

Companies like Kickstarter, Indiegogo and GoFundMe allow aspiring entrepreneurs to crowdsource and crowdfund new business models and ideas online. Browse any of these sites to see the thousands of entrepreneurs who are starting innovative new businesses.

Unlike one-time campaigns on sites like Kickstarter, Indiegogo and GoFundMe, the crowdfunding website and app Patreon allows people to pay monthly subscriptions to support their favorite artists, painters, podcasters, dancers, singers, photographers, writers and game designers. Patreon announced that it expects to process more than $500 million in payments to the artists and creators on its platform in 2019.

Fans, or "Patreons," get to support artists and causes they deem worthy. They may get exclusive access to artists for Q&A sessions, invitations to private exhibitions, or early previews of their work. Artists and creators get a steady and predictable stream of income to support their work.

Patreons sign up for tiers of support ranging from one dollar to ten dollars, plus more for special perks. Some Patreon artists make more than thirty thousand dollars per month. Patreon takes ten percent of each pledge. The site is in English and only accepts United States dollars yet forty percent of Patreons are outside the United States.

You now have the ability to connect with complete strangers over the internet who may have an interest and an ability to invest in your business. That's an incredibly empowering development.

TODAY, SUCCESS HAS LESS TO DO WITH WHO YOU ARE OR WHO YOU KNOW AND MORE TO DO WITH THE QUALITY OF YOUR IDEAS.

Some of the most significant barriers to entry that once stood in the way of the average person's success have been eliminated and replaced by new opportunities. Increased access to capital is one of the most important of these new opportunities. Take advantage of your increased access to capital by creating your own business. You do that by creating and offering others something of value; something that enriches their life. When you can deliver true value, at a profit, you have a business.

BECOMING AN ONLINE SENSATION

There are currently more than one billion smartphone users. Apps like Periscope and Meerkat are being used to create live videos that are quickly and easily broadcast on Twitter, Facebook and YouTube.

YouTube is the world's second-largest search engine. It draws millions of viewers who watch creative videos showing everything you can imagine. Advertisers and sponsors want to capture those viewers. Google bought YouTube in 2006 and holds regular workshops for promising YouTubers to help them create content and grow their brands.

The deal is; you generate original content and get half of the ad revenues your videos attract. The bigger the audience you build, the more money you stand to make.

THE KEY IS TO ADD VALUE.

A simple video offering solutions for common storage issues became the most popular Facebook video of all time. My first book, *Seize Your Destiny,* available on Amazon, provides more detailed information on becoming an online sensation. If this is something that interests you, you should read it.

GOOGLE'S TOP SEVEN SKILLS

*In 2013, Google decided to test
its hiring hypothesis.*

Project Oxygen looked at hiring, firing and promotion data accumulated since the company's founding in 1998. The results surprised everyone by concluding that, among the eight most important qualities of Google's top employees, STEM expertise comes in dead last.

THE SEVEN TOP CHARACTERISTICS OF SUCCESS AT GOOGLE ARE ALL SOFT SKILLS.

They are:

1. Being a good coach
2. Communicating and listening well
3. Possessing insights into others
   (including others' different values and points of view)
4. Having empathy toward and being supportive of one's colleagues
5. Being a good critical thinker
6. Being a good problem solver
7. Being able to make connections across complex ideas

These are some of the most important 21st Century skills.

DIGITAL NOMADS

Wandering the globe while doing
internet-enabled work is now a common
fantasy among traditional workers.

R esearch by MBO Partners and Emergent Research, found that 4.8 million Americans described themselves as digital nomads. Among traditional American workers, twenty-seven percent said they might become digital nomads in the next two to three years and eleven percent said they planned to.

The report points out that, "Most of these people will not become digital nomads. Instead, they will continue to be what we call armchair digital nomads—those who follow the exploits of others instead of becoming digital nomads themselves."

Nonetheless, the researchers concluded, "this data shows the extent of the interest in this work and lifestyle. It also shows that the number of digital nomads will likely grow substantially over the next few years."

One thing that unites digital nomads—as their name implies—is their reliance on technology. They can work whenever and wherever they want, thanks to the internet and a proliferation of cloud-based tools. The growth of supportive services such as shared working spaces, online talent marketplaces and job sites, digital nomad tour services and online information sites such as Nomad List (which offers data on the cost of living in various locales) have helped the movement grow.

Many are freelancers in creative-class jobs like writers and designers, marketing and communications professionals, IT professionals and ecommerce pros. Others may supplement their digital work with more traditional jobs.

DIGITAL NOMADS ARE LEADING THE SHIFT TO MOBILE AND DISTRIBUTED WORK.

The report notes, "Workers in general are increasingly working remotely and spending more of their time away from the office. It's important to recognize that the way we work is changing and that remote, dispersed work, including digital nomadism, will only continue to grow in the future."

#Vanlife is a lifestyle hashtag that has come to signify the digital nomad lifestyle. It's both a mentality and a movement. Using the hashtag has enabled people to leverage their travels into a sponsored product.

There are now professional "vanlifers" who get sponsors to underwrite their travels, which are then played out on social media. Vanlifers get paid to post sponsored images on Instagram (on behalf of companies whose products they use on their trips) and tag their sponsors who benefit from the exposure to the vanlifer's followers.

Sponsors include companies like Kettle Brand potato chips, Clif Bars and Synergy Organic Clothing.

One vanlife couple, traveling under @WheresMyOfficeNow, has over one hundred eighty thousand Instagram followers and a dozen corporate sponsors. Even Volkswagen and Nissan have announced new vans aimed at vanlifers.

Their income is all over the map. Among them, thirty-eight percent report earning less than ten thousand dollars per year from this work but sixteen percent—or about seven hundred and ninety thousand vanlifers—say they earn seventy-five thousand dollars a year or more.

The trend shows no signs of slowing down with more and more people valuing this lifestyle and companies offering increased flexibility to attract and retain workers.

eSPORTS

*eSports have been around for the past decade but
have recently exploded in popularity.*

e Sports organizations typically fund multiple teams for a variety of games. They normally pay for player amenities such as housing, food, utilities, coaches and trainers as well as the team's gaming computers and peripherals.

Organizations have agreements with different leagues to share media rights and generate sponsorships. eSports teams partner with sponsors that advertise on player jerseys or through digital media. Teams produce content that features those products and services and this content is distributed through streaming communities such as Twitch. This creates substantial revenue. Teams also generate prize money and additional revenue from the sale of merchandise such as hats and t-shirts.

eSports salaries vary by teams and players. According to the professional eSports organization Riot, each team in the League of Legends Championship Series receives a designated amount of money to provide salaries and help with operating expenses; and each player must be paid a minimum of $12,500 for the twenty-eight-match season. A select group of highly successful players receive much greater compensation.

In addition to basic compensation, teams and players can earn additional money by winning or placing in competitions. Below is an example of recent team and player earnings for one of the top teams - Team Liquid.

Team Liquid 2018:

Total Prize Money Earned: $18,231,389.11
Total Tournaments Played: 1,130

Top Games:

- *Dota 2* (Prize Money Earned: $14,258,294)
- *StarCraft II* (Prize Money Earned: $1,268,979)
- *Counter-Strike: Global Offensive* (Prize Money Earned: $949,121)

Top Earning Players:

- Kuro Takhasomi aka KuroKy (Prize Money Earned: $2,831,532)
- Ivan Ivanov aka MinD_ContRoL (Prize Money Earned: $2,816,032)
- Lasse Urpalainen aka Matumbaman (Prize Money Earned: $2,811,532)

These figures are in no way representative of average earnings. These are the earnings of those at the top of their game and, like any professional sport, reaching that pinnacle of performance is not easily achieved. It requires a level of talent and an intensity of dedication that few can or will ever achieve. Yet for some, it is clearly possible.

128

FAB LABS

In 2018, there were over
one thousand two hundred fab labs worldwide.

A fab lab is essentially a room full of computer-guided fabrication tools like lasers, cutters, mills for carving materials and 3-D printers that allow people to create things with a precision normally reserved to large companies.

In the book *Designing Reality*, Neil Gershenfeld, an MIT professor who created the first fab lab in 2003, describes a world where fab labs will become ubiquitous. Big fabrication firms may be a thing of the past, perhaps making a shift to selling designs and raw materials. Products made at fab labs may eventually be made from locally sourced raw materials that have been recycled from used and discarded products.

In the not-too-distant future, rather than go to a large fabrication facility to create a prototype for your new invention, spare parts for your car, or replacement parts for your dishwasher, you may use your own computer-guided fabrication tools and/or those of your neighbors, using recycled materials from your local community.

This emerging area; along with other innovative resources like crowd-funding, co-work spaces and social media platforms; creates amazing opportunities for enterprising entrepreneurs.

ISSUES THAT MATTER

129

PUBLIC CORRUPTION

*"Power tends to corrupt and
absolute power corrupts absolutely."*

—*John Acton, English historian, politician and writer.*

James Wolfensohn, the former chairman of the World Bank, warned in his farewell speech to the bank two decades ago that the problem that disturbed him the most when contemplating the future of the world economy was corruption.

We often hear of large capital outflows from countries like Russia that go into offshore banking centers that act as money launderers. We've also seen the rapid rise in crypto currencies that facilitate such transfers.

Leaders like Putin, Xi, Mugabe, Chavez and Maduro have ignored, modified, or circumvented their own constitutions in order to enrich and entrench themselves at the expense of those they claim to represent. Billions of dollars in oil money are unaccounted for in Russia, Venezuela, Brazil, Nigeria and a number of Middle Eastern nations. These national resources are not optimally allocated for the benefit of society as a whole. They are simply stolen by the ruling elite.

Public corruption in the United States is no better. The cost per mile to extend the New York Second Avenue subway was four times the cost per mile to construct the new Cross-Rail Underground in London. Why? Why must contractors in New York pay thirty percent more for concrete than anywhere else? The answer is unethical and/or illegal agreements between construction contractors, public sector unions, criminal organizations and government agencies. The costs of these practices to consumers is not only higher construction costs, but also significant and often even more costly delays, some that can last for decades.

Elected officials are rarely held accountable for such corruption. Other forms of corruption are explained away as policy ignorance on the part of our legislators.

One of the greatest economic problems confronting the United States today is the problem of unfunded entitlements—benefits which, having been granted, can never be retracted. This is true for the federal government and for state and local governments, many of which are or could be facing bankruptcy due to their inability to fund these ever-increasing deficits.

When officials are asked how this could happen, the most frequent explanation is;

"WE DIDN'T REALIZE HOW BAD THE SITUATION WAS."

This is either a lie or evidence of gross negligence. Many have been shouting warnings for more than forty years.

The reality is that legislators bought votes from the public by promising ever-increasing benefits that succeeding generations can never afford to pay. In doing so, they created unfunded pensions and liabilities whose present value is around eighty trillion dollars, or four times the nation's current twenty-one-trillion-dollar Treasury debt.

"WHAT PEOPLE FAIL TO APPRECIATE IS THAT THE CURRENCY OF CORRUPTION IN ELECTED OFFICE IS NOT MONEY, BUT VOTES."

—James L. Buckley, American jurist, politician and author.

The public treasury, and with it our future economic security, has been traded for votes. This has been happening for decades, if not centuries, and it's continuing at our collective expense.

There is also the discrepancy in retirement benefits paid to government workers versus private sector workers. The benefit increases that public sector employees enjoy has risen at three times the rate of those in the private sector. The benefit packages for members of the United States Congress are even worse. They receive lavish lifetime retirement benefits, including very low-cost comprehensive healthcare coverage, not to mention exemption from regular

FICA taxes. For decades, we have acquiesced to this outright theft from the public treasury.

What we have been allowing to happen is nothing short of the wholesale mortgaging of our future and our children's future by corrupt and/or incompetent politicians.

"THE MORE YOU OBSERVE POLITICS, THE MORE YOU HAVE TO ADMIT THAT EACH PARTY IS WORSE THAN THE OTHER."

—Will Rogers, American humorist, newspaper columnist and social commentator.

Democratic politicians buy votes by approving public sector pension and retirement packages that are unsustainable and by promising their constituents entitlements that require ever increasing taxation. While Republicans allow their contributors to strip the nation of its natural resources by allowing unrestricted environmental exploitation. In both cases, these concessions are traded for financial contributions and political support. And in both cases, this is outright fraud. No political party should be allowed to use the public treasury to solicit or secure votes. And no political party should be allowed to mortgage our children's future to get elected.

Politicians who engage in these activities need to be held accountable and restrained.

"THE WORST DISEASE IN THE WORLD TODAY IS CORRUPTION. AND THERE IS A CURE: TRANSPARENCY."

—Bono, Irish singer-songwriter and philanthropist.

Millennial Samurai will need to address the issue of public corruption by making structural changes to our political system, that promote greater transparency and accountability.

ECONOMIC INEQUALITY

*America is experiencing the biggest income
and wealth disparity in nearly 100 years.*

S even of the richest men in America are among the ten richest people in the
world. Bill Gates, Warren Buffett and Mark Zuckerberg now control more
wealth than the bottom 150 million Americans.

Nearly half of men ages 18-34 now live with their parents—the highest
level since the Great Depression. Seventy eight percent of the United States
population now lives paycheck to paycheck with essentially zero savings.

In 2018, according to the Federal Reserve Bank of New York, a record
number of Americans—seven million—were ninety days or more behind on
their auto loans. This is a troubling statistic. Auto loan payments, like rent, are
usually prioritized. People need their cars to get to work and people can sleep
in their cars if necessary.

America has historically experienced rising wages; it was the foundation
of the middle class. For millions of Americans, life got better with each year
as the value of their wages increased and our economy grew. This is no longer
happening. The middle class is disappearing. For most Americans, real wages
have been stagnant or falling for decades.

LOW INCOME EARNERS NOW MAKE LESS
IN REAL TERMS THAN THEY DID IN 1980.

And middle income earners make just six percent more than they made
then, in real terms. Instead of earning more over time, people are actually
earning less in terms of what their wages can actually buy.

Investments in financial assets have dramatically increased the wealth and incomes of the wealthiest Americans while average Americans are worse off than they were decades ago. Many blame private equity. Since 2008, private equity has quintupled to five trillion dollars. Diane Standaert of the Center for Responsible Lending says, "Their superpower is their obscurity."

Private equity firms borrow heavily to buy companies. They then often sell off company assets or cut jobs, to generate the cash required to repay the loans and pay shareholder dividends to investors. Workers are typically harmed by these actions.

At Toys "R" Us, thirty thousand workers lost their jobs in 2018. Many had worked at the company for years. Sears, Radio Shack and Claire's were all gutted by private equity in the same year.

Life is hard for millions of Americans. Most people are forced to borrow just to keep up. Historically, the average American had very little debt outside of a mortgage on their first home. But after almost forty years of declining real wages, Americans now have to go into serious debt for just about everything they buy.

AMERICANS NOW HAVE NEARLY THIRTEEN TRILLION DOLLARS IN TOTAL DEBT.

More than one and a half trillion dollars in college debt, over one trillion dollars in credit card debt, and more than one trillion dollars in auto loan debt—all record highs. The debt load for the working poor has nearly quadrupled in the past twenty years as a percentage of their income.

AND MOST OF THIS DEBT WILL NEVER BE REPAID.

We now have the highest-ever percentage of people on food stamps—double the historical rate. In some states, nearly ten percent of working age adults receive disability payments. From 1973 to 2016, net productivity rose 73.7 percent while hourly wages essentially stagnated—increasing only 12.5 percent over forty three years.

AMERICANS ARE WORKING MORE PRODUCTIVELY THAN EVER WHILE THE FRUITS OF THEIR LABOR HAVE ACCRUED TO CORPORATE OFFICERS, DIRECTORS AND THEIR SHAREHOLDERS.

Even though there's been an enormous amount of wealth created by our economy, life for average Americans hasn't improved. The average worker has gotten poorer while the cost of just about everything has gone up.

Moreover, no matter how big the gains in productivity have been, the government and the Federal Reserve have continuously created more money. They've done it by creating new credit and by simply printing trillions of new dollars out of thin air.

This new money has caused prices to rise more than productivity. Because wages are no longer connected to gains in productivity, there's nothing the average American can do to stay ahead of inflation. So, most Americans have been forced to borrow—in a way that is unprecedented in our history. For those who have taken on these incredible new debt loads, life is very stressful.

THIS GROUP IS GROWING
AND THIS STRESS AND ANGER IS BUILDING...
ULTIMATELY FUELING MANY OF TODAY'S BIGGEST ISSUES.

We've seen protests all over the country. Groups like Antifa, the New Black Panthers and White Supremacists are on the rise. We've seen NFL players refusing to stand for the national anthem. Mass shootings are occurring with alarming and unprecedented frequency. This isn't just about race, Donald Trump, or police brutality.

IT'S ABOUT MONEY, UNEMPLOYMENT,
FRUSTRATION AND HOPELESSNESS.

Tens of millions of people in America are desperate. They have no way out. Deaths by drugs and suicide, for the bottom sixty percent of America's population, have doubled since 2000. Sooner or later, this hopelessness and despair is going to find an outlet - quite possibly a violent one.

Millions of Americans are already calling for the government to "do something." Some are calling for a "universal basic income."

Democratic Presidential candidate United States Senator Elizabeth Warren, is proposing a new annual tax on assets of the seventy-five thousand wealthiest Americans. She has proposed a 2% tax on assets above fifty million and an additional 1% "billionaire surtax" on households with a net worth exceeding one billion.

Jeffrey Sachs, a professor of sustainable development at Columbia University, proposes a single-payer healthcare system modeled on countries like Canada and Australia, overhauling the economics of higher education, better school-to-work transition programs, a wealth tax and an infrastructure program that would increase employment and training opportunities for workers.

Others are calling for a clean slate; to wipe out their debts. The idea of erasing debts to reset the financial system is not new. In fact, in the Bible, it's referred to as a "Jubilee." If you're unfamiliar with the term, it comes from The Old Testament, the Book of Leviticus, Chapter 25. Pope Boniface VIII proclaimed the first Christian Jubilee in 1300. Since then, it's been used dozens of times when anger among a population hits extreme levels.

Carla Reinhart of Harvard University and Stephen Roach of Yale have already advocated for a debt Jubilee in the United States.

London School of Economics Professor David Graeber, says, "we are long overdue for some kind of biblical-style Jubilee... it would relieve so much genuine human suffering."

Paul Kedrosky, a senior fellow at the Kaufman Foundation (a liberal think tank), says, "we need a fresh start and we need it now... we need... a Jubilee."

A JUBILEE, WHICH WIPES THE SLATE CLEAN FOR MILLIONS OF THE MOST INDEBTED AMERICANS AND "RESETS" THE FINANCIAL SYSTEM, MAY BECOME THE LEADING POLITICAL ISSUE IN YEARS TO COME.

Iceland used a Jubilee in 2014 to restructure mortgages that were under water. Croatia used a Jubilee in 2015 to wipe out millions in consumer debt. The idea of a debt Jubilee has become the de facto solution when debts can't be paid. President Trump even suggested a debt Jubilee for all of Puerto Rico's bond debt after Hurricane Maria.

In 1841, the laws in America were temporarily changed so that debtors could be discharged of their debts - without the consent of their creditors.

It must be understood that a Jubilee does not come without cost. It would redistribute trillions of dollars from those who have invested and saved to those who can no longer pay their debts. The stock market would experience huge losses. Some banks would close. Many companies would go bankrupt. Millions would lose their savings overnight.

And while the cost of a Jubilee would be high, it must be understood that inaction also has a cost. Barbara Ehrenreich, who wrote *Nickel and Dimed: On (Not) Getting By in America*, is concerned by what she sees; the street protests and the increased anger toward immigrants. She says;

"PEOPLE DON'T ALWAYS ACT RATIONALLY WHEN THEY SEE THEIR OWN LIFE CHANCES DIMINISHING."

Millennials are now our country's largest generation (eighty five million), outnumbering Baby Boomers (eighty million). They will have an enormous stake in whether or not a national debt Jubilee is declared. According to a recent Harvard study, more than fifty percent of Millennials do not believe in capitalism. How they address the issue of income inequality will have significant and lasting consequences for the global economy. Those who emerge as Millennial Samurai will play an important role in this debate.

131

STUDENT DEBT

*Millennials face the greatest student debt crisis ever
faced by any generation.*

S tudent debt now exceeds all credit card debt. No other generation has had the level of debt that Millennials now have and Millennials have even less opportunity to retire that debt than any prior generation due to stagnating wages and inflation.

A thirty-year-old today makes no more money than a thirty-year-old did thirty years ago. Unfortunately, prices have continued to increase during those thirty years so the same salary buys far less. Rent, in some instances, is ten times higher than it was thirty years ago.

Finally, forty-five percent of Millennials get out of college, burdened by that crushing debt, only to learn that they can't get jobs that require a college degree. So where does that leave them? They've taken on massive debt that they can't pay off for a degree that doesn't enhance their earning capacity.

Essentially, Millennials have been screwed by a for-profit educational system that prior generations created. It served those prior generations well but the same cannot be said for Millennials. Add to that the depressing reality that our educational system was designed for the industrial revolution and is ill-suited to the technological revolution and you have a recipe for failure.

This crushing debt prohibits many Millennials from saving money for retirement, to buy a home, or to start a business. This has never happened before on such a large scale. Ultimately, as this situation becomes increasingly untenable, we will likely see more and more calls for student debt forgiveness. Something needs to change.

THE CURRENT FOR-PROFIT EDUCATION SYSTEM ISN'T SERVING US WELL.

Certain services should not operate exclusively under a for-profit model. Education is one of those services. Healthcare is another. These are necessities of life that have an enormous impact not only on quality of life but on society as a whole. New solutions need to be developed to provide these essential services to more people at lower costs.

Student debt may be one of the first issues addressed by Millennial Samurai since it affects their generation most directly. How they address it will impact all of us.

132

MODERN MONETARY THEORY

*If you haven't heard about Modern Monetary Theory
(MMT), you will. It's the economic theory du jour
and it will be all over the news in the months to
come—leading up to the 2020 election.*

H arvard economist John Kenneth Galbraith once said;

**"THE ONLY FUNCTION OF ECONOMIC FORECASTING IS
TO MAKE ASTROLOGY LOOK RESPECTABLE."**

MMT is a new way of looking at the economy. It's very seductive (everyone gets a job) and very different from conventional economic theory.

Most economists believe that macroeconomic policy should stabilize the economy with the lightest possible touch—that it's better to let markets allocate resources.

That's been the prevailing economic theory for decades, as popularized by Ronald Reagan's "trickledown" theory—the idea that less government and lower taxes will stimulate the economy. I'm not a fan of "trickledown." We need more than a "trickle" to help those who are struggling. But is MMT the answer? Is it real?

Relying on the fact that governments control their own currency, MMT argues that governments can spend untold sums to create jobs—since they can always create more money to pay off debts in their own currency. They simply print it.

The theory suggests that government spending can be used to grow the economy to its full capacity, fuel the private sector, reduce unemployment and finance major programs such as universal healthcare, free college tuition and the "Green New Deal."

Sounds great. No need to focus on deficits, we are told. Focus instead on the private sector surplus that deficit spending creates.

Congresswoman Alexandria Ocasio-Cortez likes MMT. According to Business Insider, she believes that MMT can fund the Green New Deal, and should be "a larger part of the conversation."

United States Senator and Presidential candidate, Bernie Sanders, retains Stephanie Kelton as an economic advisor. She's a professor of public policy and economics at Stony Brook University and one of the primary proponents of MMT.

Kelton argues, "the best way to stabilize the economy and ensure full employment is to have the federal government guarantee every American a job."

Those that agree with Kelton argue that increasing the deficit, so that the government can invest in infrastructure and the labor force, should not make anyone bearish on the stock market. It should make them bullish.

Traditionally, economists have a very different view of money creation or "money printing." They view it as being inherently bad for the economy.

Paul Krugman, a Nobel prize winning economist, says MMT's proponents engage in "Calvinball" (a game in the comic strip "Calvin and Hobbes" in which players may change the rules on a whim).

Larry Summers, a former United States Treasury Secretary, now at Harvard University, recently called MMT the new "voodoo economics."

United States Federal Reserve Chairman, Jerome Powell, recently told Congress that MMT is "just wrong."

Many of us are old enough to remember learning about the Weimar Republic in which the German government, in defeat after World War I, printed money to pay its bills. And we know how that turned out. It resulted in hyperinflation. People needed wheelbarrows full of cash just to buy loaves of bread.

More recent examples of governments running the printing presses to pay for the promises of misguided politicians (resulting in hyperinflation and economic collapse) include Venezuela, Zimbabwe and Argentina.

But MMT proponents point to Ben Bernanke's bailouts of the banks in 2008 and ask; why was there no inflation when Bernanke created one trillion dollars by printing money to bail out the banks?

MMT proponents argue that by insisting on balanced budgets, we're handicapping ourselves with an underperforming economy, increased unemployment and lost opportunities.

They point to Japan which, in 2019, is running a government debt of close to 240% of their GDP and has not experienced runaway inflation. The inflation rate in Japan is currently 0.29%.

It's not the printing of money that causes inflation, MMT advocates argue; it's the lack of goods, or labor, or capacity that triggers inflation, they say.

Only when the supply of labor, goods, or services becomes restricted will inflation become a threat, MMT proponents argue.

MMT economists like Warren Mosler and Stephanie Kelton believe that the government should use its position as a monopoly issuer of the currency to ensure full employment.

And they have some support on Wall Street—which we know is always looking out for the little guy.

MMT proponents support the idea of a "jobs guarantee" program, which provides government-funded jobs to everyone who wants or needs one. They argue that the existence of unemployment is de facto evidence that net government spending is "too small."

IF MMT BECOMES UNITED STATES ECONOMIC POLICY, THE STAKES COULD NOT BE HIGHER.

As Paul Krugman recently wrote in the *New York Times*, "Do the math and it becomes clear that any attempt to extract too much from seigniorage (printing money)—more than a few percent of GDP, probably—leads to an infinite upward spiral in inflation. In effect, the currency is destroyed."

The United States now has a deficit of twenty-two trillion. And we're currently adding a trillion a year. MMT advocates say no problem. As long as there is a supply of labor, goods and services, we can just print more money.

BIG PROMISES, WHICH ALIGN WITH WHAT WE WANT TO BELIEVE, ARE HARD TO RESIST.

Bad Blood: Secrets and Lies in a Silicon Valley Startup, tells the story of the fraud and over-promising that brought down a Silicon Valley sensation—Theranos and its CEO, Elizabeth Holmes.

The company had assembled a "who's who" board of directors and raised more than $700 million in funding on the promise of new technology that would revolutionize the blood-testing industry.

Theranos provides a cautionary tale of the perils of over promising, the risks of confirmation bias and (above all) the lure of a big idea.

Holmes built her company on the promise of revolutionizing an entire industry. She claimed that the company's miniLabs were "the most important thing humanity has ever produced." Her claims generated incredible interest in and support for Theranos.

Her board included former Secretary of State Henry Kissinger, former Secretary of State James Mattis, former Wells Fargo CEO Richard Kovacevich and Bechtel Group chairman Riley Bechtel.

The problem was; the company wasn't actually able to deliver on its claims.

What all of these brilliant people bought into, according to the book's author, was "little more than digital snake oil."

Is MMT any different?

And will politicians like Maxine Waters (who serves as Ranking Member of the House Financial Services Committee) and Congresswoman Alexandria Ocasio-Cortez (who serves with her) be better at making these kinds of assessments than those who were wrong about Theranos? Unlikely.

So, as "Auntie Maxine" says, "stay woke."

133

SOCIAL MEDIA

*Social media represents the first wave of
the technological revolution and it's
already causing significant disruption.*

A study published in the American Journal of Preventative Medicine found that social media use is linked to greater feelings of social isolation.

RESEARCHERS DISCOVERED THAT THE MORE TIME PEOPLE SPENT ON SOCIAL MEDIA SITES, THE MORE SOCIALLY ISOLATED THEY PERCEIVED THEMSELVES TO BE.

And perceived social isolation is one of the worst things for us, both mentally and physically.

Seventy-five percent of teenagers in America currently have profiles on social networking sites. While social networking undoubtedly plays an important role in broadening social connections; sexting, cyberbullying, internet addiction and sleep deprivation can have devastating effects.

The American Psychological Association defines bullying as aggressive behavior by an individual that causes discomfort to another. The Pew Research Center found that nearly thirty-nine percent of teens on social networks have been cyberbullied.

Trolling—the act of deliberately inflicting hatred, bigotry, racism, misogyny and/or just simple bickering between people (often anonymously) is also pervasive in social networks. Sexting—the act of sending sexually revealing pictures or sexually explicit messages to another individual or group—is another common activity among teens using social media.

A nationwide survey by the National Campaign to Prevent Teen and Unplanned Pregnancy found that twenty percent of teens have participated in sexting. While teenage boys resort to sending sexually explicit or suggestive messages, teenage girls are more likely to send nude photos of themselves, mostly to their boyfriends. Beyond the personal trauma and humiliation that the unwanted disclosure of sexting may cause, there are legal ramifications as well. Some states consider such activities as misdemeanors; others treat sexting as a felony.

DIGITAL FOOTPRINTS CREATE A PERMANENT TRAIL. THIS DIGITAL FOOTPRINT CAN HAVE SERIOUS REPERCUSSIONS IN THE FUTURE, BOTH PERSONALLY AND PROFESSIONALLY.

A survey conducted by the Royal Society for Public Health, asked fourteen to twenty-four-year-olds in the U.K. how social media platforms impacted their health and wellbeing. The survey results found that Snapchat, Facebook, Twitter and Instagram all led to increased feelings of depression, anxiety, poor body image and loneliness.

Another problem with social media is that modern teens are learning to do most of their communication while looking at a screen, not another person. "As a species, we are very highly attuned to reading social cues," says Dr. Catherine Steiner-Adair, a clinical psychologist and author of *The Big Disconnect*. "There's no question kids are missing out on very critical social skills. Texting and online communicating… puts everybody in a nonverbal disabled context, where body language, facial expression and even the smallest kinds of vocal reactions are rendered invisible." She also notes, "Part of a healthy self-esteem is knowing how to say what you think and feel even when you're in disagreement with other people or it feels emotionally risky."

When friendship is conducted online and through texts, teens are doing this in a context stripped of many of the most personal—and sometimes intimidating—aspects of face-to-face communication. When you're texting, less is at stake. You don't hear or see the effect that your words are having on the other person and because the conversation isn't happening in real time, each party can take more time to consider a response.

IF TEENS AREN'T GETTING ENOUGH PRACTICE RELATING TO PEOPLE FACE-TO-FACE AND IN REAL TIME, MANY OF THEM WILL GROW UP TO BE ADULTS WHO ARE ANXIOUS ABOUT OUR PRIMARY MEANS OF COMMUNICATION—TALKING.

This can cause social interactions and negotiations to become more difficult, especially as people get older and begin navigating personal and professional relationships and employment.

THE OTHER BIG DANGER THAT COMES FROM KIDS COMMUNICATING MORE INDIRECTLY IS THAT IT HAS GOTTEN EASIER TO BE CRUEL.

"Kids text all sorts of things that you would never contemplate saying to anyone's face," says Dr. Donna Wick, a clinical and developmental psychologist who runs Mind to Mind Parent, which teaches reflective rather than reactive parenting. She says that this seems to be especially true of girls, who typically don't like to disagree with each other in real life. "You hope to teach them that they can disagree without jeopardizing the relationship, but what social media is teaching them to do is disagree in ways that are more extreme and do jeopardize the relationship. It's exactly what you don't want to have happen," she says.

Dr. Steiner-Adair agrees that girls are particularly at risk. "Girls are socialized more to compare themselves to other people, girls in particular, to develop their identities so it makes them more vulnerable to the downside of all this." She warns that a lack of solid self-esteem is often to blame;

"WE FORGET THAT RELATIONAL AGGRESSION COMES FROM INSECURITY AND FEELING AWFUL ABOUT YOURSELF AND WANTING TO PUT OTHER PEOPLE DOWN SO YOU FEEL BETTER."

When kids scroll through their feeds and see how great everyone seems to be doing, it only adds to the pressure. Social media also raises other profound social issues that may be far more consequential than we realize.

Suicide rates for girls age fifteen to nineteen are now the highest in forty years. The country is currently experiencing the greatest political division in over 160 years. Both of these social phenomena have been fueled by the rise of social media.

People are being influenced by what they see on social media and some are being motivated to act.

"WE ARE A BEHAVIOR CHANGE AGENCY."
—Alexander Nix, CEO of Cambridge Analytica.

In 2016, "Project Alamo" (the digital arm of the Trump presidential campaign), worked with Cambridge Analytica, to identify people, in select geographic areas throughout the United States, whose views could be influenced or manipulated. These groups were identified using information obtained from over 87 million Facebook users.

"IN 2018, DATA SURPASSED OIL AS
THE MOST VALUABLE ASSET ON EARTH."

—Brittany Kaiser, Cambridge Analytica.

These targeted groups came to be known as "the Persuadables". Project Alamo spent over a million dollars a day bombarding the Persuadables with highly targeted, social media messaging. Employing what Brittany Kaiser, of Cambridge Analytica, described as "weapons grade communication tactics", Project Alamo was instrumental in helping Trump win the 2016 U.S. presidential election.

It should be noted, that these tactics were not unique to the Trump campaign. Brittany Kaiser previously worked for the Obama campaign and Cambridge Analytica used these same "weapons grade communication tactics" in elections all over the world.

None of us fully understand the implications of social media but certain things are obvious. We know that the implications are significant and we know that not all are good.

On March 14, 2019, a twenty-eight-year-old Australian citizen who had recently published an anti-Muslim, anti-immigrant manifesto on the internet committed multiple terror attacks in New Zealand that killed forty-nine and seriously injured twenty. The shooter streamed the shooting on Facebook. It was also posted on YouTube and Twitter.

Social media companies have generally erred on the side of protecting the First Amendment. In 2017, Mark Zuckerberg, describing Facebook's response to Russia's attempt to influence America's elections, said, "We don't check what people say before they say it and, frankly, I don't think society should want us to. Freedom means you don't have to ask for permission first and, by default, you can say what you want."

He's right.

WE SHOULD GENERALLY HOLD THE FIRST AMENDMENT INVIOLATE, BUT CERTAIN INCIDENTS ILLUSTRATE THAT WE ARE NOW IN UNCHARTED WATERS.

Russian hacking, increases in school shootings, increases in teen suicides, decisions like Citizens United, how we handle speech on college campuses and the evolving nature of the media—all raise important questions concerning whether we need to have an evolving or fixed view of the First Amendment.

The prevailing wisdom, which I have always believed, is that the antidote for false or hateful speech is more truthful speech and I still believe that's true. Or I want to believe it's true, but what if it's no longer true? If social media is a game changer, does that mean the rules of the game also need to change?

WHAT HAPPENS WHEN WE BECOME SURROUNDED BY FALSE AND HATEFUL SPEECH?

This is a real possibility when computers can now be used to create automated speech and when individuals, corporations and governments— who are all interested in shaping public opinion—gain access to this ominous new technology. What happens when outside actors, whose sole mission is to undermine American democracy, are using social media and the First Amendment to harm or divide us?

We have already seen state actors use social media in an attempt to influence public opinion. We know that algorithms exist that can be used to disguise computer-generated speech as an outpouring of authentic human opinion. We know that the human brain is extremely malleable with more than ninety-five percent of information entering through our unconscious brain, outside of our conscious awareness. We know that scientists and researchers are getting much closer to being able to hack the human brain. We know that we have an increasingly ignorant and easily distracted public that is highly susceptible to being misled. And we know that social media, a relatively recent phenomenon whose true impact is still unknown, will play an enormous role in shaping public opinion. These are all issues that we need to be discussing.

Old rules and perceptions may no longer apply or serve us well and we certainly shouldn't blithely assume that they will.

AMERICA'S GREATEST STRENGTH AND GREATEST LIABILITY MAY SIMULTANEOUSLY BE SPELLED OUT IN THE FIRST AMENDMENT.

The very idea that we might now have to view the First Amendment as anything but inviolate illustrates the depth of the water around us.

Limiting the amount of time you spend on your computer provides a healthy counterpoint to our growing obsession with social media and technology, but we must do more than simply self-limit our access. We must try to understand the broad implications of this powerful new technology and use it to advance our collective objectives rather than sit back and watch as it is used by others to undermine our shared interests.

134

RACISM

*Racism has existed for thousands of years
and despite the best efforts of many, it continues
to be an intensely emotional and polarizing issue
for millions of Americans.*

R acism is real. It is a dehumanizing act and experience. It is offensive not only to its intended and unintended targets, but to all those whose sense of decency and morality abhors injustice.

The idea that one man would judge another man inferior simply by virtue of the color of his skin is beyond ignorant. It is a cruel and intolerable assault on human dignity that no man or woman should be expected to endure.

America has responded to racism with a variety of measures including, but not limited, to the Thirteenth, Fourteenth and Fifteenth Amendments to the United States Constitution; the 1954 United States Supreme Court decision of *Brown v. Board of Education*; the Civil Rights Act of 1964; the Voting Rights Act of 1965; and numerous state and federal rules and regulations designed to correct past wrongs.

While helpful and well intentioned, these legal responses have not eliminated and cannot eliminate racism in America. No legislation can. Racism is an attitude grounded in bias and perception. In many cases, these biases and perceptions have been handed down within families generation after generation.

ENDING RACISM WILL REQUIRE MORE THAN CHANGES IN LAW AND SOCIAL POLICY. IT WILL REQUIRE A FUNDAMENTAL SHIFT IN OUR INDIVIDUAL BIASES AND PERCEPTIONS.

Unfortunately, biases and perceptions often prove resistant to change.

Despite the best efforts of many, racism continues to undermine our national ethos and inflict pain and suffering on millions of Americans. These are complex, emotionally charged issues that have existed for generations. Only the continuing efforts and commitment of this and future generations can resolve these issues and this will take time.

AMERICA HAS MADE GREAT STRIDES IN THIS AREA BUT MUCH MORE NEEDS TO BE DONE.

Many young African-American men and women are out of work. Although unemployment among black teens has fallen from a high of forty nine percent, in 2010, to a fifty year low of 19.3 percent in 2019, the rate of unemployment for young African Americans is still substantially higher than the rate of unemployment for white teens—which in 2019 stands at 12.8 percent.

For many young men and women of color, attending college is not an option. Many of these young people have very few options. Some who lack employment opportunities may loiter and engage in mischief, as young people of all races and backgrounds are inclined to do. In other cases, young men and women of color who are generally law-abiding citizens may come into contact with police for minor traffic violations such as speeding or expired license plates. Some young people who are unable to find work and are lured by the lucrative underground economy, may turn to selling drugs or prostitution. Some get involved in more serious crimes.

ONE IN FOUR BLACK MALES WILL GO THROUGH THE CORRECTIONS SYSTEM IN HIS LIFETIME.

Arrests and incarceration have a devastating effect on the lives of those involved, often leading to unemployment or increased criminality. This, in turn, perpetuates the stereotypes and public perceptions that fuel racism when the true causes of increased crime in America's inner-cities have nothing to do with race and instead result from a lack of economic opportunity, a lack of education and a lack of family or community support.

In the final analysis, racism is nothing more than a lie. It is a lie that some people cling to out of their own insecurity and impaired self-image. Much like drowning victims will pull down those around them to save themselves, racists attempt to reduce the stature of those whose skin color is different from their own in a misguided attempt to somehow elevate their own stature by comparison.

Racists are fundamentally insecure; they have a low self-image and they overcompensate for their insecurity by attempting to diminish others. Those whose victim mentality causes them to see racism around every corner are equally insecure.

Today, the term racism has become completely untethered from it's historical roots. Instead of being used to describe someone who believes in racial inferiority or superiority, the term "racist" is now being used, by those on both sides of the political spectrum, as a political weapon. This deliberate and irresponsible misuse of the term is not contributing to an end of racism. Instead, it is fueling and increasing our division and it should not be encouraged or tolerated.

TRUTH IS THE ONLY MEANS CAPABLE OF ENDING RACISM AND TRUTH REQUIRES HONESTY AND OBJECTIVITY.

All people need to be treated equally, fairly and objectively regardless of race, color, creed, or national origin.

To think highly of others—you must first think highly of yourself.

135

INCARCERATION

*The United States is the biggest jailer on the planet.
We have only five percent of the world's
population but twenty-five percent of the
world's prison population.*

**WE SPEND SEVENTY-FIVE BILLION DOLLARS
PER YEAR ON INCARCERATION—
ONE HUNDRED THOUSAND DOLLARS PER PRISONER.**

This does not factor in the true social costs of incarceration, which is believed to be over one trillion dollars annually. That's more than the annual operational costs of the United States government. These costs are reflected in less human capital, lower wages, reduced earnings, increased dependency and increased crime.

**IN CONTRAST, WE SPEND ONLY SIXTY-FIVE BILLION
DOLLARS ON UNIVERSITIES—
TEN THOUSAND DOLLARS PER STUDENT.**

A greater investment in education could result in massive decreases in the cost of and the need for incarceration. Children of incarcerated people are five times more likely to go to prison than their peers.

WE MUST REVERSE THIS CYCLE OF POVERTY AND HOPELESSNESS AND THE WAY TO DO THAT IS THROUGH INCREASED INVESTMENT IN EDUCATION AND INNER-CITY ECONOMIC DEVELOPMENT.

For generations, we have resisted this line of reasoning, instead buying into the ideology of personal responsibility and self-sufficiency. These are great ideals—when they work. But they don't always work. In many of our economically depressed communities, these ideologies (without assistance) have not worked. And their failure has created tinder boxes of discontent—that are highly susceptible to manipulation and organized agitation, which is already happening.

The greatest threat facing America is not an invasion by a foreign power. It is a domestic revolution—surreptitiously inspired and encouraged by foreign powers or domestic actors who are targeting these communities through the use of social media.

136

GLOBAL WARMING

Global warming is a term used to describe a gradual increase in the average temperature of the earth's atmosphere and its oceans.

Global warming is a major issue for this and future generations. Many believe that global warming is leading to permanent changes in the earth's climate. They believe that it is an "existential threat." A threat to our existence.

97% of climate scientists looking at the data agree on three critical facts:

1. The planet is warming;

2. Humans are the primary cause; and

3. This phenomenon is already creating significant adverse consequences for the planet.

Changes resulting from global warming include rising sea levels due to the melting of the polar ice caps, as well as an increase in the occurrence and severity of storms and other severe weather events.

MANY BELIEVE THIS TO BE ONE OF THE MOST IMPORTANT ISSUES FACING OUR PLANET. OTHERS DISAGREE.

Some argue that the science surrounding the likely impact of climate change is uncertain and that restrictions on energy production will do more harm than good. This is likely to be a major issue in the 2020 election.

Using a simple risk/reward analysis, the potential risks of ignoring global warming seem to dwarf the potential rewards of decreased regulation. If we are to err on this issue, it seems that the logical and responsible thing to do would be to err on the side of caution.

WE CAN SURVIVE DOING TOO MUCH; THE SAME MAY NOT BE TRUE OF DOING TOO LITTLE.

This will continue to be a major issue during your lifetime. Millennial Samurai will need to educate themselves on the critical issues surrounding global warming and climate change. They will need to develop a consensus as well as solutions that will help to reduce global warming and enable humanity to better control and manage our environment.

All issues having a significant and lasting impact on our environmental resources should be addressed with one overriding consideration. And that is; that we are the stewards of these environmental resources not only for each other but for future generations yet unborn.

137

THE SECOND AMENDMENT

"A well-regulated militia being necessary to the security of a free State, the right of the people to keep and bear arms shall not be infringed."

The Second Amendment is one of the most important yet, at the same time, one of the most divisive and misunderstood Amendments to the U.S. Constitution.

Many passionately believe that our right to bear arms makes us safer, rather than less safe. Others reject that assertion and claim the opposite is true.

In *District of Columbia v. Heller*, 554 U.S. 570 (2008), Justice Scalia, writing for a 5-4 majority, stated that the Second Amendment *"protects an individual right to possess a firearm unconnected with service in the militia."* This clearly establishes that the right to bear arms is an individual right.

But what is the scope of that individual right? Is it the right to own and use any weapon for any purpose whatsoever? No. It is not. Nor should it be.

In *Heller*, Justice Scalia, writing for the majority, stated;

"LIKE MOST RIGHTS, THE RIGHT SECURED BY THE SECOND AMENDMENT IS NOT UNLIMITED. IT IS NOT A RIGHT TO KEEP AND CARRY ANY WEAPON WHATSOEVER IN ANY MANNER WHATSOEVER AND FOR WHATEVER PURPOSE... THE SECOND AMENDMENT DOES NOT PROTECT THOSE WEAPONS NOT TYPICALLY POSSESSED BY LAW-ABIDING CITIZENS FOR LAWFUL PURPOSES."

Under our system of government, this is the law.

In considering how we as a society should exercise and apply our rights under the Second Amendment, it is important to understand that the right to bear arms, like any other Constitutional right, is not an unlimited right.

In any society, all individual rights are subject to certain inherent limitations, that are required to protect the rights of others.

The question that we should be asking is; should "military style assault weapons" and high capacity magazines be the means by which we protect ourselves? Do these "military style assault weapons" and high capacity magazines make our families, and society as a whole, safer or less safe? Do any of us even want to live in a neighborhood where our neighbors and their children may have access to an AR15, without having undergone any meaningful training, certification and/or background checks?

Based on a fair reading of *Heller*, this is not what the Second Amendment requires nor what sound policy dictates.

THE AMERICAN BAR ASSOCIATION REPORTS THAT AMERICAN CHILDREN ARE TWELVE TIMES MORE LIKELY TO DIE FROM GUN RELATED INJURIES THAN ARE YOUTH IN ALL OTHER INDUSTRIALIZED COUNTRIES COMBINED.

So why is it that we can't get Congress to pass any meaningful gun control legislation? Why don't we, at minimum, require universal background checks and some basic training, licensing and/or certification, to own a "military style assault weapon" and/or high capacity magazines?

Why are sensible solutions demonized as insurrection worthy assaults on the Second Amendment?

THE LATIN PHRASE *CUI BONO,* ASKS *WHO STANDS TO BENEFIT?*

And that is precisely what we should be asking when we see common sense solutions being ignored or vilified.

In 2011, NRA CEO Wayne La Pierre told a conservative audience that President Obama, once re-elected, planned to "erase the Second Amendment from the Bill of Rights and exorcise it from the U.S. Constitution."

The 2008 and 2012 elections of Barak Obama and the panic created by gun advocates, surrounding Obama's efforts at gun legislation, triggered unprecedented increases in gun sales and profits. *"Cui Bono?"* The gun industry benefits.

From Obama's first inauguration to the day before Newtown, the share price of Sturm Ruger (RGR), the largest publicly traded gun manufacturer, increased by **729%**. The S&P 500 increased only **67%** during the same period.

INCREASED HYSTERIA = INCREASED SALES AND PROFITS

Successfully resolving these issues will not be easy. It will require education, understanding, engagement, accountability and compromise. Above all compromise. This is not an all or nothing issue.

THOSE WHO CALL FOR WIDE RANGING RESTRICTIONS ON GUNS ARE AS WRONG AS THOSE WHO CALL FOR NO RESTRICTIONS ON GUNS.

Educating yourself with regard to these issues will allow you to deal with these issues more intelligently and effectively.

Understanding and appreciating alternative perspectives will allow you to engage in a dialogue aimed at constructive compromise. Increased engagement will allow all positions to be heard and ultimately force responsible, elected representatives to take appropriate corrective action.

Unfortunately, not all elective representatives are responsible or responsive. Therefore, in the final analysis, requiring accountability from those that you elect to represent your interests is the only thing that will create real change.

We must learn to reject hyperbole and avoid derision. We must examine issues rationally and objectively. We must recognize the dangers created by misinformation while respecting, considering and being open to discussing alternative views.

WE MUST LOOK BEYOND OUR DIVERGENT POSITIONS AND SEARCH FOR COMMON INTERESTS.

Fortunately, our most fundamental interest—the safety and security of our families—is a shared interest. We simply have differing views on how to advance that shared interest.

Society needs and deserves intelligent decisions. We don't need hyperbole, rigidity, hysteria or deception. These are difficult questions upon which reasonable minds may differ. We all need to recognize that there are very compelling arguments on both sides of this issue.

138

HUNGER

Hunger is a global problem.
Over eight hundred million people on the planet—
one out of nine—suffer from chronic hunger.

T he UN recently warned that twenty million people are at immediate risk of dying from hunger. Four countries face extreme risk. Tens of millions are affected in Yemen, Nigeria, South Sudan and Somalia alone. Eighteen additional countries are suffering from a high level of food insecurity. The U.N. forecasts that an additional two billion people will be lacking food by 2050.

One in three people suffer from some form of malnutrition, meaning they lack sufficient vitamins and minerals in their diet which can lead to health issues such as stunted growth in children. Each year, poor nutrition kills 3.1 million children under the age of five.

Chronic hunger is caused by poverty. According to the Hunger Project, hunger exists "when people lack the opportunity to earn enough income, to be educated and gain skills, to meet basic health needs and to have a voice in the decisions that affect their community." Droughts, a lack of clean water and poor sanitation are major causes of disease and death.

Norman Borlaug, an American agronomist, was a pioneer in this area. He spent years crossing thousands of strains of wheat from across the globe, ultimately developing a high-yielding, disease-resistant variety. Where the variety was planted, yields soared. Mexico became self-sufficient in grain. Yields doubled in India and Pakistan. Borlaug was not only a famous scientist, he was one of only seven people to have won the Nobel Prize, the Presidential Medal of Freedom and the Congressional Gold Medal.

As Borlaug said;

"THE FIRST ESSENTIAL COMPONENT OF SOCIAL JUSTICE IS ADEQUATE FOOD FOR ALL MANKIND."

Borlaug's Green Revolution helped to avoid famine. He saved over a billion lives and prevented a big part of the underdeveloped world from starving to death.

However, food supplies still can't keep pace with rising population. Borlaug's battle may never be completely won. We still face unprecedented challenges in attempting to eradicate hunger. Increases in population will continue to present new challenges in this area going forward.

Access to clean water, fertilization and education remain critical challenges. But the major causes of famine are dysfunctional governments and natural disasters.

Investing in agriculture, markets, roads, communications, public works programs, emergency food aid and buffer stock management is required to ensure that systems are in place to help vulnerable people. This needs to be done before famine catalysts; such as civil conflict, bad harvests, transportation disruption, or droughts occur.

TO FEED THE WORLD'S NINE BILLION PEOPLE IN THIRTY-FIVE YEARS, WE'RE GOING TO HAVE TO DOUBLE THE AMOUNT OF FOOD AVAILABLE.

Existing technology makes that possible, but not without some increased thought and effort.

Millennial Samurai will need to contribute to that increased thought and effort.

139

WATER

Water is likely to be a major issue in your future.

W illem Buiter, Citigroup's chief economist, says;

"WATER AS AN ASSET CLASS WILL, IN MY VIEW, EVENTUALLY BECOME THE SINGLE MOST IMPORTANT PHYSICAL-COMMODITY-BASED ASSET CLASS, DWARFING OIL, COPPER, AGRICULTURAL COMMODITIES AND PRECIOUS METALS."

Access to clean water ought to be a human right, but as global populations continue to grow, waste and misuse of this precious resource may challenge that assumption.

Seventeen countries now face severe water shortages. India and Iran are currently using almost all the water they have, according to World Resource Institute (WRI) data.

Among cities with over three million people, thirty-three face "extremely high water stress" according to the WRE report. By 2030, forty-five cities are expected to be in this category—affecting 470 million people.

Desalination plants, grey-water recycling systems, efforts at conservation and repairs of leaky municipal water pipes will all need to be considered as possible solutions.

The United States currently has sixteen seawater desalination plants in some stage of planning, along the west coast. The billion-dollar mega plant near San Diego has been operating for several years and has already purified over forty billion gallons of ocean water.

One of the most talked about new technologies, developed at the Massachusetts Institute of Technology (MIT), is being studied in laboratories in the U.K., Saudi Arabia, South Korea and elsewhere. It is composed of one-atom-thick perforated graphene membranes that can cut reverse osmosis desalination to a fraction of its current cost. The membrane's pores can be tuned to optimize permeability. The challenge now is how to mass produce the material.

Other technologies may include products like those being developed by NBD Nanotechnologies, based in Boston. NBD stands for Namib Beetle Design, referring to an insect that captures moisture on its body from surrounding fog. The company makes coatings that can be added to plastic and metal surfaces enabling them to then pull water out of thin air.

A residential option (or an option for those who want to live off the grid) is available from Zero Mass Water based in Scottsdale, Arizona. It is a two-thousand-dollar hydro panel that captures water vapor from air. One panel can produce up to five liters a day. Two of them can produce enough for a family's daily cooking and drinking needs.

140

LONELINESS

*In the past fifty years, rates of loneliness
have doubled in the United States.*

A ccording to data from the General Social Survey (GSS), the number of Americans who say they have no close friends has roughly tripled in recent decades and "zero" is the most common response when people are asked how many confidants they have. These are alarming statistics.

Former United States Surgeon General Vivek Murthy stated, "Loneliness and weak social connections are associated with a reduction in lifespan similar to that caused by smoking fifteen cigarettes a day, and even greater than that associated with obesity."

IN A SURVEY OF OVER TWENTY THOUSAND AMERICAN ADULTS, ALMOST HALF OF RESPONDENTS REPORTED FEELING ALONE, LEFT OUT OR ISOLATED.

One in four Americans, who participated in the survey, shared that they rarely feel understood.

Loneliness is a subjective experience and a common human emotion. When fleeting, an individual may not be impacted. However, persistent and pervasive feelings of loneliness can be very harmful to our health. Lonely individuals are less likely to get quality sleep. They typically experience reductions in reasoning and creativity, reduced productivity and decreased job satisfaction. Loneliness can also lead to anxiety, depression, even suicide.

According to a recent study published in the Harvard Business

Review, workers who experienced higher levels of loneliness also reported fewer promotions, less job satisfaction and a greater likelihood for frequently changing jobs.

The quality of our relationships appears to be a significant factor in loneliness. Adult men seem to be especially bad at keeping and cultivating friendships. The study also found that lawyers, doctors and engineers were the occupations reporting the highest levels of loneliness.

Surprisingly, Dr. Douglas Nemecek, the chief medical officer for behavioral health at health insurer Cigna, told NPR;

"OUR SURVEY FOUND THAT THE YOUNGER GENERATION WAS LONELIER THAN THE OLDER GENERATIONS."

So, what's making Americans lonely? The survey found that working too often, or not enough, contributed to loneliness. Workplaces are a significant source for fostering social relationships and ensuring a work-life balance.

Dr. Nemecek says, "There is an inherent link between loneliness and the workplace, with employers in a unique position to be a critical part of the solution."

Katie Acheson, CEO of Youth Action NSW, says, "There's a whole bunch of older people living with a disability who are trying to stay at home longer and wanting to stay out of care facilities."

As a solution, she says, "We're suggesting that the government put together a pilot program where young people live with older people, or people with a disability, in exchange for about ten hours of support around the home."

Programs like this are being started all over the world. Daycare facilities for children are also being paired with eldercare facilities. The concept of "non-familial intergenerational interactions" is based on the simple yet powerful idea that old and young can bring new energy, knowledge and enthusiasm to each other's lives. This concept has been gaining traction, particularly in the United States where more and more shared-care facilities are being opened.

A new initiative, The U.K.'s Commission on Loneliness, will invest millions of pounds on ways to connect people with community support that can restore social contact in their lives. The new initiative, described by the U.K. government as "social prescribing," will enable the country's doctors to prescribe therapeutic art or hobby-based treatments for ailments ranging from dementia to psychosis, as well as lung conditions and mental health issues. It will allow doctors to prescribe art classes, dance classes, singing lessons and museum visits as treatments.

Under the plan, general practitioners across the country will be equipped to guide patients to an array of hobbies, sports and arts groups.

The initiative will embrace multiple disciplines from various walks of life, including social activities like cooking classes, playing bingo and gardening to more culturally focused activities including library visits, art, dance, singing classes and concerts. Social prescribing is intended to complement rather than replace more traditional forms of treatment. The initiative is projected to be employed across the U.K. by 2023.

You can address the issue of loneliness in your own life by cultivating and maintaining meaningful relationships, by volunteering and by participating in programs like these.

141

MENTAL ILLNESS

*Three hundred and fifty million people worldwide
are affected by some form of depression.*

One in five people in the United States suffers from mental illness. Social anxiety (an intense fear of interacting with others) is one of the most common psychiatric conditions in the United States. It can be so debilitating that it prevents people from holding a job.

**WOMEN ARE SEVENTY PERCENT MORE LIKELY TO
EXPERIENCE DEPRESSION IN THEIR LIFETIME THAN MEN.**

In 2015, there were 44,193 reported suicide deaths in the United States. Suicide is the second leading cause of death for those between the age of fifteen and thirty-four in America.

Over fifty percent of all people who commit suicide suffer from major depression and half of Americans with major depression don't seek treatment.

Research protocols for depression typically evaluate drugs for their general effectiveness based on the "average" patient, but new approaches promise to be more targeted. Two people diagnosed with the same mental illness can respond very differently to the same treatment and pharmaceutical companies typically target the largest possible market rather than tailoring treatments to smaller groups, let alone individual needs. Drug developers also lack the information they need to tailor drug treatments to individuals. Routine medical practice doesn't include diagnostic techniques to predict whether a person will profit from a given treatment.

Other treatments that don't involve drugs also show promise for treating depression. Behavioral treatment of depression using a form of talk therapy known as cognitive behavioral therapy, or CBT, provides benefits to roughly half of the patients who receive it.

Brain-imaging techniques combined with sophisticated algorithms that track and analyze neural activity are now able to reveal brain differences that predict whether a given drug or talk therapy will effectively treat an individual patient's depression or relieve severe social anxiety. This information will allow for treatments that are specifically tailored to meet a patient's individual needs.

Genetics can also predispose a person to mental illness and experience plays a role in determining which genes are activated in the brain. The combination of breakthroughs in brain-imaging techniques and genetic research will soon allow scientists to predict with greater accuracy what treatments will be most effective.

Mental illness is an issue that will continue to affect hundreds of millions of people globally. And these numbers will only grow from the disruption caused by the technological revolution.

Millennial Samurai will need to use both technology and empathy to develop solutions that address this growing problem.

142

EMDR

Eye Movement Desensitization and Reprocessing
(EMDR) is a psychotherapy treatment that was
originally designed in the early 1990s, to alleviate the
distress associated with traumatic memories.

P ost-Traumatic Stress Disorder (PTSD) is a trauma and stress related
disorder that may develop after exposure to an event in which death or
severe physical harm occurred or was threatened. People who suffer from the
disorder include military troops, rescue workers and survivors of shootings,
bombings, violence and rape.

**PTSD AFFECTS ABOUT 8 MILLION AMERICAN ADULTS AND
CAN OCCUR AT ANY AGE, INCLUDING CHILDHOOD.**

EMDR therapy facilitates the accessing and processing of traumatic
memories and other adverse life experiences to bring these to an adaptive
resolution.

During EMDR therapy, the client focuses on emotionally disturbing
material in brief sequential doses while simultaneously focusing on an external
stimulus. Therapist directed lateral eye movements are the most commonly
used external stimulus but a variety of other stimuli including hand-tapping
and audio stimulation are often used.

**THIS PROCESS OF DUAL ATTENTION HAS BEEN FOUND TO
BE IMPORTANT IN SUCCESSFULLY HEALING A TRAUMA.**

After successful treatment with EMDR therapy, affective distress is relieved, negative beliefs are reformulated and physiological arousal is reduced.

When EMDR is successful, new associations are forged between the traumatic memory and more adaptive memories or information. These new associations are thought to result in complete information processing, new learning, elimination of emotional distress and development of cognitive insights.

EMDR therapy is recommended as an effective treatment for trauma victims by numerous organizations, including the American Psychiatric Association, the Department of Defense and the World Health Organization.

143

SUICIDE

More teenagers and young adults die from suicide than
from cancer, stroke, heart disease, birth defects, pneumonia,
influenza, chronic lung disease and AIDS combined.

E very day in America, there are an average of over fifty-four hundred
suicide attempts by young people in grades seven to twelve.

FOUR OUT OF FIVE TEENS WHO ATTEMPT SUICIDE
HAVE GIVEN CLEAR WARNING SIGNS.

Kids who are bullied are more than twice as likely to consider suicide, according to a study published in the Journal of the American Medical Association.

In another study, researchers from the Universities of Oxford and Birmingham looked at more than 150,000 children and young people across 30 countries, over a 21-year period and reached the same conclusion.

Stresses such as conflicts with parents, breakup of a relationship, school difficulties, legal difficulties, social isolation and physical ailments are commonly reported or observed in young people who attempt suicide. Even adolescents who initially may seem at low risk may be asking for help the only way they can—by joking about suicide or repeatedly seeking treatment for physical complaints. Their concerns should be assessed thoroughly and follow-up should be arranged for additional evaluation and treatment.

From 1950 to 1990, the suicide rate for adolescents in the fifteen to nineteen-year-old age group increased by three hundred percent. Adolescent males in this age group had a suicide rate six times greater than the rate for females.

The National Youth Risk Behavior survey of students in grades nine through twelve indicated that nearly one fourth (24.1 percent) of students had seriously considered attempting suicide during the twelve months preceding the survey.

The following are some of the signs you might notice in yourself or a friend that may be reason for concern:

- Talking about wanting to die or to kill oneself
- Looking for a way to kill oneself such as searching online for, or buying a gun
- Talking about feeling hopeless or having no reason to live
- Talking about feeling trapped or being in unbearable pain
- Talking about being a burden to others
- Increasing the use of alcohol or drugs
- Acting anxious or agitated; behaving recklessly
- Sleeping too little or too much
- Withdrawing or feeling isolated
- Showing rage or talking about seeking revenge
- Displaying extreme mood swings

IF YOU ARE IN CRISIS AND NEED HELP, CALL 1-800-273-TALK (8255); AVAILABLE TWENTY-FOUR HOURS A DAY, EVERY DAY.

You will reach the National Suicide Prevention Lifeline, a service available to anyone. You may call for yourself or for someone you care about and all calls are confidential. You can also visit the Lifeline's website at http://www.suicidepreventionlifeline.org.

If you've been the subject of bullying, reach out to counselors at the above number. Talk to a professional. Most importantly, realize that whatever you may be feeling will pass. You are living in the most extraordinary period in human history. Don't let the actions of others control your emotions or your life. Take control of your life and experience the incredible journey that awaits you. Believe in yourself. You have the ability to live a happy, successful and meaningful life.

If you're engaged in bullying, stop and seek help. You're not only harming others; you're harming yourself. Talk to a professional. Only the weak, who try in vain to compensate for their own weaknesses, resort to bullying.

Millennial Samurai are not bullies. They're guardians, defenders and friends of those in need.

144

*The threat of misinformation, fake news, and mass
manipulation may be the single most significant
threat to society you will face during your lifetime.*

FAKE NEWS

In 2017, the term "fake news" increased in usage by 365 percent, causing it to become "word of the year," according to the Collins English Dictionary, which described it as "false, often sensational information disseminated under the guise of news reporting."

The indictment of twenty-six Russian nationals by Robert Mueller, the special counsel investigating Russian efforts to influence America's 2016 Presidential election, detailed the secret workings of the Internet Research Agency, a Russian organization that disseminated false information online in an effort to erode public faith in American democracy. According to American intelligence officials, the Kremlin oversaw this operation.

After the Mueller indictment, Twitter issued a statement stating that technology companies "cannot defeat this novel, shared threat alone" and that "the best approach is to share information and ideas to increase our collective knowledge, with the full weight of government and law enforcement leading the charge against threats to our democracy."

Whether on social or mainstream media, stories that are repeatedly reported can quickly gain widespread acceptance as being factual. "When you see the fact for the second time, it's much easier to process—you read it more quickly, you understand it more fluently," says Vanderbilt University psychologist Lisa Fazio. "Our brain interprets that fluency as a signal for something being true whether it's true or not."

Fact checkers at Snopes.com, FactCheck.org, OpenSecrets.org and PolitiFact.com increase our collective knowledge and can help to combat the spread of fake news. But in the end, we must all be vigilant in our search for the truth.

Harvard University psychologist Steven Pinker tells us in his book *Enlightenment Now: The Case for Reason, Science, Humanism and Progress*, "The human brain is capable of reason given the right circumstances; the problem is to identify those circumstances and put them more firmly in place."

TEACHING PEOPLE TO THINK CRITICALLY, RIGOROUSLY DISCUSSING AND DEBATING ISSUES AND COMMUNICATING EFFECTIVELY ARE ALL REQUIRED TO OVERCOME FAKE NEWS AND COGNITIVE BIASES.

Given the inherent vulnerability and malleability of the human brain, the opportunities for manipulation (brought about by advances in technology and the democratization of media) are certain to become some of the most important and defining issues of our age.

145

TECHNOLOGY AND EMPLOYMENT

*Technological change has been redefining the
workplace since the Industrial Revolution, but
the speed of technological innovation and the
scale at which it will disrupt the current nature of
employment are entirely unprecedented.*

N ew technologies like robotics and artificial intelligence will radically change the nature of employment. They will allow for improvements in productivity, efficiency, safety and convenience. They will also create downward pressures on wages and an urgent need for education and retraining.

Economist John Maynard Keynes made the prediction decades ago that society is heading toward a period of technological unemployment. Keynes predicted that society would discover ways to increase labor efficiency more rapidly than it would find new uses for labor.

In *The Second Machine Age*, Erik Brynjolfsson and Andrew McAfee of the Massachusetts Institute of Technology (MIT) asked what jobs will be left once computing power enables inexpensive, computerized solutions to problems that previously required costly human engagement.

**AS MACHINES EVOLVE AND ACQUIRE GREATER
PERFORMANCE CAPABILITIES THAT MATCH OR
EXCEED HUMAN CAPABILITIES, THE ADOPTION OF
AUTOMATION WILL INCREASE.**

Some estimate that about sixty percent of all occupations have at least thirty percent of activities that can be automated based on currently available technologies.

In *The Future of Employment: How Susceptible Are Jobs to Computerization?* Carl Benedikt Frey and Michael A. Osborne estimate that forty-seven percent of total United States employment is in the high-risk category of potentially becoming automated over the next several decades.

On a global scale, McKinsey & Company (the global consulting firm) estimates that the adaptation of currently demonstrated automation technologies could affect fifty percent of the world economy, or 1.2 billion employees and $14.6 trillion in wages over the next two decades. By replacing human workers, machines often reduce labor costs, liability, management duties and space requirements. It will be hard for employers to resist these increased efficiencies.

Target, CVS and Kohl's are all deploying more self-checkout machines. More than 150 companies like Amazon, Zippin, BingoBox and Standard Cognition are developing cashier-free retail options. Walmart is deploying floor-cleaning robots. In the financial sector, "robo-advisors" are already making investment decisions which means that wealth managers everywhere may soon need to find new work. Journalists will be replaced on a massive scale. Algorithms already exist that can write articles and even books with minimal human involvement. By the end of 2020, it is expected that machines will publish a fifth of all business content.

Adidas has opened a robotic manufacturing plant in Germany called the Speedfactory. It eliminates the six-week shipping time from suppliers in Asia to Europe. More than nine million people across Southeast Asia are dependent on textiles, clothing and footwear jobs. Technology like the Speedfactory will put millions out of work. It will also make goods more accessible and reduce costs.

A significant percentage of the current 3.6 million fast food workers will be impacted by the use of machines designed to do their jobs faster, more efficiently and more cost effectively. Calls for increases in the minimum wage will only accelerate the transition to increased automation. A study at the University of Washington found that an increase in Seattle's minimum wage resulted in workers receiving fewer hours, resulting in a net loss of income for the worker.

Educational systems have not kept pace with the changing nature of work or technology, resulting in many employers already saying they cannot find enough workers with the skills they need. In a McKinsey survey of young people and employers, forty percent of employers said "lack of skills" was the main reason for entry-level job vacancies. The survey identified gaps in technical skills such as STEM subject degrees and deficiencies in soft skills such as communication, teamwork and punctuality.

Today, thirty to forty-five percent of the working-age population around the world is underutilized—unemployed, inactive, or underemployed.

SEVENTY-FIVE MILLION YOUTH
ARE UNEMPLOYED GLOBALLY.

Advances in automation will increase these numbers.

Many are concerned about their children's economic prospects. It is no longer an article of faith that every generation will enjoy a higher standard of living than their parents. And there's good reason for concern; real wages have been stagnating for decades while the costs of goods and services have continued to increase.

The American Dream, for many, has become increasingly out of reach. Many blame governments, corporations and establishment "elites" around the world. And the principles of free trade and open borders are under attack. From 2000 to 2014, migration provided about forty percent of labor force growth in Canada, Spain, the United Kingdom and the United States. Migrant workers, on average, earn wages that are twenty to thirty percent lower than those of comparable native-born workers.

Popular sentiment has moved against immigration. Surveys suggest that a significant proportion of middle and low-income groups in the United States are pessimistic about the future and likely to hold particularly negative views about immigrants.

Greater interaction between humans and machines will increase productivity but will require different skills, different wage models and different types of investments in education to allow workers to acquire the skills required to interface and keep pace with changing technology. Increased emphasis will need to be placed on job creation, digital jobs in particular.

Brynjolfsson emphasizes that the commitment to education needs to continue. He also argues that lifelong learning will be essential for people to keep pace with the changing demands of roles constantly being reshaped by technology. "We have to reinvent education and reskilling," he says.

Brynjolfsson says, "People are going to have to take it upon themselves to more aggressively learn these skills... it's going to be a case of lifelong learning and continuously reskilling."

Machines are not good at everything. As Brynjolfsson notes, machines are not very good at motivating, nurturing, caring for, or comforting people. Human interactions are important and, so far at least, machines are far less capable than humans are for those tasks.

According to the research firm Oxford Economics, employers' top priorities already include relationship building, cultural sensitivity, brain-storming, co-creativity and the ability to manage diverse employees—essentially, the right-brained skills of social interaction. Meg Bear, Oracle group vice president, says;

"EMPATHY IS *THE* CRITICAL 21ST CENTURY SKILL."

As technology continues to advance, the demand for these uniquely human skills is only going to increase.

Those who can build and maintain relationships, collaborate and lead and those who can engage clients with humor, energy, sensitivity and generosity will be tomorrow's most sought-after employees.

We need to be thinking about how humans will continue to add value in a world where computing power and the opportunities made possible by that computing power double every two years. Adding value in the machine age will require that we learn to dance with machines. It will require that we leverage our strengths by developing all the qualities that make us uniquely human—the ability to lead, the ability to collaborate and the ability to empathize. It will require that we remain flexible, adaptive and multidimensional.

We will also find that machines are not infallible. The failure of the MCAS (Maneuvering Characteristics Augmentation System) on Boeing's 737 MAX 8 jetliner may have resulted in the March 2019 Ethiopian airline crash that killed 157 people. According to the *New York Times*, the same faulty systems may have also been responsible for the Lion Air crash that killed 189 people in October 2018. False information from the plane's sensors may have caused the MCAS to change the angle of the plane's flight. This could have resulted in either or both of these aviation disasters.

Similar issues may arise in other uses of technology like self-driving vehicles. Faulty software, sensors, or connections can exist in any environment that employs them.

Policy makers working with education providers will need to do more to improve basic STEM skills, prepare children for the technological revolution and foster adaptive, lifelong learning. Companies will need to play a more active role in educating and training workers and consumers. This training will not only need to train workers and consumers to use and work with technology; it will also need to prepare them to respond to failures in technology.

New forms of entrepreneurship that emerge will need to be nurtured and encouraged. Finally, as automation creates increased unemployment and greater pressure on wages, ideas such as a universal basic income will need to be considered and tested.

These changes in technology will require lifelong learning and continuous adaptation.

Millennial Samurai will forever need to be sharpening their swords.

POLITICAL DYSFUNCTION

*"Just because you don't take an interest
in politics doesn't mean that politics
won't take an interest in you."*

—Pericles, Greek philosopher.

2016 marked the first time in the forty-plus-year history of the Gallup Poll that public confidence in government was measured in the single digits.

ACCORDING TO PUBLIC POLICY POLLING, AMERICANS LIKE WITCHES, THE IRS AND EVEN HEMORRHOIDS BETTER THAN CONGRESS.

Eighty-five percent of registered voters polled disapprove of the job Congress is doing; only eight percent approve.

Our political finance system, in which candidates are funded by deep-pocketed special interests, has eroded public confidence in our system of government. In 2014, Arianna Huffington wrote *Pigs at the Trough: How Corporate Greed and Political Corruption Are Undermining America*. In it, she details how politicians have been complicit in facilitating massive transfers of wealth from taxpayers to corporate special interests.

MANY OF AMERICA'S LARGEST CORPORATIONS PAY ZERO IN FEDERAL INCOME TAXES.

The richest 0.1% of Americans pay a lower percentage of income taxes, as a share of net worth, than the bottom 99.9%. All of this is due to lobbying and special interest influence. Provisions of the tax code are often written by special interests and then submitted to legislators who then present these bills to Congress as proposed legislation, which are then voted upon by representatives who have received campaign contributions from the very same special interests.

GERRYMANDERING, THE MEANS BY WHICH POLITICAL PARTIES DETERMINE ELECTORAL DISTRICTS, HAS BECOME SO PERVERTED THAT EVEN HOLDING ELECTIONS NOW SEEMS POINTLESS.

Through the use of gerrymandering, the boundaries of electoral districts have been specifically designed by incumbent politicians in both parties to be overwhelmingly Republican or Democrat. Under this system, only the most highly partisan candidates of the Democratic or Republican party can win. The consequence is a polarized government, paralyzed by partisan gridlock and unable to govern effectively.

Political scientists Nolan McCarty, Keith Poole and Howard Rosenthal have examined the attitudes of our political parties going back to 1879 and have found party polarization in recent years to be greater than at any time in the last 160 years.

YOU HAVE TO GO BACK TO THE CIVIL WAR TO FIND A LEVEL OF POLITICAL POLARIZATION EQUAL TO WHAT WE ARE SEEING TODAY.

Ideological polarization, the rise of social media, targeted mainstream media (designed to play to the public's confirmations biases) and the radicalization of both the Republican and the Democratic base—have all contributed to our current state of political dysfunction.

THE POLITICAL SYSTEM ITSELF HAS COME TO BE SEEN AS ILLEGITIMATE. THESE ARE DANGEROUS AND UNCHARTED WATERS FOR MODERN AMERICAN DEMOCRACY.

American families, undercut by globalization and technological change, have suffered stagnant or declining incomes for years. Income inequality in the United States now exceeds anything seen in our history and anything seen in other industrialized nations.

In 1990, the United States was ranked sixth in education and health care. In 2018, according to a study out of the University of Washington, it was ranked twenty-seventh.

The total of our public debt is now almost half a million dollars for every American family. Healthcare costs have risen out of control putting it out of reach for millions of Americans.

OUR SYSTEM OF GOVERNMENT IS BROKEN.

We are sending the most partisan candidates from both parties to Congress—the exact opposite of who we should be sending.

So, what do we do? Given the influence of special interests, party reformation hardly seems like a viable option. And anyone who believes that their party (the one that half the country now despises) is the answer, is obviously wrong (in the opinion of half the country). What the entire country thinks may not matter to some, but it should. Not caring what the other half of the country thinks (the half that doesn't agree with you) is incredibly selfish. Worse, it's counter-productive. It doesn't offer a viable path forward. It guarantees continued polarization and deadlock and therefore undermines all of us.

Extreme partisanship identifies people who don't care about the views of those they disagree with. They want things to be the way they believe they should be, the way they see the world. These people are a big part of the problem on both sides of the political spectrum. You don't want to be one of those people.

Each of us represent only one of 330 million people in the United States What any one of us thinks, about any of the major issues facing all of us, is insignificant. You're just one piece of the puzzle and so is everyone else you meet. Our combined views are and should be what matter.

CONSENSUS IS WHAT MATTERS.

Understanding that is the first step toward progress.

So, what is the answer? Is it additional new parties that would require coalition building to obtain a majority? Possibly. But that doesn't address the flawed historical performance of the incumbent players or the fact that these major players are hopelessly compromised by special interests. So, a new party (or parties) is not enough. In my view, absent the removal of money and special-interest influence, the only viable response to the existing two-party system is circumvention. The answer is to work around the current system.

THE ANSWER IS TO DENY BOTH MAJOR POLITICAL PARTIES THE BRAND LOYALTY THAT THEY CURRENTLY ENJOY.

We can do this simply by refusing to support—financially or otherwise—either Republican or Democratic candidates. By supporting and voting only for moderate, intelligent, open-minded, non-partisan candidates, you take away the power of the incumbent political parties.

If the incumbent parties are seen as tarnished brands and their candidates can't win elections, special interest money and influence will abandon those parties like rats abandoning a sinking ship. This will then allow for true moderates to reach compromise. It will allow for the best ideas from both sides of the political spectrum to be leveraged and employed. And it will allow for legislation to be passed that provides for true campaign finance reform and an end to gerrymandering. It will allow for shared governance, an end to gridlock and increased collaboration and efficiency.

Political dysfunction seems to be a highly complex and seemingly insurmountable problem. In truth, there's a very simple fix. It doesn't require a revolution. It doesn't even require legislation. It simply requires a shift in mindset. It's true, that a shift in mindset isn't easy. It's just easier than any other alternative.

THE FIX IS TO TREAT THE ESTABLISHED BRANDS AS THEIR PERFORMANCE DICTATES—BY REJECTING BOTH OF THEM. IF ENOUGH PEOPLE WERE TO DO THIS, BOTH PARTIES WOULD LOSE THEIR POWER.

Others will disagree. Those who are involved in, invested in, or benefiting from the current system will disagree most strenuously. The party faithful will object out of ignorance and ingrained bias, the party apparatus will object out of self-interest and the special interest influencers will object because fixing the system (by limiting their disproportionate influence) will cost them billions.

You need to understand that there are those who like the current system; they manipulate the current system, they leverage the dysfunction and they profit from it—some very significantly. My response to these incumbent forces is simple: you have failed us, your time is up.

For some, who cling to their misplaced party loyalty, this may seem like a radical proposition. In truth, it's not. Faced with the radical dysfunction we now labor under and the absence of campaign finance reform and increased transparency, it may be the most sensible solution available, short of revolution.

THE END OF THE TWO-PARTY SYSTEM

"Every valuable human being must be a radical and
a rebel, for what he must aim at is to make
things better than they are."

—Neils Bohr, Danish physicist.

George Washington, 1st President of the United States, in his farewell address to the nation on September 19, 1796, said, "I have already intimated to you the danger of parties in the state, with particular reference to the founding of them on geographical discriminations. Let me now take a more comprehensive view and warn you in the most solemn manner against the baneful effects of the spirit of party, generally. This spirit, unfortunately, is inseparable from our nature, having its root in the strongest passions of the human mind. It exists under different shapes in all governments, more or less stifled, controlled, or repressed; but, in those of the popular form, it is seen in its greatest rankness and is truly their worst enemy."

Ironically, the entire speech is still read aloud on the floor of the Senate every year on his birthday. Unfortunately, his advice hasn't been heeded. Today, very few elected leaders think for themselves and party has, as Washington said it would, become a major source of political dysfunction.

THIS COUNTRY IS CONTROLLED BY SPECIAL INTERESTS AND THEY ARE RESPONSIBLE FOR THE GREATEST TRANSFER OF WEALTH IN HUMAN HISTORY.

You pay taxes into the system and your elected representatives transfer those funds (your money) to America's politically connected corporate elite and/or to the constituents that support their election and reelection. This has been happening for decades and it's never been worse.

"We must never judge political movements by their aims, no matter how loudly proclaimed or how sincerely upheld, but only by the means they use to realize these aims."—Warner Heisenberg, physicist.

THE PROBLEM WITH THE AMERICAN POLITICAL SYSTEM IS SYSTEMIC. THE TWO-PARTY SYSTEM IS FATALLY FLAWED—IT NO LONGER REPRESENTS OR SERVES THE AMERICAN PEOPLE.

Abraham Lincoln, 16th President of the United States, said, "If you once forfeit the confidence of your fellow citizens, you can never regain their respect and esteem."

Through decades of abuse and neglect, both the Republican and Democratic parties have forfeited that confidence.

The world is awash in a sea of social, economic, religious, technological and political change. Individual empowerment is greater than at any other time in human history.

NO DYSFUNCTIONAL POLITICAL SYSTEM CAN LONG ENDURE.

This is especially true in a world where people are educated, connected and empowered.

What you are seeing today, in the dysfunction that paralyzes Congress, is an unraveling of the existing political system. It's only a matter of time before complete failure occurs. How much time is anyone's guess but I would take the under on thirty years. It is inconceivable to me that major structural political change will not occur in the United States before 2050. I believe it must and will happen much sooner.

The major political parties, supported by the media, are attempting to accumulate and maintain political power by dividing and appealing to us along racial, social, economic, political and ideological lines. Stop and think about it.

BOTH PARTIES PROFIT FROM DIVISION.

It's Business 101—product differentiation. By defining your offering in stark terms, you give people a clear choice. Chocolate or vanilla. And remember, you don't need one hundred percent of the people to achieve your objective. You only need fifty-one percent. You can effectively ignore the other forty-nine percent. This is how our political parties think. Once elected, they reward their voters, constituents and donors with jobs, contracts, public works projects and favorable legislation.

Both political parties encourage division, if for no other reason than to make the competition's offering seem unacceptable and to underscore the value of their own offering. Creating division also serves both political parties in another important way. It's a major source of distraction. If Party A's leadership keeps their constituents focused on the threat posed by Party B, the constituents of Party A will be less likely to focus on the deficiencies of Party A's leadership. No matter how bad either party is, it will always be better than the alternative—so long as the alternative is always portrayed in starkly unfavorable terms.

COMPROMISE AND COLLABORATION
DON'T WIN ELECTIONS—DIVISION DOES.

The people in this country who profit from division are the people who are creating it—aided by the ignorant and the uninformed whom they skillfully manipulate with false information and carefully crafted and choreographed narratives that encourage division. This tactic will eventually lose its appeal. Millennials are far more educated, empowered and diverse than any prior generation. Their children will be even more educated, empowered and ethnically diverse. Millennials are also more networked and now have access to a democratized media, which will make them more decentralized and far more difficult to control.

Income inequality, unemployment, economic uncertainty and continued political polarization will cause Millennials to become increasingly dissatisfied with the current system. They will come to see it for what it is—unsustainable—and they will act. They will begin to rise up and demand change. It's already happening.

Richard Hass, President of the Council on Foreign Relations, tells us that history suggests that world orders die long before anyone notices. The world order that we grew up with is gone.

THE TWO-PARTY SYSTEM IS THE WALKING DEAD.

It's just a matter of time before it's replaced by something else—hopefully something better.

The political mayhem that we are witnessing is far from over. Our children and our grandchildren will be dealing with it; and the people who are causing mayhem will continue blaming it on others.

THE ANSWER IS FOR PEOPLE FROM ALL WALKS OF LIFE, ALL RACES, ALL CREEDS, ALL RELIGIONS AND ALL BELIEFS TO RECOGNIZE THAT THEIR COMMON CONDITION CREATES MORE THAT UNITES THEM THAN DIVIDES THEM.

People on all sides of the political spectrum need to focus on what unites them and elect candidates who embrace and are committed to advancing their shared values of liberty, equality, opportunity and justice for all.

It may take decades before all vestiges of the two-party system are gone—but dramatic and systemic change is inevitable and necessary, if we are to preserve the greatest experiment in democracy the world has ever known.

148

CAMPAIGN FINANCE REFORM

*Special interests have a stranglehold on politicians
and it is inconceivable that these same politicians
will ever vote to loosen that grip. Therefore, the
most viable solution, short of revolution, is to elect
nonpartisan candidates that work exclusively for and
are funded exclusively by the American people.*

B y raising eight million donations, averaging twenty-seven dollars each, Bernie Sanders has already shown a path forward that doesn't require government involvement. That path is the use of broad-based, grassroots, public financing of elections that does not rely on large contributions.

Candidates who can unite the people, on both sides of the political spectrum, can use that independent campaign finance model to create a broad and diverse coalition of public support, uncorrupted by party influence and special interests.

THAT NEW AND SUPERIOR MODEL OF INDEPENDENT GRASSROOTS CAMPAIGNS FINANCED BY, FROM, AND FOR THE PEOPLE, WILL RENDER THE EXISTING TWO-PARTY SYSTEM OBSOLETE.

Strong candidates who can develop a broad following will be able to raise small contributions, potentially from millions of people, to finance their campaigns. These candidates will not need the major political parties.

To facilitate this alternative finance model, America needs a new online system for vetting and electing candidates for public office. A system that empowers both the public and the candidates. It could be as simple as a nonprofit or government-funded Facebook-like platform—a platform that would allow candidates to: communicate with and raise small donations from their supporters; recruit, organize and empower volunteers; make real-time financial disclosures of contributions; and disseminate substantive information on the site including bios, degrees, licenses, certifications, blogs, vlogs, interviews with media and detailed positions on issues. This same site would allow people and the press to learn about; research, interview comment on and communicate with candidates, with equal opportunity for the candidates to respond.

The same platform, supported by blockchain technology, could allow people to verify their identity and even vote for candidates while on the site. It could provide a platform that lobbyists might be required to use when communicating with candidates and/or elected officials to create increased transparency and accountability. It could eliminate the need for costly primaries. People could potentially vote at any time throughout the year.

This is all entirely possible with existing technology. This could be done through an open-source, free public site available to the general public and to all candidates for public office, including both state and federal elections. A platform like this would empower both the public and candidates for public office. It would eliminate the need for political parties altogether and it would reign in the perverse influence of lobbyists and special interests. This is an obvious opportunity made possible by advances in technology that can create increased transparency and accountability. Other solutions exist as well. And all of them should be considered.

Those who create and champion this type of platform, freeing the public from the limitations of the current systems, will rightfully be regarded as having made one of the greatest contributions to American democracy ever made.

The goal must be to limit the corrupting influence of money in politics and empower candidates to serve their constituents and the public interest without relying on a party apparatus or hierarchy that is funded and irredeemably corrupted by special interests. My hope is that Millennial Samurai will be dedicated to achieving this goal. The incumbent players will never create such a system—but a Millennial Samurai could—in their garage.

149

THE ELECTORAL COLLEGE

Some have claimed that the electoral college is one of the most dangerous institutions in American politics. They argue that the electoral college system, as opposed to a simple majority vote, distorts the one-person, one-vote principle of democracy because electoral votes are not distributed according to population.

It is accurate to say that the electoral college gives citizens of smaller states disproportionate weight in a Presidential election. For example, Vermont, a state with a population of about six hundred thousand, has one member in the House of Representatives and two members in the United States Senate, which gives the citizens of Vermont three electoral votes, or one electoral vote per two hundred thousand people. California, our most populous state, has more than thirty-nine million people and fifty-five electoral votes, or approximately one vote per 715 thousand people. Therefore, individuals in Vermont have nearly four times the voting power in the electoral college as Californians. The question remains; is this a good thing or a bad thing?

F. Scott Fitzgerald, American fiction writer, said;

"THE TEST OF A FIRST-RATE INTELLIGENCE IS THE ABILITY TO HOLD TWO OPPOSING IDEAS IN THE MIND AT THE SAME TIME, AND STILL RETAIN THE ABILITY TO FUNCTION."

I have two opposing views on the electoral college. One is predicated on the notion that the American dream is alive and well. And the other assumes the opposite—that the party is over and the dream is dead. If you still believe in the American dream, then you should believe in the electoral college. If you believe that the American dream is dead and that economic inequality will continue to increase, leading to obscene concentrations of wealth and the disappearance of the middle class (which is what we are now seeing), then democracy may be a better choice going forward and the electoral college may have outlived its usefulness.

I want to believe that the American dream is alive and well, or at least salvageable, but evidence is mounting that it isn't.

Many argue that using the electoral college instead of the popular vote and majority rule is undemocratic. That is accurate. What they fail to understand or acknowledge is that our founders went to great lengths to ensure that America is a republic and not a democracy. In fact, the word democracy does not appear in the Declaration of Independence, the Constitution, or any of our founding documents. Why is that?

John Adams, 2nd President of the United States, warned in a letter;

"REMEMBER, DEMOCRACY NEVER LASTS LONG. IT SOON WASTES, EXHAUSTS AND MURDERS ITSELF. THERE NEVER WAS A DEMOCRACY YET THAT DID NOT COMMIT SUICIDE."

It's hard to argue for democracy with that admonition.

John Marshall, former Chief Justice of the United States Supreme Court, observed, "Between a balanced republic and a democracy, the difference is like that between order and chaos."

Some argue that these were simply the positions of a wealthy, white, land-owning class of elites that designed a system 240 years ago in order to serve their own social, political and economic interests. For the purpose of argument, let's assume that's true. That doesn't alter the fact that this system, imperfect as it might be, has allowed for the orderly and peaceful transition of power and the peaceful cooperation of all fifty states for most of our 240-year history as a nation. In sum, the system that these men devised has worked. It has balanced the rights of majority and minority interests in a way that has promoted equilibrium, stability and prosperity. Some will say, "not prosperity for all." True, but relative prosperity for most.

The question therefore becomes: would a radical and sweeping change from a republic to a democracy increase equilibrium, stability and prosperity or decrease it? Given the widespread absence of thoughtful and informed critical thinking among the majority of our citizens, I fear the latter.

On September 14, 2012, the 225th anniversary of the Constitution, former United States Supreme Court Justice David Souter said that our republican government wasn't threatened by foreign invasion or a military coup, but by civic ignorance.

He said;

"I DON'T BELIEVE THAT THERE IS ANY PROBLEM OF AMERICAN GOVERNMENT AND AMERICAN PUBLIC LIFE WHICH IS MORE SIGNIFICANT THAN THE PREVALENCE OF CIVIC IGNORANCE OF THE CONSTITUTION OF THE UNITED STATES AND THE STRUCTURE OF GOVERNMENT."

With Justice Souter's comments in mind, is America ready for democracy? I think not. Moreover, before abandoning the electoral college, one should also ask; is it worth taking the risk of abandoning a system that has worked successfully, albeit not perfectly, for more than 240 years to try a new system—one advanced by those allegedly advocating on behalf of the majority, that is entirely untested and that will decrease state participation?

I'M NOT CONVINCED THAT THE PEOPLE ARE READY FOR PURE DEMOCRACY ANY MORE THAN THEY WERE 240 YEARS AGO.

And, like James Madison, I don't think that the majority can be relied upon to protect the rights of the minority. In Federalist Paper No. 10, Madison wanted to prevent rule by majority faction, saying, "Measures are too often decided, not according to the rules of justice and the rights of the minority party, but by the superior force of an interested and overbearing majority."

The founders were concerned about the tyranny of majority rule. So, throughout our Constitution, they placed impediments to that tyranny. Two houses of Congress pose one obstacle to majority rule. That is, fifty-one senators can block the wishes of 435 representatives and forty-nine senators. The President can veto the wishes of 535 members of Congress. It takes two-thirds of both houses of Congress to override a Presidential veto. To change the Constitution requires not a majority but a two-thirds vote of both houses and if an amendment is approved, it requires ratification by three-fourths of state legislatures.

The electoral college is yet another measure that thwarts majority rule. It makes sure that the highly-populated states—roughly ten states on the east and west coasts—cannot alone control who is elected POTUS. That forces a Presidential candidate to take into consideration the wishes of the other forty states.

Those who argue for majority rule might want to get rid of the Senate as well, where states, regardless of population, have two senators. Or they might argue that we should change representation in the House of Representatives to a system of proportional representation and eliminate the guarantee that each state gets at least one representative. Currently, seven states with populations of one million or fewer each have one representative, thus giving them disproportionate influence in Congress.

IT IS IMPORTANT TO UNDERSTAND THAT WE ARE NOT SIMPLY A NATION OF CITIZENS. WE ARE ALSO A NATION OF STATES.

And if we are to maintain our strength and unity as the United States of America, then we must have a system that balances the needs of both our majority and minority elements. The needs of our small states must be balanced with those of our larger states. The needs of the majority must be balanced with the needs of the minority.

Spain, which has proportional representation, was unable to even form a coalition government for almost a year. Setting a world record, Belgium, with its proportional representation voting system, did not have an elected government for 589 days.

Professor Charles R. Kesler of Claremont McKenna College explains, "In truth, the issue is democracy with federalism (the electoral college) versus democracy without federalism (a national popular vote). Either is democratic. Only the electoral college preserves federalism, moderates ideological differences and promotes national consensus in our choice of a chief executive."

The electoral college encourages national participation and engagement in government by all fifty states. This in turn promotes unity, something our country desperately needs. Absent such a system, the residents of smaller states would feel disenfranchised. They would rightly feel that their votes do not count. They might disengage, believing that the new President will have little or no regard for their interests. Secession by some states could easily follow. America has already seen the consequences of such disengagement. It resulted in the Civil War. And in a country that is now equally and sharply divided, that could happen again.

AN ABANDONMENT OF THE ELECTORAL COLLEGE COULD DIVIDE THE NATION ALONG STATE LINES.

We might cease to be one powerful nation made up of fifty states and instead end up with regional democracies or other smaller coalitions of like-minded communities. The founders saw and anticipated this possibility more than 240 years ago and they designed our republic to address the inevitable majority/minority imbalance that they anticipated.

The founders created a stable, well-planned and carefully designed system that has operated smoothly and successfully for almost two and a half centuries. It preserves federalism, encourages broad state participation and unity, prevents chaos, creates definitive electoral outcomes and prevents tyrannical or unreasonable rule.

Alexander Hamilton, American statesman and one of the country's founding fathers, was right when he described the electoral college in Federalist Paper No. 68;

"PERHAPS THE ELECTORAL COLLEGE IS IMPERFECT, BUT A PERFECT SOLUTION IS DOUBTLESS UNACHIEVABLE. NEVERTHELESS, THE PRESIDENTIAL ELECTION PROCESS DEVISED BY THE FRAMERS IS CERTAINLY EXCELLENT."

One has to ask why someone would argue for a democracy when the founders warned that it would fail and went to great lengths to avoid it? When you ask the question, one answer becomes obvious—power and control. I'm not choosing sides here; I view both of America's political parties as fundamentally flawed. However, it is painfully clear that some within the leadership of the Democratic Party want to abandon the electoral college because they want the power and control that a popular vote would provide them. In essence, they want the masses (the majority) to be in control—so long as they control the masses.

What they fail to realize, is that they will never be able to maintain that control. They can't even control their own party. And as John Adams warned, "There never has been a democracy that didn't commit suicide." I would therefore urge caution in abandoning something that does work for the promise of something that never has worked. A better option would be to address the deficiencies that exist within our current system of government before abandoning it, especially for an alternative that is likely to be inferior.

But what if we are unable—or those in power are unwilling—to address our existing deficiencies? What if economic inequality continues to increase and the nation's wealth continues to be concentrated in the hands of the few? What if the middle class continues to shrink and the nation's natural resources continue to be plundered and put at risk?

WHAT IF THE NEEDS OF SOCIETY CONTINUE TO BE UNMET BY AN ELITIST CLASS THAT ONLY GROWS MORE POWERFUL AND MORE CONCENTRATED?

If these trends continue, then at some point, change must occur. And at that point, democracy and an end to the electoral college may be the best vehicle to facilitate that change, short of revolution.

150

AMERICAN EXCEPTIONALISM

*America is and always has been exceptional.
Since its founding in 1776, America has been
built on the principles of liberty, equality,
self-government and social mobility. These
principles have defined America for 240 years.*

Amerca is not without fault. Like all other countries, we have made many mistakes. That is undeniable.

WHAT MAKES AMERICA EXCEPTIONAL IS NOT THAT IT IS FREE FROM ERROR, BUT THAT ITS PROMISE IS UNPARALLELED.

And that promise has already shown itself to be not simply a major force for good in the world, but *the* major force for good in the world.

History is filled with examples of Americans rising to meet great challenges. Americans fought against fascism and mass genocide during WWII; rebuilt Europe after WWII; stood up to the spread of communism; brought down the Berlin Wall; negotiated nuclear weapons reductions with Russia and facilitated the peace accord between Egypt and Israel. When the need arose, Americans answered the call.

For more than two centuries, America has been revered in the world. Americans could go almost anywhere and be welcomed. This was a reflection of the status our country held around the world.

Today, that is no longer the case. We stand at a turning point. The decisions we make as a nation will determine whether the 21ˢᵗ Century will be another era of American leadership or if our global leadership will come to an end as it has for other major powers throughout history.

Our political dysfunction is not only affecting our status in the world, it is also limiting our ability to pursue our national goals. Our system of self-government has been compromised by a campaign finance system that allows special interests to corrupt politicians and buy elections. These special interests have increased the costs of healthcare, education and our nation's public works projects. They have created financial markets that generate obscene profits for those who can manipulate the markets rather than increased value for the small investors who fund those markets, or the labor that makes such markets possible.

Other special interests are responsible for demanding unsustainable entitlements that are capable of bankrupting state and local governments. Still others are responsible for orchestrating and encouraging America's involvement in foreign wars and global conflicts in a reckless pursuit of corporate profits and political power. Together, these special interests are responsible for the greatest transfer of wealth in human history and untold suffering.

Social mobility, once a source of national pride, is no longer available to millions of Americans. In America today, if you're born in the bottom twenty percent of the economy, the likelihood is that you will die there.

MILLENNIAL SAMURAI WILL HAVE THE OPPORTUNITY TO REDEFINE AND RESTORE AMERICAN EXCEPTIONALISM, AND TO ONCE AGAIN LEAD THE WORLD COMMUNITY.

I hope and trust that they will seize that opportunity and that the new definition of American Exceptionalism will include a recognition of the need for global unity, compromise, collaboration and compassion.

THE BYSTANDER EFFECT

*The more people present in a given situation,
the less likely we are to intervene when
someone needs help.*

In 1968, psychologists John Darley and Bibb Latane did pioneering research on a phenomenon that has come to be known as the "bystander effect." In their experiments, they tricked research subjects into thinking that another participant in the room was having a seizure. They found that participants who believed that they were alone in the room with the "victim" were far more likely to seek help and to do so more quickly than when participants were seated in the room with three or four others. The finding was that the presence of other people reduces our own sense of responsibility for a given situation.

This partly explains our abstention from politics and other pressing issues.

**WE ASSUME THAT WE DON'T NEED TO ADDRESS CERTAIN
MATTERS BECAUSE OTHERS WILL.**

Unfortunately, because this is a shared assumption, it becomes a de facto false assumption.

Your involvement is required in all matters affecting your life and the lives of those you love.

YOU DON'T HAVE THE LUXURY TO BE A BYSTANDER.

Not in today's world and certainly not in tomorrow's.

HOW TO BUILD CONSENSUS

Unity is the only way forward.

O ur government is paralyzed. Republicans and Democrats are so ideologically polarized that they can't get anything done. Both parties have shut down the government on nineteen separate occasions since 1977. Republicans and Democrats also have significant divisions among themselves.

Democrats include far-left liberals and Republicans include far-right conservatives.

THE PEOPLE ON THE FAR LEFT AND THE FAR RIGHT ARE CONTRIBUTING TO THE PROBLEMS WE NOW FACE.

They are creating and maintaining the polarization and division. These are the people who refuse to work together and refuse to compromise. If you are voting for these people, then you too are part of the problem. The good news is, you are also the solution.

It doesn't matter if you are a Democrat or a Republican. If you are ideologically driven and you are helping to elect ideologically driven zealots, then you need to stop. Why? Because the people you are sending to Congress can't build consensus. Consequently, they can't govern. All they can do is obstruct—and obstruction hurts all of us.

You wouldn't allow your employees to engage in a level of competition against one another that impairs the company's ability to meet its objectives. So, why would you allow it in your government?

We all need to stop being intellectually lazy and selfish.

IT'S NOT ALL ABOUT YOU, YOUR PASSION FOR CRIMINAL JUSTICE REFORM, YOUR SEXUAL ORIENTATION, YOUR VIEWS ON ABORTION, OR YOUR GUNS. IT'S ABOUT US—ALL OF US.

So, what can you do? How can you help to create positive change? You can begin by losing the "D," the "R," and the "Me" and shift your focus and your allegiance to "Us." Understand that both political parties care first and foremost about themselves. They care about their survival, their growth and their quest for power and control.

MILTON FRIEDMAN, NOBEL PRIZE WINNING ECONOMIST, SAID, "THE WORLD RUNS ON INDIVIDUALS PURSUING THEIR SELF-INTERESTS."

Not your interests, their interests. Politicians on both sides of the aisle care about who and what will get them elected and then reelected. They operate out of self-interest. As Friedman notes, that's human nature. And in today's political environment, getting elected takes money—lots of it. If you're not giving your elected representatives money, ask yourself who does, because I can promise you that your representatives care more about them than they do about you.

But you're a voter, you say. They need you. No, they don't. What they need is your vote—and you give that freely. You give it to the candidates who say what you want to hear. You give it to people you know little, if anything, about. You vote for your United States senators with less reflection than you exercise when deciding what movie to see. And you vote along party lines, just like your representatives do.

Why? Because they carry a brand—an "R" or a "D"—that you have been made to believe means that they are somehow qualified to lead? Or is it because their false narrative appeals to your confirmation bias and therefore seems comforting? And how have they demonstrated their qualifications—through decades of incompetence and dysfunction?

You vote for candidates who you believe are on your "team." Rather than think for yourself, you allow your "team" to think for you. Why? Because you're either too busy, too trusting, too uniformed, or too lazy to think for yourself.

And how's that been working out for you? Are you willing to accept the constant infighting in Congress, the lack of progress on critical issues, or our lessening stature and increased vulnerability domestically and internationally?

Aren't you tired of the dysfunction and paralysis? Are you ready for change—real change? Then here's what you need to do.

Reject both political parties. Reject both brands. Reject ideology. Reject identity politics. Embrace unity. Elect people who can work with one another.

ELECT SMART PEOPLE—PEOPLE WHO CAN BUILD CONSENSUS.

Elect people whose priority is to reach across the aisle, form alliances and make real progress. Not the people who are singing your singular tune or the people who are feeding your confirmation biases. Not the people who are fueling your distrust, resentment and division. And not the people who have consistently failed to deliver for decades.

Reach across the aisle yourself when selecting candidates to support. Don't limit yourself to one "team" or the other. Don't be lured by tarnished brands. Look for smart, ethical, consensus builders, regardless of party affiliation. And understand that if they're not talking about the need to build consensus, then they are not consensus builders. If they're not saying that they will vote across party lines, then don't expect them to do so. Make certain that the need for compromise and consensus building is at the core of who they are and what their message is, or don't vote for them.

First, learn to compromise yourself. Then send people to Washington who will do the same. Understand that party officers are their party's stewards. They are not America's stewards, just as corporate officers are their shareholder's stewards, not the public's stewards. Understand that at this moment in history, the two-party system has reached a stalemate; it's become a liability rather than an asset.

THE PEOPLE THAT YOU ELECT SHOULD HAVE ONLY ONE ALLEGIANCE, ONLY ONE PRINCIPAL AND ONLY ONE DUTY OF FIDELITY, NOT TO YOU, NOT TO ME, NOT TO THEMSELVES, BUT TO "US."

America needs a course correction. We are a ship adrift and ships adrift eventually crash upon the shore. We need to chart a new course and we can't rely on maps that have already run us aground.

Look for honest, hardworking and intelligent people regardless of party affiliation. That path provides an immediate and accessible course correction available to all of us, that can create real, lasting and positive change.

And for those of you who think you're clever—the fringe elements who think they can let the other side elect centrists while they send more ideologues to Congress—think again. That door swings both ways. The other side will then do the same and when that happens, we will be back to where we are now—hopelessly divided and dysfunctional. More importantly, that outdated and myopic mentality has no future.

The world is changing rapidly and radically. If we are to survive as a species, distrust and division will need to be replaced by cooperation and collaboration. And those who fail to recognize that, or worse continue to foster increased division, will see their base of support erode with increasing frequency. They will come to be seen as obstructionists and will become marginalized and disenfranchised. They will ultimately come to be seen as the illiterate of the 21st Century.

ALL THAT IS REQUIRED FOR REAL AND SUSTAINABLE CHANGE IS FOR A MAJORITY OF "US" TO RECOGNIZE AND ACT ON THIS SOLUTION.

This simply requires a change in mindset followed by action. Be part of the solution by recognizing our profound interdependence, by speaking out for unity and by seeking and building consensus.

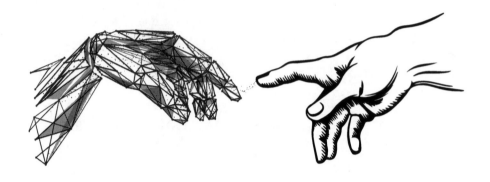

THE FUTURE IS HERE

153

CHANGES IN HUMANITY

*Advances in technology will
redefine life as we know it.*

Forty years ago, the first human was conceived in a petri dish using in vitro fertilization. At the time, the editors of *Nova* magazine complained that in vitro fertilization was;

"THE BIGGEST THREAT SINCE THE ATOM BOMB."

The American Medical Association wanted to halt research altogether.

Since then, millions of babies have been conceived using in vitro fertilization. We are now on the brink of a new ethical dilemma caused by another revolution in reproduction. Scientists working in the field of in vitro gametogenesis (IVG) are learning how to convert adult human cells, taken from a piece of skin on an arm or leg, into artificial gametes (lab-made eggs and sperm) that could be combined to create an embryo and then implanted into a womb.

The possibilities are extraordinary. Adults with no sperm or egg could become biological parents. A child could have a single biological parent, because a skin sample, taken from a single individual, could be used to make both the egg and the sperm.

A SAME-SEX COUPLE COULD HAVE A CHILD THAT IS BIOLOGICALLY RELATED TO BOTH OF THEM.

Even fresh hair samples of someone who recently passed away might be used to create the egg and/or the sperm. Modern gene editing technologies like Crispr-Cas9 can already be used to repair, add, or remove genes.

Eli Akashi, former dean of medicine at Brown University, says;

"WHAT RESEARCHERS HAVE ACHIEVED
SO FAR IS MIND-BOGGLING."

In 2006, a Japanese researcher named Shinya Yamanaka reported that he had induced adult mouse cells into becoming pluripotent stem cells. In 2007, he demonstrated that he could do the same with human cells. Unlike most cells, pluripotent stem cells can develop into any type of cell.

In 2016, two Japanese scientists, Mitinori Saitou and Katsuhiko Hayashi, turned cells from a mouse's tail into induced pluripotent stem cells (iPSCs) and from there, into eggs. This was the first time artificial eggs had been made outside of an organism's body. Using the artificial eggs, Saitou and Hayashi then created eight fertile pups.

According to an article from *Science News*, a research team from the Chinese Academy of Sciences has successfully produced healthy mice from parents of the same sex. The report states that offspring from a pair of female mice are still thriving and continued to reproduce on their own afterward.

Scientists are now working on transforming human cells into gametes. Once that happens, and existing research suggests that it will, editing the stem cells will be possible with existing technology. According to Eli Akashi;

"TO SUGGEST THAT THIS WON'T BE
POSSIBLE IN HUMANS IS NAIVE."

The implications of this new technology are beyond extraordinary and raise a host of moral and ethical questions that society will need to consider.

Studies using germline editing in rats, cattle, sheep and pigs have indicated that it is possible to disable or delete genes in an embryo. This is only possible in some cells and is still not a perfect method, but it is much simpler than trying to correct DNA sequences. Germline editing brings up various legal and ethical concerns because the edits cannot be reversed and the effects would continue through generations.

This is a fascinating area that will redefine life as we know it. Millennial Samurai will provide the technological, moral and ethical leadership required to navigate this emerging and extraordinary field.

154

ARTIFICIAL INTELLIGENCE

"I don't know why more people aren't talking about it."

—Bill Gates, founder of Microsoft and philanthropist.

Artificial Intelligence (AI) is a machine learning system that will eventually be capable of thought or behavior based on natural processes including vision, language processing, reasoning and learning. AI incorporates research from computer science, psychology, mathematics, linguistics and neuroscience and is supported by large data sets and modern distributed computing platforms to develop problem-solving applications that supplant or augment human intelligence.

RAY KURZWEIL, THE HEAD OF AI FOR GOOGLE, SAYS THAT AI WILL ECLIPSE HUMAN INTELLIGENCE BY 2029. HE PREDICTS THAT BEFORE 2050 AI WILL BE A BILLION TIMES MORE CAPABLE THAN HUMAN INTELLIGENCE.

In July of 2017, China announced its ambition to become the world leader in AI. The United States and China are currently considered the leaders in this space. Vladimir Putin says, "Whoever becomes the leader in this sphere will become the ruler of the world." Putin believes that future wars will be fought with drones. "When one party's drones are destroyed by the drones of another, it will have no choice but to surrender." Putin says.

Many are expressing concern that AI will transform the face of warfare. AI can be used to develop cyber weapons like drone swarms (fleets of drones with a shared "brain") that can be used for attacking opponents. Both the United States and China are currently working on this technology.

In 2017, 116 technology leaders signed a letter calling on the United Nations for regulations on how AI weapons are developed and a ban on autonomous weapons known as "killer robots." The group stated that the introduction of autonomous technology would be tantamount to a "third revolution in warfare" following the development of gunpowder and nuclear weapons.

AI also has huge implications for employment. With innovations like self-driving vehicles and stores without clerks or cashiers just around the corner, we are rapidly moving into what could be an era of mass unemployment and with it, an increased likelihood of social unrest. As a result, some are proposing a universal basic income plan which would give every American adult as much as one thousand dollars a month to guarantee them a minimum standard of living while they retrain themselves for new kinds of work.

At the same time, AI is also certain to yield incredible, even unimaginable benefits in all areas of human endeavor. Ray Kurzweil has predicted that by the 2040s, nanotechnology will be incorporated into many of our internal organs and we will have nanobots travelling through our bloodstream curing all or most of our diseases.

AI IS CERTAIN TO HAVE A PROFOUND IMPACT ON YOUR LIFE.

The more you know about AI, the better. It will radically change the world we live in and create unprecedented opportunities and challenges. What most people don't realize, is that this is going to happen over the next twenty to thirty years.

Millennial Samurai will be at the forefront of the technological revolution as we encounter what has been described as the most significant event in human history—"The Singularity".

THE SINGULARITY

"Singularity" represents a school of thought that believes that accelerating progress in technologies will cause a runaway effect, wherein artificial intelligence will exceed human intellectual capacity and control, thus radically changing or even ending civilization in an event called "The Singularity".

The capabilities of such a technology-based intelligence may be impossible for humans to even comprehend. The technological singularity is an occurrence beyond which events may become unpredictable or even unfathomable.

In 2014, theoretical physicist Stephen Hawking, said;

"SUCCESS IN CREATING AI COULD BE THE BIGGEST EVENT IN THE HISTORY OF OUR CIVILIZATION. BUT IT COULD ALSO BE THE LAST, UNLESS WE LEARN HOW TO AVOID THE RISKS."

Hawking believed that in the coming decades, AI could offer "incalculable benefits and risks" such as "technology outsmarting financial markets, out-inventing human researchers, out-manipulating human leaders and developing weapons we cannot even understand." Hawking believed that, "full development of AI could spell the end of the human race." Clearly, more should be done to analyze, plan and prepare for The Singularity.

As technology continues to evolve in areas like AI, advanced genomics, biotechnology, nanotechnology, space travel, renewable energy, 3-D printing, cloud computing and the internet of things, we will gain increased perspectives and our perceptions are certain to undergo radical transformations. We really have no way of knowing how limited and inaccurate our current perceptions may be.

SPACE TRAVEL

"Humanity has the stars in its future."

—Isaac Asimov, American writer and futurist.

According to Dr. Michio Kaku, American theoretical physicist and futurist, the stars we see at night are about fifty to one hundred light years from us and our galaxy is one hundred thousand light years across. The nearest galaxy is two million light years away. Many people believe that the universe is simply too big for interstellar travel to be practical.

According to Einstein's theory of Special Relativity (1905), no usable information can travel faster than light locally, hence it would take centuries to millennia for an extra-terrestrial civilization to travel between the stars.

Within the Milky Way galaxy alone, there are over one hundred billion stars and there are an uncountable number of galaxies in the universe. Although none of the over one hundred extra-solar planets so far discovered in deep space resemble ours, it is inevitable, many scientists believe, that one day we will discover small, earth-like planets that have liquid water—the "universal solvent" that made the first DNA in our oceans possible perhaps 3.5 billion years ago.

**DR. KAKU BELIEVES THAT THE DISCOVERY OF
EARTH-LIKE PLANETS MAY TAKE PLACE WITHIN
THE NEXT TWENTY YEARS, WHEN NASA INTENDS TO
LAUNCH THE SPACE INTERFEROMETRY SATELLITE INTO
ORBIT, WHICH MAY BE SENSITIVE ENOUGH TO DETECT
SMALL PLANETS ORBITING OTHER STARS.**

So far, we have no hard evidence of signals from extra-terrestrial civilizations from any Earth-like planet. The SETI project (the search for extra-terrestrial intelligence) has yet to discover any reproducible evidence of intelligent life in the universe from such Earth-like planets, but the matter is still receiving ongoing scientific study.

According to Dr. Kaku, the key is to reanalyze the objection to faster-than-light travel. Special Relativity was superseded by Einstein's own theory of General Relativity (1915), in which faster-than-light travel is possible under certain rare conditions. The principal challenge is amassing enough energy of a certain type to break the light barrier.

Dr. Kaku believes that one must therefore analyze extra-terrestrial civilizations on the basis of their total energy output and the laws of thermodynamics.

The first realistic attempt to analyze extra-terrestrial civilizations from the point of view of the laws of physics and the laws of thermodynamics was by Russian astrophysicist Nicolai Kardashev. He based his ranking of possible civilizations on the basis of total energy output, which could be quantified and used as a guide to explore the potential of advanced civilizations. Dr. Kardashev breaks civilizations into three types:

- **Type I:** this civilization harnesses the energy output of an entire planet.

- **Type II:** this civilization harnesses the energy output of a star and generates about ten billion times the energy output of a Type I civilization.

- **Type III:** this civilization harnesses the energy output of a galaxy, or about ten billion times the energy output of a Type II civilization.

A Type I civilization would be able to manipulate planetary energies. They might, for example, control or modify their weather. They would have the power to manipulate planetary phenomena such as hurricanes, which can release the energy of hundreds of hydrogen bombs.

A Type II civilization may resemble the Federation of Planets seen on the TV program Star Trek, which is capable of igniting stars and has colonized a tiny fraction of the nearby stars in the galaxy.

A Type III civilization may resemble the Borg, or perhaps the Empire found in the Star Wars saga. They may have colonized the galaxy itself, extracting energy from hundreds of billions of stars.

By contrast, we are a Type 0 civilization which extracts its energy from dead plants (oil and coal), growing at the average rate of about three percent per year. Based on our current growth rate, one might calculate that our own civilization may attain Type I status in about one hundred to two hundred years, Type II status in a few thousand years and Type III status in about one hundred thousand to a million years. These time scales may be accelerated by advances in technology like artificial intelligence or quantum computing.

According to Dr. Kaku;

"TO GO FASTER THAN LIGHT, ONE MUST GO BEYOND SPECIAL RELATIVITY TO GENERAL RELATIVITY AND THE QUANTUM THEORY. ONE CANNOT RULE OUT INTERSTELLAR TRAVEL IF AN ADVANCED CIVILIZATION CAN ATTAIN ENOUGH ENERGY TO DESTABILIZE SPACE AND TIME."

Perhaps only a Type III civilization can harness Planck energy, the energy at which space and time become unstable. Various proposals have been given to exceed the light barrier including wormholes and stretched or warped space, but all of them require energies found only in Type III civilizations.

157

THE WISDOM OF CROWDS

In 1906, the polymath Francis Galton asked 787
farmers to guess the weight of an ox. Their guesses
varied widely, but the average of all of them was only
a single pound off the correct answer of 1,197 pounds.

A Silicon Valley startup called Unanimous AI has built a tool to support human decision-making by crowdsourcing opinions online. It lets hundreds of participants respond to a question, pooling their collective insight, biases and varying expertise into a single answer. Unanimous AI has registered around fifty thousand users and answered 230 thousand questions. Much of the decision making in nature follows the same swarm approach. Birds, insects and fish work together to make better decisions by combining the information they have.

Unanimous AI's "hiveminds" have had remarkable success at predicting a number of events, including the winners of the 2015 Oscars; the winners of the 2016 National Hockey League's Stanley Cup; and the first four winning horses (in order) of the 2016 Kentucky Derby (the odds were 542 to one), converting a twenty-dollar bet into $11,800.

They also predicted not only the winning team in baseball's 2016 World Series, the Chicago Cubs (who took the prize for the first time since 1908), but also the Cub's opponent in the final series, the Cleveland Indians, as well as all eight of the teams to make the playoffs. These accurate predictions were published four months in advance in the Boston Globe.

Even small swarms consistently outperform much larger crowds.

According to Louis Rosenberg of Unanimous AI, we tend to make better decisions as a group than as individuals.

Rosenberg says;

"SWARMS WILL OUTPERFORM VOTES AND POLLS AND SURVEYS BECAUSE IT'S ALLOWING THE GROUP TO CONVERGE ON THE BEST ANSWER RATHER THAN SIMPLY FINDING THE AVERAGE SENTIMENT."

Picking an answer all at once is important because it prevents those who get in first from swaying others. This is very different from groupthink, where the group is being lead by the group's leader or leadership, to a position which may not reflect actual group consensus.

Rosenberg, who worked on building augmented reality systems at the United States Air Force's Armstrong Labs in the early 1990s, found his inspiration in bees. When a swarm of bees wants to set up a new colony, it must come to a collective decision about where to build it. A few hundred scout bees will set off in different directions to look for potential locations . When they return, they perform a waggle dance to communicate information about what they have found to the swarm. Different scouts attempt to pull the swarm toward or away from their preferred direction and eventually the colony decides as a group which scout to follow.

Members of a swarm must vie with others in the group to pull them toward their preferred solution. Rosenberg is trying to capture the same dynamic with his human swarms. Answering a question with the Unanimous AI tool involves moving an icon to one corner of the screen or the other—pulling with or against the crowd—until the hivemind converges. Individuals must constantly vie with other members of the group to persuade them to move toward their preferred solution.

Experiments have shown that this approach outperforms existing crowd-based predictions using polls.

GLASS INFORMATION STORAGE

5-D is humanity's new way of storing information.

COMPUTERS HAVE LEARNED TO READ INFORMATION BASED ON THE BENDING OF LIGHT INSIDE GLASS.

R esearchers at the U.K.'s University of South Hampton have created a glass disk that reads information in five dimensions of space. These glass disks create a nano structure that only lasers can read.

A normal CD holds 128 GB of data. A glass disk of the same size can contain up to 360 TB of data. A glass disk can store three thousand times more data than a CD.

MOREOVER, IT IS ESTIMATED THAT THESE GLASS DISKS WILL LAST 13.8 BILLION YEARS, WHICH IS THE AGE OF THE KNOWN UNIVERSE AND THREE TIMES THE AGE OF EARTH.

They can also survive the intense heat of one thousand degrees Celsius, which would destroy all other storage devices.

ASTEROID MINING

*Water, while abundant on Earth, is rare
in space and that makes it extremely valuable.*

In November 2015, President Obama signed the Space Act into law that recognizes the property rights of private companies over the resources they mine in space. Companies like Planetary Resources, with founding investments from Google founder Larry Page and chairman Eric Schmidt, among others, now plan to mine speeding asteroids.

There are five thousand near-Earth asteroids that have orbits that are easier to get to than landing on the moon. Many are made of pure metal—usually nickel, iron and platinum.

Chris Lewicki, CEO of Planetary Resources, says, "Having an abundant source of platinum group metals from space can transform the way our world works."

AN ASTEROID CALLED DAVIDA HAS BEEN IDENTIFIED, WHICH IS BELIEVED TO CONTAIN OVER ONE HUNDRED TRILLION DOLLARS WORTH OF PLATINUM GROUP METALS. THAT'S MORE THAN THE WORLD'S CURRENT GDP.

An estimated eighteen near-Earth asteroids could also supply water for space fuel. "We currently pay fifty million dollars a ton just to get payloads out of Earth's gravity and up to the ISS," Lewicki says. This water won't be used solely for life support, but also as rocket fuel. "We can convert it into liquid oxygen and hydrogen," Lewicki says. "These are the same ingredients that fueled all 135 NASA space-shuttle missions."

Spacecraft currently need around ten tons of fuel for every ton of mass that you want to transport. For every ton of additional propellant required for an onward Martian transfer, you would need another ten tons of fuel just to carry that up from the earth's surface.

Now imagine if you didn't have to carry that fuel up with you. "It blows the mind how much this changes things," Lewicki says. "If you could take the amount of energy you had in that rocket to get out to space and refill it again, you could get to Pluto."

Lewicki also says;

"ASTEROIDS ARE THE MOST ACCESSIBLE FORM OF RESOURCES THAT WILL ALLOW US TO EXTEND FURTHER INTO SPACE, TO SET UP INFRASTRUCTURE ON THE WAY TO MARS AND THEN ON MARS ITSELF— INFRASTRUCTURE THAT DOESN'T REQUIRE ONE HUNDRED PERCENT OF ITS RESUPPLY FROM EARTH. THIS IS HOW COLONIZATION TAKES OFF."

Asteroid mining is certain to be an emerging industry for Millennial Samurai.

160

GENOMICS

The future is beyond our ability to comprehend.

A dvances in genomics will impact virtually all aspects of life on the planet. The availability of genetic information and understanding the role of genes and DNA, in disease and health, will usher in a far more personalized approach to diagnosis, treatment and prescription in managing our health.

Pharmacogenetics—the identification of specific patient groups who will respond in a particular way to a medicine or treatment, as a consequence of their genetic makeup, will drive clinical practice and the discovery and development of new medicines.

Genes that point to potential health issues will be identified and tests will be widely available. Personalized genomic information will give individuals greater awareness of genetic predispositions they may have. You will have an increased ability to manage your health and prevent disease, as opposed to the classical doctor/patient relationship. Better health will lead to greater longevity for many people.

English gerontologist Aubrey De Grey says;

"THE FIRST PERSON WHO WILL LIVE
TO ONE THOUSAND IS ALIVE TODAY."

Pharmaceutical companies will develop molecules that are targeted at subsets of the population who are identified through specific biomarkers.

Genomic sciences will enable significant advances in the farming of crops and plants for food and fuels. Foods with health benefits will be designed for targeted use in conjunction with an individual's genetic makeup. Improved breeding approaches for animals and plants will enable increased efficiency and output.

Greater understanding of which genes contribute to unwanted human characteristics, as well as to desired ones, will create pressures to deliberately eliminate undesirable genes from an individual and possibly to introduce desired ones.

Human genetic engineering will be available; it's simply a matter of time. Society will have to address the related moral and ethical issues in preparation for the scientific possibilities. In short, advances in genomics will radically change life as we know it.

161

ANTIBIOTIC-RESISTANT SUPERBUGS

*Superbugs are strains of bacteria that
are resistant to antibiotics.*

E ach year, these drug-resistant bacteria infect more than two million
people nationwide and kill at least twenty-three thousand, according to
the United States Centers for Disease Control and Prevention (CDC).

For more than a century, antibiotics have helped to control and destroy
many of the harmful bacteria that can make us sick. But in recent decades,
antibiotics have been losing their effectiveness against some types of bacteria.
Drug-resistant forms of tuberculosis, gonorrhea and staph infections are just a
few of the dangers we now face.

Unfortunately, the way we've been using antibiotics is helping to create
these new superbugs. Antibiotics are some of the most commonly prescribed
drugs. They're also given to livestock and poultry to prevent disease in animals
living in cramped and unhealthy conditions, as well as to promote growth.
Unfortunately, many antibiotics prescribed to people and to animals are
unnecessary.

The overuse and misuse of antibiotics helps to create drug-resistant bacteria.
The FDA estimates that animal agriculture accounts for seventy percent of
all antibiotic use in the United States. The overuse of antibiotics in the meat
and poultry industry is contributing to the rise of antibiotic-resistance in the
United States and around the world.

When used properly, antibiotics can help destroy disease-causing bacteria. But if you take an antibiotic when you have a viral infection like the common cold, the drug won't destroy the virus that's making you sick. Instead, it'll destroy the good bacteria in your body that help you digest food, fight infection and stay healthy. Bacteria that are tough enough to survive the drug will have a chance to grow and multiply. These drug-resistant strains can become superbugs that can no longer be controlled by antibiotics.

Scientists have been trying to keep ahead of newly emerging drug-resistant bacteria by developing new drugs, but it can take years to develop new antibiotics. You can help slow the spread of drug-resistant bacteria by taking antibiotics properly—only when needed. Don't insist on an antibiotic if your health care provider advises otherwise.

One common superbug is methicillin-resistant Staphylococcus aureus (MRSA). These bacteria don't respond to methicillin and related antibiotics. MRSA can cause skin infections and, in more serious cases, pneumonia or bloodstream infections. The CDC estimates that more than eighty thousand aggressive MRSA infections and eleven thousand related deaths occur each year in the United States.

Clostridium difficile is one of the deadliest antibiotic-resistant superbugs. It can strike patients after a course of antibiotics wipes out their existing intestinal bacteria.

THE BEST WAY TO PREVENT BACTERIAL INFECTIONS IS BY WASHING YOUR HANDS FREQUENTLY WITH SOAP AND WATER.

It's also a good idea not to share personal items such as towels or glasses. Antibiotics should be used only as directed. Finally, it is a good idea to eat yogurt while taking antibiotics and to take probiotics after taking antibiotics to replace your body's good bacteria. Always consult with your medical professional before taking antibiotics.

162

CYBERSECURITY

I n April of 2015, the United States Office of Personnel Management (OPM) was hacked. This attack continues to have potentially devastating consequences for America's national security. Evidence suggests that the attack was state-sponsored and that the sponsor may have been China.

CHINA'S MILITARY ALLEGEDLY HAS OVER ONE HUNDRED THOUSAND DEDICATED HACKERS THAT MAKE UP THEIR CYBERESPIONAGE DIVISION WITH UNITS LIKE UNIT 61398.

Five members of 61398 were indicted by a grand jury in Pennsylvania for stealing trade secrets from United States companies like Westinghouse and United States Steel. All defendants still remain at large.

Although American companies and government agencies experience tens of millions of attempted digital intrusions per month, OPM's data is especially sensitive. OPM processes over two million sensitive background investigations per year involving everyone from contractors to federal judges.

OPM's digital files contain over eighteen million copies of Standard Form 86, a 127-page questionnaire required for federal security clearance that includes questions about the applicants, personal finances, past substance abuse and psychiatric care.

THE AGENCY ALSO COLLECTS AND WAREHOUSES DATA ON APPLICANTS FOR SOME OF THE NATION'S MOST SENSITIVE AND SECRETIVE JOBS.

The data includes everything from lie detector tests to information on sexual activity and partners.

The hackers obtained millions of personnel files and millions of digital images like photos and fingerprints.

THIS INFORMATION COULD BE USED TO RECRUIT AND COMPROMISE UNITED STATES MILITARY, GOVERNMENT PERSONNEL AND CONTRACTORS, EVEN JUDGES.

Fingerprints could be grafted onto foreign agents to defeat biometric sensors. The potential risk is alarming and unprecedented.

The United States needs to build better networks that can limit, detect and prevent these intrusions in the future. This will require the combined efforts of our best and our brightest talent. It will require that our government is able to recruit some of that talent away from lucrative opportunities at technology startups and Silicon Valley. It will require that some of that talent decides that defending America, by battling foreign cyberespionage forces, is more important than money or fame. Some of that talent will be Millennial Samurai. If that happens to be you, let me be one of the first to say thank you.

163

THE FUTURE OF WAR

AI could speed up warfare to a point where
unassisted humans can't keep pace.

In July of 2017, China announced plans to become the world's dominant power in "all aspects" of artificial intelligence—including military—by 2030.

In January of 2018, China reported that they had made a breakthrough in building a conventional supercomputer that is ten times faster than today's supercomputers. It's scheduled for completion in 2020. That's a revolutionary leap in computing power.

China is also making advances in quantum information sciences, a field that could accelerate AI and have profound military applications. This research leverages the ability of subatomic particles like photons to exist in multiple states simultaneously and to mirror each other across vast distances. Breakthroughs in this field could change the world as we know it.

China began work last year on a one-billion-dollar national quantum-information-sciences laboratory. China already leads the world in transmitting information with unbreakable quantum encryption.

In January of 2018, China's military TV network broadcast footage of researchers testing swarm intelligence, which could ultimately link dozens of armed drones into an automated attack force.

THESE DRONES COULD BE DESIGNED IN VARYING SIZES RANGING FROM FLYING INSECT-SIZED ATTACK DRONES, ARMED WITH MINIATURIZED EXPLOSIVES OR POISONS, TO LARGER MORE HEAVILY WEAPONIZED ATTACK DRONES.

In December of 2018, Russian President Vladimir Putin announced that deployment of a hypersonic glide vehicle called Avangard, which is launched from intercontinental ballistic missiles (ICBMs), will begin in 2019. It can carry conventional or nuclear weapons and maneuver past defenses, according to Russian officials. Putin said, Avangard "heads for its target like a meteorite." Russia is also focused on creating autonomous weapons powered by AI.

All major powers are now focused on having their military robotized, which will radically transform the nature of warfare. In the future, AI programs will identify threats and weaknesses in enemy infrastructure that humans are currently unable to detect and then devise attack scenarios—conventional and cyber—against multiple targets. Strikes could be launched within nanoseconds of identifying the targets if nations were willing to turn over the decision-making to machines.

Retired United States Marine General John Allen calls this new phenomenon "hyperwar." According to General Allen, "In a hyperwar, the side that will prevail will be the side that is able to respond more quickly." A pentagon directive from 2012 currently restricts autonomous weapons. AI may assist with targeting but a military commander must decide what and when a warhead strikes.

Some United States officials believe that the Chinese or the Russians may not feel similarly constrained. Both sides would no doubt prefer maximum human control, but the realities and emerging necessities of conflict will make all governments face hard choices going forward.

According to Dr. Michio Kaku;

"THE THREAT OF MILITARY DRONES IS ABSOLUTE."

He says, "We have drones that a human supervises and says, 'kill that target.' In the future, the drone will recognize the human form and have permission to kill the target. It may go crazy one day—a mistake; a short circuit could take place—and it just keeps shooting that human form independent of any instructions. Automatic killing machines are the one thing we have to worry about today, not tomorrow."

In April of 2018, more than three thousand Google employees signed a letter asking management to end Google's involvement in Project Maven, a Defense Department drone surveillance project. The employees argued that Google's involvement violated the company's "Don't Be Evil" policy. The company countered that Google's involvement was for "non-offensive purposes."

Google is at the leading edge in developing artificial intelligence and it relies heavily on its seventy-eight thousand employees. How these employees react to certain initiatives may have far-reaching consequences including, but not limited to, influencing the future nature of war and the global balance of power.

Other more novel and cost-effective ways to disrupt and destabilize governments will also be used to wage social, economic and political warfare.

FUTURE WARS WILL NOT BE WAGED USING AIRCRAFT CARRIERS AND CRUISE MISSILES. THEY WILL BE WAGED ON LAPTOP COMPUTERS.

A new computer program created at OpenAI, the San Francisco AI lab, produces remarkably human-sounding prose. Write the first sentence of an article and the computer does the rest. "There are probably amazingly imaginative and malicious things you could do with this technology," says Kristin Hammond, a Northwestern professor and the CEO of AI company Narrative Science. Knowing what we now know, about the malleability and susceptibility of the human brain, that's clearly an understatement.

Richard Fontaine and Kara Frederick of the Center for New American Security, writing in the Wall Street Journal, state;

"AI-DRIVEN APPLICATIONS WILL SOON ALLOW AUTHORITARIANS TO ANALYZE PATTERNS IN A POPULATION'S ONLINE ACTIVITY, IDENTIFY THOSE MOST SUSCEPTIBLE TO A PARTICULAR MESSAGE AND TARGET THEM MORE PRECISELY WITH PROPAGANDA."

They go on to state, "Bots will soon be indistinguishable from humans online."

AI-generated images have already reached the point where they are indistinguishable from real photographs. Highly realistic videos have also been created in which President Obama is seen delivering a speech that he never gave. The quality of these computer-generated instruments of fake news is only going to increase as computing power continues to increase.

This new technology creates the possibility of fake news being circulated on an industrial scale—a scale that could create massive social, political and economic disruption—at a cost of less than a single cruise missile.

Insects may also play a role in modern warfare, as they have in the past. Ryan C. Gott, PhD, writing in Entomology Today, tells us that, "Humans have waged entomological warfare—the use of insects and other arthropods as part of wartime tactics—for thousands of years."

In 190 B.C., Hannibal won a naval victory over King Eumenes of Pergamon by firing earthen vessels full of snakes into King Eumenes' ships. In 1763, Sir Jeffrey Amherst, commander in chief of the British forces in the American colonies, had two blankets and a handkerchief from a British smallpox hospital sent to Indian chiefs. A smallpox epidemic soon erupted.

Dr. Shiro Ishii was a microbiologist and a Japanese army medical officer during World War II. He was in charge of building and running Unit 731, a top-secret biological weapons research and development facility. Ishii and others working at Unit 731 would eventually kill well over ten thousand Chinese citizens and prisoners of war over the years.

In 1951, biological weapons and chemical warfare were incorporated into official strategic planning by the United States armed forces. In 1953, United States Brig. General Rothchild, chemical officer of the Far East command, wrote that biological weapons could have played a vital role in the Korean War by distributing anthrax or yellow fever pathogens into the cold air flows that travel from Siberia through the populated areas of China.

By the end of the 1950s, labs in Camp Detrick, Maryland, were set up to breed 130 million yellow fever mosquitoes a month. The plan was to infect them with yellow fever and deliver them to the enemy via cluster bombs or warheads. By 1960, the labs were experimenting with malaria, dengue, cholera, anthrax, dysentery, relapsing fever and tularemia.

In 1972, the United States signed the Biological Weapons Convention Treaty, which banned the development, production, stockpiling, transfer and acquisition of biological weapons. In 1975, the United States also signed the Geneva Protocol of 1925, which also banned the use of these weapons in war.

The use of insects to destroy crops would be banned under the above conventions, but countries can ignore these conventions and not all countries subscribe to them. Moreover, the treaties do not ban research on biological weapons.

Here's what the Defense Advanced Research Projects Agency (DARPA) has to say about the current Insect Allies Program:

"The Insect Allies Program is pursuing scalable, readily deployable and generalizable countermeasures against potential natural and engineered threats to the food supply with the goals of preserving the United States crop system. National security can be quickly jeopardized by naturally occurring threats to the crop system, including pathogens, drought, flooding and frost, but especially by threats introduced by state or non-state actors. Insect Allies seeks to mitigate the impact of these incursions by applying targeted therapies to mature plants with effects that are expressed at relevant timescales—namely, within a single growing season...To develop such countermeasures, Insect Allies performer teams are leveraging a natural and efficient two-step delivery system to transfer modified genes to plants: insect vectors and the plant viruses they transmit.

THE PROGRAM'S THREE TECHNICAL AREAS—VIRAL MANIPULATION, INSECT VECTOR OPTIMIZATION, AND SELECTIVE GENE THERAPY IN MATURE PLANTS— LAYER TOGETHER TO SUPPORT THE GOAL OF RAPIDLY MODIFYING PLANT TRAITS WITHOUT THE NEED FOR EXTENSIVE INFRASTRUCTURE.

Since the start of the program, Insect Allies teams with expertise in molecular and synthetic biology have demonstrated mounting technical breakthroughs that are providing foundational knowledge in plant virus gene editing and disease vector biology from which the program will continue to build."

This release speaks of a defensive strategy which may well be necessary. What the United States and/or other countries may be planning in terms of offensive strategies is likely highly classified information that we won't learn about until it's too late.

OTHER WORLDS

"It is far better to grasp the universe as it really is than to persist in delusion, however satisfying and reassuring."

—Carl Sagan, American astronomer and astrophysicist.

N ASA's planet-hunting satellite, the Kepler spacecraft, is preparing to shut down, but several new satellites targeting exoplanets launched in 2018. The Transiting Exoplanet Survey Satellite (TESS) and the Characterising Exoplanet Satellite (CHEOPS) are now both searching for signs of new planets and other worlds. Both of these satellites will bring us closer to answering two important questions: are there other habitable worlds and is there life in the universe beyond Earth?

THE MERGER OF MAN AND MACHINE

*Singularity University co-founder, Google AI
Director and noted futurist Ray Kurzweil believes that
the next evolutionary leap for our neocortex won't be
inside of our skulls, but rather outside of them.*

According to Kurzweil, we will have brain-computer interfaces by the 2040s that allow us to connect the neocortex in the cloud to our human brains.by creating neocortex-like objects in the cloud, we will be able to connect them to each other and to our own brains. This is not far off.

Understanding what intelligent life will be like in the future is incomprehensible. It would be like asking one of our prehistoric ancestors to imagine today's technologies.

The key to uploading the human brain into a computer is the ability to reverse engineer how neurons encode cognition. Randal Koene, a Dutch computational neuroscientist, former director of the department of neuroengineering at the Fatronik Technalia Institute in Spain and the founder of carboncopies.org, is working in this area. Koene believes that;

**"ADVANCES IN NEUROSCIENCE MAY MAKE IT POSSIBLE
WITHIN OUR LIFETIMES TO RECORD THE UNIQUE
ARRANGEMENT OF NEURONS AND SYNAPSES THAT CONTAIN
YOUR MEMORIES AND BACK THAT UP TO A COMPUTER."**

"This sounds like science fiction," Koene says, "but we believe the road to whole-brain emulation is composed of difficult, but tractable, engineering challenges."

Researchers also believe that advances in technology will allow our minds to control equipment with thought alone or even carry on conversations telepathically, without speaking a word. Scientists are already experimenting with brain implants that allow quadriplegics to send signals from the brain's motor cortex that move prosthetic limbs.

At DARPA (Defense Advanced Research Projects Agency), researchers are working on augmented cognition systems that monitor the flow of information to different parts of the brain and change the delivery of that information in real time so that no region of the brain is overtaxed. Pilots in one study conducted by Boeing, used the system to fly twelve drones simultaneously with few mistakes.

Bioengineer Gerwin Schalk, of the Wordsworth Center of the New York State Department of Health, believes it will one day be possible to seamlessly integrate not just the human mind, but all human minds, with computers. Schalk says;

"YOU WOULD EVENTUALLY BECOME PART OF THE MACHINE. YOU DON'T NEED TO TYPE ANYMORE. YOU DON'T NEED TO DO ANYTHING TO COMMUNICATE EXCEPT THINK. YOU WOULD HAVE COMPLETE BARRIERLESS ACCESS TO ALL THE INFORMATION THAT'S AVAILABLE TO GOOGLE."

Schalk says, you would have access to a hive-mind conceivably shared by everyone on the planet who is "hooked in." He believes that we will create a "supersociety" that will completely transform not only humanity but what it means to be human.

You would not only have the ability to calculate complex equations—like 1,376 x 682,900,442,538—you would have the ability to access every fact available on the Internet, or in the "hivemind," instantaneously.

166

READING MY MIND

Our thoughts will not remain private.

Psychologists from the University of Toronto have created AI that can essentially read your mind with astonishing accuracy. The algorithm is able to recreate images seen by humans based on their brain activity as collected using electroencephalogram (EEG) sensors. The team fed a neural network huge numbers of pictures of faces, which taught it to spot characteristics and patterns in the photos. After it had learned to distinguish these characteristics, it was then taught to match these characteristics with patterns of brain activity recorded in EEG scans while observing the same.

"When we see something, our brain creates a mental percept, which is essentially a mental impression of that thing," Dan Nemrodov, who works at the lab, explained in a statement. "We were able to capture this percept using EEG to get a direct illustration of what's happening in the brain during this process."

EEG sensors were attached to volunteers in the experiment before they were shown images of faces. The AI was then able to reconstruct these faces using information read from these EEG scans with astonishing accuracy. Nemrodov explained, "It could also have forensic uses for law enforcement in gathering eyewitness information on potential suspects rather than relying on verbal descriptions provided to a sketch artist." Rather than describe a crime you witnessed, you could have your brain scanned as you remember the events. The crime and the criminal's face could then be reconstructed from your brainwaves.

Researchers at Columbia University and the Feinstein Institute for Medical Research are working to develop a brain-computer interface that can turn thoughts into speech. By monitoring signals produced in study participants' brains while listening to words and phrases, the researchers have begun to create a kind of brain-to-speech translation dictionary, which they believe could be used to interpret and vocalize the brain signals of those who cannot speak due to illness or injury.

More and more experts think a system that decodes whether a person is silently saying "yes" or "no" or "hungry" or "pain" or "water" is now within reach thanks to recent advances in neuroscience, engineering and machine learning. "We think we're getting enough of an understanding of the brain signals that encode silent speech that we could soon make something practical," says Brian Pasley, a neuroscientist at the University of California, Berkeley. Pasley says, "I'm convinced it's possible."

Further in the future, others envision similar technology facilitating consumer products that translate thoughts into text messages and emails. No typing or Siri necessary.

ARCHIVING YOUR MIND

Your consciousness will one day reside in the cloud.

D r. Eric Leuthardt, a brain surgeon at Washington University, is confident that in the future, humans will be able to get brain implants that will allow them to share information with others. In an in-depth interview with MIT Technology Review, he explains how chips implanted in our brains will one day give humans a computer-like interface in their head. According to Dr. Leuthardt, "A true fluid neural integration is going to happen. It's just a matter of when."

A Silicon Valley startup has claimed that they will be able to take your memories and upload them to a computer allowing you to live on (in some digitized form) after you're dead.

NECTOME, A COMPANY STARTED BY TWO FORMER MIT STUDENTS, IS STILL IN ITS EARLY STAGES OF DEVELOPMENT, BUT THEIR END GOAL IS CLEAR; THEY ARE "COMMITTED TO THE GOAL OF ARCHIVING YOUR MIND."

In short, they're planning to upload the things that make you you into the cloud so that scientists in the future can essentially recreate a digital version of your consciousness.

The Brain Preservation Foundation awarded Nectome an eighty thousand dollar prize for successfully preserving the connectome—the trillions of neural connections within the brain—of a pig. This was the first time the connectome of a brain had been preserved. The company has also been given more than a million dollars in grant money from the United States National Institute of

Mental Health and was working closely with MIT's top neuroscientists until MIT terminated their relationship due to certain scientific claims being made by the company.

Though the technology to reanimate humans doesn't yet exist, Nectome has come closer than anyone so far. Their website claimed that as soon as 2024, give or take a year, a biological neural network could be fully simulated. After the split with MIT, some of their claims have been withdrawn although their outlook remains incredibly optimistic.

AUGMENTED REALITY

In decades to come, we will control
computers with our minds.

The European Union and the United States are committing hundreds of millions of dollars to map the neural pathways of the brain. It is only a matter of time before we will be able to experience telepathy (mind-to-mind contact) and telekinesis (mind controlling matter), allowing us to upload memories, create a brain-net (memories and emotions sent over the internet) and record thoughts and even dreams.

**BASIC PROOFS OF PRINCIPLE FOR ALL OF THIS
HAVE ALREADY BEEN DEMONSTRATED.**

This will have an enormous social impact. If memories can be uploaded, unemployed workers might one day be retrained to learn new skills. Students could take college courses while sleeping. Movies may offer emotions, feelings, sensations and memories, not just images and sound.

Scientists working in these areas believe that the internet will one day be accessible via contact lenses. If so, profiles will appear next to the faces of the people we talk to and we'll see subtitles if they are speaking in a foreign language. These lenses would revolutionize the lives of actors, politicians, surgeons, tourists, soldiers and astronauts by delivering maps, scripts, speeches, translations, biographies and charts with the blink of an eye.

169

BLOCKCHAIN TECHNOLOGY

*Blockchain has the potential to become the system
of record for all global transactions.*

B lockchain is a peer-to-peer network that sits on top of the internet. It was introduced in October 2008 as part of a proposal for "bitcoin," a virtual currency that operates without a central authority. Blockchain is an open distributed ledger, that can record transactions between two parties in a verifiable, efficient and permanent way. The ledger itself can also be programmed to trigger transactions automatically.

With blockchain, contracts can be embedded in digital code and stored in shared databases where they can be identified and validated and where they are protected from deletion, tampering and revision.

Blockchain is a disruptive technology. If contracts are automated, it would radically change the roles of intermediaries like lawyers and accountants. Therefore, the process of adoption will be gradual. It will take decades for widespread global adoption, just as the internet did. However, it is already clear that it will happen. And the changes will be profound.

TODAY, A DECENTRALIZED SYSTEM OF CURRENCY IS THE MOST VISIBLE OPPORTUNITY FOR BLOCKCHAIN, BUT THAT IS JUST ONE OF MANY POTENTIAL APPLICATIONS.

Today, a typical stock transaction can be executed within seconds. However, transfer of ownership of the stock can take days, while a series of intermediaries act as guarantors of the assets and while others update records of the transaction. In a blockchain system, the ledger is replicated in a large number of identical databases, each hosted and maintained by an interested party. When changes are entered in one copy, all the other copies are simultaneously updated. There is no need for third-party intermediaries to verify or transfer ownership. A stock transaction on a blockchain-based system can be settled within seconds, securely and verifiably.

"Smart contracts" are another transformative blockchain application. A smart contract can send a payment to a supplier as soon as a shipment is delivered, or the product could have GPS technology, which could automatically log a location update that could trigger a payment.

BLOCKCHAIN ALSO HAS THE POTENTIAL TO COMPLETELY TRANSFORM LARGE-SCALE PUBLIC IDENTITY AND/OR IMMIGRATION SYSTEMS.

These are just some of the potential applications of this transformative technology. Others are certain to be discovered and pursued. Millennial Samurai are already involved in this new technology.

170

MINIATURIZED COMPUTERS

*At IBM Think 2018, IBM introduced the world's
smallest computer. It's the size of a grain of salt
(one millimeter by one millimeter) and it has
the same power as an x86 chip from 1990.*

I BM believes that the tiny computer will become a crucial element in attempts to apply blockchain technology to supply-chain management by collecting, processing and communicating data on goods and materials being shipped around the world.

AND THE TINY COMPUTER COSTS LESS
THAN TEN CENTS TO MANUFACTURE.

IBM envisions the device being embedded into products as they move around the supply chain. The computer's sensing, processing and communicating capabilities could turn every item in the supply chain into an internet of things device. Increased supply-chain data could streamline business operations, reduce waste and cut costs. Even more importantly, the computer could be a critical element of IBM's efforts to apply blockchain technology to the supply chain.

THIS COULD HAVE ENORMOUS IMPLICATIONS
FOR SUPPLY-CHAIN MANAGEMENT.

Today, you have multiple stakeholders from suppliers to couriers to clients all using different ways of tracking items, processes and transactions. With blockchain technology, all of this can be recorded in a shared ledger. Updates can be generated in real time and provide every participant with the same visibility, which is entirely traceable.

For blockchain to work with supply-chain management, the goods themselves need to interact with the blockchain. This is where IBM's computers come in.

IBM has been working on what it calls crypto-anchors, which it describes as "tamper-proof digital fingerprints, to be embedded into products, or parts of products and linked to the blockchain." These anchors carry a cryptographic message linked back to the blockchain that can be used to identify and authenticate the product. The implications of this new technology will likely be profound.

171

3-D PRINTING

3-D printing will transform retail consumption.

3-D printing is essentially the machine layering of materials (such as plastic resin) until the layers add up to an object. It sounds simple, but this ability to produce objects of any shape or configuration, as needed, will democratize production and transform entire industries.

THINGS THAT TOOK WEEKS TO PRODUCE AND COST TENS OF THOUSANDS OF DOLLARS IN COSTLY TOOLING WILL BE PRODUCED IN HOURS AT A FRACTION OF THE COST.

As applications of 3-D printing technology expand and prices drop, more goods will be manufactured at or close to their point of purchase or consumption. Goods that previously required large, centralized plants will be produced locally in our homes. Cars that today are made by just a few manufacturers might one day be made in every city. Parts will be made at dealerships and repair shops, as needed. Goods will be infinitely more customizable. Businesses throughout the supply, manufacturing and retailing chains will need to rethink their strategies and operations. 3-D printing will have far-reaching implications.

**IT WILL DRAMATICALLY CHANGE
THE FACE OF RETAIL CONSUMPTION.**

When you need a pair of shoes for your child, you won't need to go to the mall. You'll take a picture of your child's foot with your phone, upload it to your 3-D printer and select from a menu of shoes that can be printed on your kitchen table.

It will create an unprecedented level of selection and customization for consumers. It will mean that countries with low cost labor will no longer dominate global manufacturing. It will create businesses that never existed before and usher in a new technological revolution.

THE PRICE OF THE CHEAPEST 3-D PRINTER CAME DOWN FROM EIGHTEEN THOUSAND DOLLARS TO FOUR HUNDRED DOLLARS WITHIN TEN YEARS. IN THAT SAME AMOUNT OF TIME, IT BECAME ONE HUNDRED TIMES FASTER.

All major shoe companies have already started 3-D printing shoes. Some spare airplane parts are already 3-D printed in remote airports. The space station now has a 3-D printer that eliminates the need for the large amount of spare parts that they used to have in the past. New smart phones already have 3-D scanning features. In China, they've already 3-D printed and built a complete six-story office building.

By 2027, it is estimated that ten percent of everything that's being produced will be 3-D printed. Millennial Samurai are already creating 3-D printing fabrication facilities.

172

THE INTERNET OF THINGS

It is estimated that there will be fifty billion connected devices by 2020.

The internet of things (IoT) converts environmental information into a digital format and transmits data to a central hub for further analysis and action. The environmental data can be motion, temperature, visual, sound, geolocation, tilt, energy, pressure, moisture, force, flow, vibration, chemicals and a host of other sensory inputs that can provide deeper insights about the environment of the object or how it is being used.

THIS EMERGING TECHNOLOGY IS EXPECTED TO GROSS OVER NINETEEN TRILLION DOLLARS IN THE NEXT SEVERAL YEARS.

An IoT device has three basic building blocks:

1. Sensors
2. Computing
3. Connectivity

These three building blocks of IoT are not new, but the combination of the three creates a very powerful tool.

Sensors and microprocessors are becoming smaller, faster, cheaper and more powerful and high-speed connectivity is pervasive across the globe. This progress means we can now plug in from any corner of the world and get virtually unlimited insights in real time. This ability to capture any form of sensory information will create a new form of intelligence that never existed before. More than eighty percent of cars are expected to be connected to the internet by 2021.

Data-driven systems will be integrated into the infrastructure of "smart cities" making it easier for municipalities to manage traffic flows, reduce fuel consumption, diagnose and predict pending maintenance issues, reduce waste, improve law enforcement performance and operate other programs more efficiently.

Bridges will be built with smart cement (cement equipped with sensors to monitor stresses, cracks and warps). These sensors will alert us to fix problems at the earliest opportunity. If there's ice on the bridge, the same sensors in the concrete will detect it and communicate that information via the wireless internet to your car. Once your car knows there's a hazard ahead, it will instruct the driver to slow down and if the driver doesn't, then the car will slow down on its own.

When you're on your way home from work, you'll get an alert from your refrigerator reminding you to stop by the store to pick up specific items. Your home security system can already be enabled to remotely control your locks and thermostats, heat or cool your home, open your windows, or turn on your lights, based on your preferences.

All businesses want to minimize revenue losses that occur due to outages or downtime. In the oil and gas industry, a typical crude oil well can lose seven million dollars per week if it goes out of service. Installing a two-hundred-dollar device with a thirty-dollar-per-month data plan to monitor the well's functions can save a company millions.

IoT will also create demand for new skillsets.

BUSINESSES WILL NEED DATA SCIENTISTS WHO CAN CREATE ACTIONABLE INTELLIGENCE FOR THEIR PARTICULAR BUSINESS NEEDS.

IoT has incredible potential to disrupt both business-to-business (B2B) and business-to-consumer (B2C) business models. It will create and transform entire industries.

INVISIBLE CHECKOUT

Don't bother training to be a cashier.

Through the use of an integrated system of computers, cameras, weight sensors and deep learning (similar to that being used in self-driving cars), Amazon and other companies have been able to eliminate the need for checkout lines. Soon, you will be able to walk into a store, scan a QR code at the turnstile, pick up whatever you want and walk out the door. Cameras and sensors will monitor your shopping and record your departure. Minutes later, the store will charge your account and send you a receipt via an app.

ACCORDING TO BLOOMBERG, AMAZON PLANS TO OPEN ANOTHER THREE THOUSAND CASHIER-FREE STORES BY 2021.

And according to CB Insights, more than 150 companies like Zippin, BingoBox and Standard Cognition are also developing cashier-free retail options.

MEDICAL BREAKTHROUGHS

*Billions of people across the world lack access to
adequate healthcare. Many live in remote areas that
make access to medical services extremely difficult.*

Doctors Without Borders is already using drone technology to reach remote villages, reducing the time to deliver essential medicines and vaccines and transport diagnostic samples back to its labs for testing.

Zipline has announced what it claims to be the world's fastest drone delivery service. Their drones can reach eighty miles per hour with a roundtrip range of one hundred miles carrying 1.75 kilograms of cargo. One blood pack weighs approximately 0.5 kilograms.

Companies are testing smart-phone-based eye exam kits to diagnose eye diseases in remote settings.

JAPANESE RESEARCHERS HAVE DEVELOPED "ELECTRONIC SKIN" THAT CONTAINS SENSORS THAT MONITOR ALL YOUR BIOMETRICS.

It's called "nanomesh electrodes" and it's an elastic skin that contains displays that are ten times thinner than human skin. It sticks to your own skin for seven days allowing doctors to remotely monitor your biometrics.

Today, neuroscientists have incredible tools that allow them to examine and understand our brain function. Techniques like fluorescent microscopy and electrophysiology allow them to trace neural pathways with incredible precision, turning scans and bits of data into images that reveal the structures and signals that make our brains function.

MEDICAL STUDENTS AT STANFORD AND A GROWING NUMBER OF HOSPITALS AND MEDICAL SCHOOLS CAN NOW LEARN ANATOMY BY WALKING AROUND A LIFELIKE DIGITAL HOLOGRAM OF A LUNG, A KIDNEY, OR A HEART PUMPING BLOOD.

According to Mark Griswold, a radiology professor at Case Western Reserve University's Case Center for Imaging Research, students who used Microsoft HoloLens VR headsets to learn part of the human anatomy acquired that knowledge in nearly half the time compared with students who studied the same area of the body only on cadavers. Johnson & Johnson is currently spending millions of dollars on establishing twenty-four virtual reality training centers worldwide for surgeons.

Eric Dishman heads the Precision Medicine Initiative Cohort Program at the National Institutes of Health. He is recruiting one million Americans to share their DNA and medical histories for a massive DNA study. He's looking for links between genetic variation and disease so that doctors can one day look up a patient's DNA and use it to prescribe custom treatments for cancer, heart disease, diabetes and other life-threating conditions.

THE TRICORDER X TAKES YOUR RETINA SCAN, YOUR BLOOD SAMPLE AND YOUR BREATH SAMPLE.

It then analyzes fifty-four biomarkers that will identify nearly any disease. The company expects that it will be cheap enough in mass production to eventually enable virtually everyone on the planet to have access to world-class medical analysis at little or no cost. Animated doctors will soon give instant and reliable advice, any time of day or night.

Japan, which makes thirty percent of all robots, is already building robot nurses to prepare for an aging population. Failing body parts will be replaced just as we now replace auto parts. Already, scientists can grow skin, cartilage, noses, blood vessels, bladders and windpipes from your own cells. In the near future, scientists will grow more complex organs like livers and kidneys.

Parents will be able to choose many of the genetic characteristics of their future children. Damaged and dysfunctional genes in our genome will be cured using gene therapy, possibly leading to genetic enhancement. Genes have already been isolated that can create mice with superior memory and strength and these genes have human counterparts. Life spans might be extended by repairing or modifying mechanisms naturally found in our cells.

With nanotechnology, scientists will be able to target individual cancer cells and kill them, one by one, which may one day render chemotherapy obsolete. MRI machines that once filled entire rooms have been miniaturized to the size of briefcases. Eventually, they will be the size of cellphones, capable of analyzing diseases with a simple wave over a body.

With increased access to genetic testing, pharmacogenomics is poised to make significant inroads into precision medicine. Pharmacogenomic testing, which uses a patient's genetic makeup to predict an individual's metabolism of drugs, is now being used to avoid adverse reactions and eliminate unnecessary and ineffective prescriptions, replacing them with more effective medications.

Cancer immunotherapy is a technique that uses the body's own immune system to fight cancer. Scientists are creating new cancer immunotherapy treatments through the use of engineered T-cells. The discovery of new immunotherapeutic targets and biomarkers will allow for more effective therapies.

Utilizing 3-D printing technology, medical devices are now being made to match the exact specifications of a patient. These 3-D printed devices are specifically designed to be more compatible with an individual's natural anatomy. Devices modeled from patient-specific dimensions have shown greater acceptance by the body, increased comfort and improved performance. This technology has already been used for many complicated heart surgeries and even for the Cleveland Clinic's most recent total face transplant.

Hemorrhagic strokes, during which blood escapes from a ruptured blood vessel in the brain, are responsible for nearly forty percent of stroke deaths. Rapid diagnosis is necessary for effective treatment as uncontrolled bleeding can lead to brain damage. The hemorrhage scanning visor, which can detect bleeding in the brain, speeds up diagnosis and the time to treatment.

Robots in the operating room are currently being used to guide surgeons in achieving extreme precision in surgery. Shortened recovery time and limited pain after surgery are just a few of the patient benefits seen with minimally invasive robotized surgery.

RNA-based therapies (interfering with genetic data at the ribonucleic acid level) have shown immense potential. They have given scientists the ability to intercept a patient's genetic abnormality before it is translated into functioning (or nonfunctioning) proteins. These new therapies are being explored in a variety of rare genetic diseases such as Huntington's disease as well as in cancer and neurologic diseases.

In 2018, Stanford University researchers announced that they were recruiting lymphoma patients in a clinical trial to test a potential cancer vaccine. The treatment involves injecting immune-stimulating agents into solid tumors.

IN TRIALS ON MICE, THIS HAS BEEN SHOWN TO ELIMINATE "ALL TRACES OF CANCER IN THE ANIMALS" WITHOUT THE SIDE EFFECTS OF TRADITIONAL IMMUNOTHERAPY.

If human trials are successful, the vaccine could potentially treat multiple types of cancer tumors.

Hyperkalemia is a condition where the potassium level in your blood is higher than normal. It normally results from kidney troubles, diabetes, or as a side effect of some blood pressure medications. When levels of this electrolyte mineral increase, it can be dangerous for the heart. For those with chronic kidney disease, it can be deadly. Typically, a blood test would be needed to detect elevated potassium. A new technology, AliveCor's KardiaK Software Platform, developed with the Mayo Clinic, detects potassium levels using artificial intelligence through electrocardiograms (ECG). It has been called a breakthrough device and is being fast-tracked for FDA clearance.

The Apple Watch Series 4 includes an ECG app. According to Apple, the app "is capable of generating an ECG similar to a single-lead electrocardiogram." Electrodes built into the back of the watch take data on your heart's electrical impulses to detect abnormalities that may suggest an irregular heart rhythm like atrial fibrillation. Data is saved over time and you can then take that information to your doctor. The watch also has an accelerometer and gyroscope that detects falls and can automatically call emergency services.

When a child is diagnosed with type 1 diabetes, they need to continuously monitor their blood sugar (glucose). A glucose monitoring device called the MiniMed 670G hybrid closed-loop system can dose out insulin automatically to regulate levels around the clock and prevent dangerous highs and lows in glucose levels.

Approximately forty million Americans suffer from migraines. Aimovig is the first-of-its-kind injectable drug that can reduce migraines. According to Eric Bastings, MD, deputy director of the Division of Neurology Products in the FDA's Center for Drug Evaluation and Research, "Aimovig provides patients with a novel option for reducing the number of days with a migraine."

Some of the medical advances, we should expect, will raise moral and ethical issues. Society will need to be prepared to debate the ethics of some of these technologies, including how and when we should be able to use them.

175

LONGEVITY ESCAPE VELOCITY

*At some point in the near future, each additional
year that you live will increase your life expectancy by
more than one year.*

L ongevity Escape Velocity (LEV) is a term used to describe a hypothetical situation in which life expectancy is being extended longer than the time that is passing. For example, in a given year in which LEV would be maintained, technological advances would increase life expectancy by more than the year that just passed.

Life expectancy increases slightly every year as treatment strategies and technologies improve. At present, more than one year of research is required for each additional year of expected life. LEV occurs when this ratio reverses, so that life expectancy increases faster than one year per one year of research, as long as that rate of technological advance is sustainable.

LEV was first publicly proposed by David Gobel, cofounder of the Methuselah Foundation (MF). The idea has been championed by biogerontologist Aubrey deGray (the other cofounder of the MF) and by, Singularity University cofounder, Google AI Director and noted futurist Ray Kurzweil. Gobel and deGray claim that by focusing scientific and medical research on expanding the limits of aging, rather than continuing along at its current pace, more lives will be saved in the future.

KURZWEIL USES THE TERM LEV TO DESCRIBE THAT POINT IN TIME WHICH, ONCE REACHED, WILL DEFINE THE ABILITY FOR SCIENCE TO INDEFINITELY PROLONG LIFE. ACCORDING TO KURZWEIL, WE'RE TEN TO TWELVE YEARS AWAY FROM REACHING THAT POINT.

DeGray claims that, "the first person who will live to one thousand is alive today." These are incredible predictions coming from some very credible sources.

One of the consequences of LEV is that retirement, as a social and economic construct, goes away. This can be good or bad depending on what you're doing during these additional years. If you have the option of continuing to create and receive value (wherever and whenever you want) for doing what you truly love, it's a good thing. If not, then it might be a less welcome development. As individuals, it will mean that many of us who are older will need to start thinking about what we will do for our third or fourth acts and how we can best leverage our knowledge.

The Social Security Act of 1935 set the retirement age at sixty-five. That's because life expectancy in 1935 was sixty-five. Expect to see a change, both in how we think about retirement and the age at which we retire. These changes will impact our lives on many levels. It will affect our work, retirement, financial planning, even our relationships.

What might you do differently if you knew you were likely to live to two hundred or three hundred years old?

PERFECT CAPITALISM

With information comes power.

One by one, multibillion-dollar industries are being digitized. The first was music, where digitization drove down costs and increased efficiency and competition. Now, media is being digitized.

IN THE COMING DECADE, EDUCATION, MEDICINE, LAW, BANKING, LOGISTICS AND TRANSPORTATION WILL ALL BECOME DIGITIZED.

We are headed toward what theoretical physicist and futurist Dr. Michio Kaku calls "perfect capitalism," when the laws of supply and demand become exact. A point where everyone will know everything about a given product, service, or customer and precisely where the supply curve meets the demand curve. This will make the marketplace vastly more efficient and will radically transform multiple industries.

MASSIVELY
TRANSFORMATIVE PURPOSE

*"All of the great empires of the future
will be empires of the mind."*

—*Winston Churchill, former British Prime Minister.*

I f your goal is to grow a business, then you need to understand and anticipate the social, economic, cultural and technological changes that will impact and fuel business over the next several decades. Larger businesses are inherently much worse at doing this because they have an industrial-era infrastructure, supply chain and distribution model, as well as generally more conservative shareholders. Forcing them to be much more short-term in their thinking. This is exactly what prevented Kodak and Blockbuster from taking advantage of the exponential technologies that they had access to—and in Kodak's case, invented.

Taking advantage of abundance and exponential growth requires a fundamental shift in how you think about your business. Peter Diamandis (founder of the XPRIZE and co-founder of Singularity University) uses the term Massively Transformative Purpose (or MTP) to describe what drives you to step out of the past and become exceptional at building the future. It is the aspirational goal that stretches you, your organization and even your market—by capturing people's hearts and minds.

An MTP can be audacious, such as the MTP for XPRIZE; "To Build a Bridge of Abundance for All." Or it could be Uber's MTP of transforming the transportation industry. The key is that the transformational forces in the foreseeable future will leverage the concepts of abundance and exponential growth.

Aligning yourself and your organization so that you can take advantage of a post-industrial way of thinking is critical in positioning your business for long-term competitive growth. So what's your MTP? Does it align with and leverage the concepts of abundance and accelerating exponential growth? Have you helped your team understand these concepts so that they can integrate them into how they support your MTP?

One thing is clear—the future will be beyond extraordinary. It will be beyond our current ability to even comprehend, which makes it all the more important that we do everything we can to keep up with the technological sea changes and the tectonic social and cultural shifts that we are certain to experience.

THE FUTURE OF FOOD

*New clean meats could reduce the land and
water use of traditional animal agriculture
by more than eighty percent.*

S cientists are creating a new food group called clean meat—edible animal protein grown in a lab. Stem cells are extracted from animals, brewed in a bioreactor, fortified with nutrients and structured around collagen "scaffolds."

**INVESTORS LIKE SERGEY BRIN, CO-FOUNDER OF GOOGLE,
ARE BANKROLLING COMPANIES LIKE MOSAMEAT, CREATOR
OF THE WORLD'S FIRST CLEAN BURGER.**

New Crop Capital partner Christopher Kerr, says, "This is potentially a trillion-dollar market opportunity." The biggest challenge is reducing the cost of clean meat to make it commercially viable.

Scientists are also experimenting with new high-tech methods of food preservation. One technique bombards fluids with high-intensity blue light, which produces a form of oxygen that's lethal to pathogens. It's being adapted for use on berries and nuts.

**FRUITS, VEGETABLES, SEEDS AND SALADS ARE
BEING PRESERVED BY BLASTS OF COLD PLASMA.
A MIX OF NITROUS OXIDES, HYDROGEN PEROXIDE,
AND OTHER MOLECULES KILL BACTERIA.**

High-energy electrons are being shot into meat, fruits and vegetables, breaking up the DNA of bacteria.

These new technologies will be used to advance food safety, making foods last longer without sacrificing quality or taste, even without refrigeration.

EAT SHIT

*"Eat shit" isn't something you would
expect to hear from your doctor.*

T hat may soon change. Companies like OpenBiome believe that fecal matter transplants could be a miracle cure for some of our illnesses. Scientists now know that the wrong balance of bacteria in your gut can lead to illness and they are working on methods to manipulate the composition of that bacteria to repair failing guts and cure diseases.

Every month, a hundred or more donors drop off sealed bags of their stool at labs for OpenBiome, where a lab technician weighs and scores the sample. Only three percent of donors are healthy enough to qualify. Donors are paid forty dollars each for their poop. Another lab technician adds a saline solution, shakes it up and freezes the bags. It is then sent to doctors and researchers across the country.

**SINCE 2012, THESE PACKAGES OF POOP HAVE
SUCCESSFULLY TREATED OVER FIFTEEN THOUSAND
PATIENTS FOR CLOSTRIDIUM DIFFICILE, ONE OF THE
DEADLIEST ANTIBIOTIC-RESISTANT GUT INFECTIONS
THAT CAN STRIKE PATIENTS AFTER A COURSE OF
ANTIBIOTICS WIPES OUT THEIR EXISTING GOOD BACTERIA.**

Vedanta Biosciences is using tabletop robots to sort through fecal samples from around the world, identify individual species of bacteria and use those samples selected to grow more of the same beneficial bacteria. Algorithms look for specific bacteria that can treat specific diseases. Vedanta already has its first drug candidate to treat ulcerative colitis and Crohn's disease.

Human excrement from healthy donors has already been shown to have significant value in treating disease.

The National Institutes of Health recently announced that it would fund a fecal transplant registry maintained by the National Gastroenterological Association.

THE IMMORTALITY DRIVE

*On October 12, 2008, a large memory device called
the Immortality Drive was taken to the International
Space Station in a Soyuz spacecraft.*

The Immortality Drive is a microchip that contains fully digitized DNA sequences of a select group of humans, such as physicist Stephen Hawking and comedian and talk show host Stephen Colbert. The microchip also contains a copy of *George's Secret Key to the Universe*, a children's book authored by Stephen Hawking and his daughter Lucy. The intent of the Immortality Drive is to preserve human DNA in a time capsule in case some global cataclysm should occur on Earth.

**THE IMMORTALITY DRIVE INCLUDES A LIST OF SOME
OF HUMANITY'S GREATEST ACHIEVEMENTS AS WELL AS
MESSAGES AND WRITINGS FROM EARTH. THE TIME CAPSULE
ALSO INCLUDES THE DIGITIZED DNA SEQUENCES OF
NUMEROUS PERSONALITIES FROM EARTH.**

Video game designer and pioneer of space tourism, Richard Garriott, developed the Immortality Drive to function as a backup of the human species, in case of extinction.

Since the Immortality Drive is stored on board the ISS, if humanity does go extinct, someone or something would actually have to enter the ISS and recover the drive before the space station goes crashing into Earth due to a lack of engine maintenance.

FLYING TAXIS

*In a few years, you may be flying
to your appointments.*

T extron's Bell division, a partner in the Uber Elevate flying car initiative, introduced its new air taxi concept called the Nexus at the 2019 Consumer Electronics Show (CES). The flying concept car uses six tilted fans to aid in takeoffs and landings, which are powered by a hybrid-electric propulsion system. Inside the vehicle, four passengers and a pilot can see their flight path projected onto a screen.

**UBER PLANS TO ROLL OUT ITS FLYING CARS
IN 2023, TARGETING DALLAS-FORT WORTH AND
LOS ANGELES AS ITS FIRST DOMESTIC MARKETS.**

Electrafly also showed off its flying car concept at CES. The concept can carry one rider, which the company said is "ideal for first responders or military special forces." Other versions will be scaled for air taxis or search-and-rescue vehicles. Smaller versions might be used for shipping and package delivery.

Uber's forecasts claim that a commute between San Francisco and San Jose, which would typically take two hours during rush hour and cost about $111, would be cut down to just fifteen minutes. That same route by flying car could initially cost about $129, with the price dropping to $43 in the near term and $20 in the long term, according to Uber.

'OUMUAMUA

On October 19, 2017, the first interstellar object,
'Oumuamua (the Hawaiian word for scout or messenger),
was discovered by the Pan-STARRS survey.

The following year, Avi Loeb, the chairman of Harvard's astronomy department, co-wrote a paper (with a Harvard postdoctoral fellow, Shmuel Bialy) that examined 'Oumuamua's "peculiar acceleration" and suggested that the object;

"MAY BE A FULLY OPERATIONAL PROBE SENT INTENTIONALLY TO EARTH'S VICINITY BY AN ALIEN CIVILIZATION."

Here are Loeb's six reasons for suggesting that possibility:

1. 'Oumuamua implies that the population of interstellar objects is far greater than expected. Each star in the Milky Way needs to eject 10^{15} such objects during its lifetime to account for a population as large as 'Oumuamua implies. Thus, the nurseries of 'Oumuamua-like objects must be different from what we know based on our own solar system.

2. 'Oumuamua originated from a very special frame of reference, the so-called local standard of rest (LSR), which is defined by averaging the random motions of all the stars in the vicinity of the sun. Only one star in five hundred is moving as slowly as 'Oumuamua in that frame.

3. If 'Oumuamua came from a typical star, it must have been ejected with an unusually large velocity kick. To make things more unusual, its kick should have been equal and opposite to the velocity of its parent

star relative to the LSR, which is about twenty kilometers per second for a typical star like the sun. The dynamical origin of 'Oumuamua is extremely rare no matter how you look at it.

4. We do not have a photo of 'Oumuamua but its brightness, owing to reflected sunlight, varied by a factor of ten as it rotated periodically every eight hours. This implies that 'Oumuamua has an extremely elongated shape with its length at least five to ten times greater than its projected width. Moreover, an analysis of its tumbling motion concluded that it would be at the highest excitation state expected from its tumultuous journey, if it has a pancake-like geometry. The inferred shape is more extreme than for all asteroids previously seen in the solar system, which have a length-to-width ratio of, at most, three.

5. The Spitzer Space Telescope did not detect any heat in the form of infrared radiation from 'Oumuamua. Given the surface temperature dictated by 'Oumuamua's trajectory near the sun, this sets an upper limit on its size of hundreds of meters. Based on this size limit, 'Oumuamua must be unusually shiny with a reflectance that is at least ten times higher than exhibited by solar system asteroids.

6. Altogether, 'Oumuamua does not appear to be a typical comet nor a typical asteroid, even as it represents a population that is far more abundant than expected. The extra push exhibited by 'Oumuamua's orbit could not have originated from a breakup (into pieces) because such an event would have provided a single impulsive kick, unlike the continuous push that was observed. If cometary outgassing is ruled out and the inferred excess force is real, only one possibility remains: an extra push due to radiation pressure from the sun. In order for this push to be effective, 'Oumuamua needs to be less than a millimeter thick but with a size of at least twenty meters (for a perfect reflector), resembling a lightsail of artificial origin. In this case, 'Oumuamua would resemble the solar sail demonstrated by the Japanese mission IKAROS or the lightsail contemplated for the Starshot initiative. An artificial origin offers the startling possibility that we discovered "a message in a bottle," following years of failed searches for radio signals from alien civilizations.

While scientists can't confirm that 'Oumuamua is in fact a scout or messenger from another civilization, the fact that this possibility is being raised by someone of Loeb's stature underscores the significance of the sighting. One thing is certain—it is something we have not seen before.

CONCLUSION

The technological revolution will create unprecedented disruption and change while presenting extraordinary opportunities and risks. These changes will affect every area of human endeavor. And how we respond and adapt to these changes will determine the lives that we lead.

Success and survival in the 21st Century will require that we continuously adapt to a rapidly and radically changing environment. It will require that we identify and leverage our unique strengths while mitigating our inherent weaknesses. It will require that we embrace the ancient core values that have allowed prior generations to succeed while developing our own moral compass—one that will allow us to navigate the ethical challenges ahead.

Success and survival will require that we learn, unlearn and re-learn. It will require that we recognize our profound interdependence and leverage our combined strengths through collaboration, community and compassion.

The tsunami of technological change that will redefine life as we know it, will require that we engage in a process of lifelong learning, critical thinking and continuous reskilling. It will require that we pivot and adapt to continuously changing circumstances while traversing an ever-evolving social, political and economic landscape.

Those who accept these challenges and commit to a life of purpose that is greater than themselves will be the Millennial Samurai. And this elite class of enlightened warriors will lead their generation and future generations into the 21st Century. It is my sincere hope that *Millennial Samurai* will assist you and future leaders in that journey by encouraging you to develop a love of learning, by alerting you to the need for continuous adaption and by inspiring you to believe in yourself and your capacity to survive and thrive in any environment.

You don't overcome challenges by avoiding them. You overcome them by identifying them and by seeking them out. Here, your challenge is unity, adaptation and personal growth. And you are more than up to that challenge.

Embrace each day with gratitude, excitement and optimism. Be vigilant in your search for the truth and never stop sharpening your sword. In sum, make the most of your one and only life while contributing to the lives of others.

That's what I intend to do. And I invite you to join me and bring your friends.

Connect with me on:

MillennialSamurai.com

Register for free interactive videos; invitations to upcoming events; notices of release parties and speaking engagements in your area.

GeorgeJChanos.com   **LimitlessThinking.com**

Follow me on:

@GeorgeJChanos   @GeorgeJChanos   @MillennialSamurai
                        @TheMillennialSamurai
                        @Limitless

PLEASE DON'T KEEP THIS IMPORTANT INFORMATION TO YOURSELF. SHARE YOUR REVIEWS ON AMAZON.COM AND ON SOCIAL MEDIA. CONNECT WITH ME AND TAG ME SO THAT I CAN THANK YOU PERSONALLY.

Together, we can be the change we want to see. Your opportunities are truly limitless. Thank you!

Resources

Millennials

◊ Mussman, Anna. January 23, 2014. "Millennials Think Authority Figures Are Untrustworthy Idiots and Modern Culture is to Blame." Thefederalist.com. At http://bit.ly/2DPC51v

◊ Twenge, Jean M. May 2, 2012. "Millennials: The Greatest Generation or the Most Narcissistic?" Theatlantic.com. At http://bit.ly/2t0NHIz

◊ Taylor, Paul and Keeter, Scott. February 24, 2010. "Millennials: Confident. Connected. Open to Change." Pewsocialtrends.com. At https://pewrsr.ch/2MKl7nW

Samurai

◊ Nitobe, Inazo. July 28, 2017. *Bushido: The Soul of Japan.* CreateSpace Independent Publishing Platform

◊ Miyashita, Koki. September 19, 2017. "Japan Timeline and History Overview." Samuraimeetups.or.jp. At http://bit.ly/2GjLU9m

◊ May 3, 2018. "Samurai." Japan-guide.com. At http://bit.ly/2S2v9H9

◊ Cartwright, Mark. April 5, 2017. "Samurai." Ancient.eu. At http://bit.ly/2To0AIw

◊ 2003. "Samurai." PBS.org. At https://to.pbs.org/2MSFzDr

◊ Martin, Alexander. March 4, 2014. "Samurai Spirit: Progeny of Japan's Warrior Elite Retain Edge Today." Wsj.com. At https://on.wsj.com/2RzQKS7

THE RIGHT MINDSET

Critical Thinking

◊ Korn, Melissa, October 21, 2014, "Bosses Seek Critical Thinking, but What Is That?" The Wall Street Journal. At https://on.wsj.com/2UKll5L

◊ Nelson, Linda B. PhD. October 4, 2018, "Teaching Critical Thinking: Some Practical Points." Faculty Focus. At http://bit.ly/2UMsiDt

Control Your Thoughts

◊ Lively, Kathryn J. March 12, 2014. "Affirmations: The Why, What, How and What if?" Pychologytoday.com. At http://bit.ly/2GlcXkD

◊ TEDxYouth. February 21, 2013. "The Neuroanatomical Transformation of the Teenage Brain: Jill Bolte Taylor at TEDxYouth @ Indianapolis." Youtube.com. At https://youtu.be/PzT_SBl31-s

◊ Peale, Norman Vincent. *The Power of Positive Thinking.* March 12, 2003. Touchstone.

Set Clear Intentions

◊ Watson, Leanne. "Why Are Intentions Important?" Selfgrowth.com. At http://bit.ly/2TP0jP1

◊ Tabaka, Marla. "Setting Goals Isn't Enough: Setting Daily Intentions Will Change Your Life." Inc.com. At http://bit.ly/2TQImPZ

◊ Downey, Jo-Ann. "Intention Series: How to Create Powerful Intentions." Verysmartgirls.com. At http://bit.ly/2TVyCUR

◊ Thompson, Brian. July 17, 2015. "The Importance of Setting Your Day's Greatest Intention." Zenthinking.net. At http://bit.ly/2TO2aU1

Believe in Yourself

◊ Canfield, Jack. "How to Believe in Yourself & Change Your Life in the Process." Jackcanfield.com. At http://bit.ly/2RyUkfl

◊ Ng, Melissa. "How to Believe in Yourself in the Face of Overwhelming Self-Doubt." Tinybuddha.com. At http://bit.ly/2BdygBq

◊ Clear, James. November 22, 2012. "Believe in Yourself (and Why Nothing Will Work If You Don't…)" jamesclear.com. At http://bit.ly/2BcAJMj

Think for Yourself

◊ Dwyer, Ron. "Setting the Record Straight." Facebook.com. At http://bit.ly/2BfMzWg

◊ Hereford, Z. "How to Think for Yourself." Essentiallifeskills.net. At http://bit.ly/2BhAXC5

Open Your Mind

◊ Operation-Meditation. 2012. "8 Benefits of Having an Open Mind and How to Get One." Operationmeditation.com. At http://bit.ly/2Bdz7lC

◊ Sonnenberg, Frank. February 7, 2017. "The Benefits of Being Open-Minded: An Open-and-Shut Case." Franksonnenbergonline.com. At http://bit.ly/2Bfz0G4

◊ Positive Psychology Center. 2004. "Open-Mindedness." Authentichappiness.sas.upenn.edu. At http://bit.ly/2BiFxjA

Intuition

◊ Marano, Hara Estroff. May 4, 2014, "Trusting Intuition." Psychology Today.

◊ http://bit.ly/2VfurXJ

◊ Bradberry, Travis. January 10, 2017, "Your Intuition is More Powerful Than Your Intellect and Just as Easily Expanded." http://bit.ly/2VTNXG5

◊ Kasanoff, Bruce. February 21, 2017, "Intuition is The Highest Form Of Intelligence." *Forbes.* http://bit.ly/2XrFJ8L

Seek the Truth

◊ Altmire, Jason. September 08, 2018. "The Importance of Fact-checking in a Post-truth World." Thehill.com. At http://bit.ly/2Bknjhv

Attitude is Everything

◊ Zahed, Hyder. September 09, 2014. "Our Attitude is Everything." Huffingtonpost.com. At http://bit.ly/2Br9n5B

◊ Harrell, Keith. September 22, 2016. "Why Your Attitude is Everything." Success.com. At http://bit.ly/2BiGU1I

◊ Tredgold, Gordon. August 24, 2016. "3 Reasons Why Attitude is More Important to Your Company Than Aptitude." Entrepreneur.com. At http://bit.ly/2BdAosU

Empathy

◊ Susan. Jaqueline Lapa, MS, LPC, "Empathy the Bridge to Understanding" Total Health Magazine. http://bit.ly/2vddkXV

◊ Cherry, Kendra, October 31, 2018, "Importance and Benefits of Empathy." At http://bit.ly/2Xv9ZQ8

◊ Rises, Helen, MD and Frankel, Richard, M. PhD, May 9, 2017, "The Science of Empathy," *Journal of Patient Experience.* http://bit.ly/2IuJw1x

Gratitude

◊ October 25, 2018. "The 31 Benefits of Gratitude You Didn't Know About: How Gratitude Can Change Your Life." Happierhuman.com. At http://bit.ly/2Bh5JLr

◊ The Positive Psychology Program. February 28, 2017. "What is Gratitude and What is its Role in Positive Psychology?" Positivepsychologyprogram. com. At http://bit.ly/2Bh6DaN

◊ Carpenter, Derrick. "The Science Behind Gratitude (and How it Can Change Your Life)." Happify.com. At http://bit.ly/2Bgpu5I

Optimism

◊ May 16, 2017, "Optimism Is a Skill That Can Be Learned." Bigthink.com. At http://bit.ly/2Tv7VWD

◊ Smith, Emily Esfahani. March 1, 2013. "The Benefits of Optimism Are Real." Theatlantic.com. At http://bit.ly/2TsjKwF

Hope

◊ Harrison, P.M. January 3, 2018. "Why is Hope Important in Life?" Thedailymeditation.com. At http://bit.ly/2TtGnRr

◊ Finley, Laura. January 16, 2015. "The Importance of Hope." Counterpunch. org. At http://bit.ly/2TtDobT

◊ August 2, 2013. "Career Coach: The Importance of Hope." Washingtonpost. com. At https://wapo.st/2TvyMlA

Passion

◊ Levoy, Gregg. February 4, 2015. "5 Keys to a Passionate Life." Psychologytoday.com. At http://bit.ly/2TP1ttR

◊ Kerpen, Dave. "15 Inspiring Quotes on Passion (Get Back to What You Love)." Inc.com. At http://bit.ly/2TMVdCI

◊ Burn-Callander, Rebecca. March 27, 2015. "Eight Ways to Find the True Passion in Life that Has Eluded You." Telegraph.co.uk. At http://bit.ly/2BxnRR5

◊ Davenport, Barrie. "Want to Find Your Life Passion? Start by Simplifying Your Life." Becomingminimalist.com. At http://bit.ly/2BCM8VZ

◊ "Attribution of a Philosophy." Answers.google.com. At http://bit.ly/2BDJqQ2

Life Isn't Easy or Fair

◊ Biswas-Diener, Robert. July 31, 2014. "What to Do When Life Isn't Fair." Psychologytoday.com. At http://bit.ly/2BhPH3H

◊ Hutson, Matthew. June 2016. "Life Isn't Fair." Theatlantic.com. At http://bit.ly/2BshgaX

◊ Bolstrom, Paula. "Life Isn't Always Fair: 5 Steps to Accept Tough Situations." At http://bit.ly/2VRvbPP

CORE VALUES

Character

◊ Hokuma. May 11, 2018. "Positive and Negative Personality & Character Traits." Positivepsychologyprogram.com. At http://bit.ly/2TssnaI

◊ Sharma, Vibha. July 2015. "20 Good Character Traits That Will Help Your Kids Grow Up to Be Happy, Successful and Loved by All." Afineparent.com. At http://bit.ly/2TriZUE

◊ Miller, Christian B. "The Character Gap: How Good Are We?" philosophy.wfu.edu. At http://bit.ly/2TvEG5W

Courage

◊ BBC Travel Show. "The Blind Backpacker Who's Visiting Every Country in the World." Facebook.com. At http://bit.ly/2Twhqow

◊ Kennedy, Tristan. August 13, 2015. "8 Stories of Courage and Determination in the Face of Disability That Will Blow Your Mind." Mpora.com. At http://bit.ly/2Tp0Sid

◊ Marcus, Bonnie. July 17, 2017. "10 Ways Your Show Courage Every Day." Forbes.com. At http://bit.ly/2TvvwX5

Commitment

◊ Laryea, Edmond. October 9, 2014. "Commitment—The Best Motivational Video (Get Up)." Youtube.com. At http://bit.ly/2Tvbkon

◊ Michael, John, Sebanz, Natalie and Knoblich, Gunther. January 5, 2016. "The Sense of Commitment: A Minimal Approach." *Frontiers in Psychology*. At http://bit.ly/2TwihWg

◊ Devalia, Arvind. October 4, 2014. "11 Key Lessons from Gandhi for Leading a Powerful Life of Commitment." Arvinddevalia.com. At http://bit.ly/2Tqqgnz

◊ Oblinger, Diana. October 7, 2010. "A Commitment to Learning: Attention, Engagement and the Next Generation." Er.educause.edu. At http://bit.ly/2TtIJzL

Compassion

◊ Dunn, Elizabeth W., Aknin, Lara B. and Norton, Michael I. March 21, 2008. "Spending Money on Others Promotes Happiness." Sciencemag.org. At http://bit.ly/2TveFnk

◊ Dunn, Elizabeth W. and Norton, Michael I. June 18, 2013. "How to Make Giving Feel Good." Berkeley.Edu. At http://bit.ly/2TveLLI

◊ Keltner, Dacher, "The Compassionate Species," July 31, 2012, Greater Good Magazine. http://bit.ly/2Gpbl83

Authenticity

◊   Ibarra, Herminia. January 2015. "The Authenticity Paradox." HBR.org. At http://bit.ly/2TuezfU

◊   Carver, Melissa. "Why Authenticity is the Key to Success in Life, Business and Relationships." Chopra.com. At http://bit.ly/2TvJVCE

◊   Wright, Karen. May 1, 2008. "Dare to Be Yourself." Psychologytoday.com. At http://bit.ly/2Tqsi7b

Choice

◊   Stanford Graduate School of Business. April 19, 2018. "Sophia Shramko: The Power to Choose." Youtube.com. At http://bit.ly/2Tpj5My

◊   "We Have the Power to Choose." Tinybuddha.com. At http://bit.ly/2TuKvRg

◊   Nelson, Michael. 2014. "The Importance of Good Thinking." Goodchoicesgoodlife.com. At http://bit.ly/2TvBvLx

◊   Brenner, Abigail. May 30, 2015. "The Importance of Learning How to Make Decisions." Psychologytoday.com. At http://bit.ly/2TtMgOx

Curiosity

◊   Latumahina, Donald. "4 Reasons Why Curiosity is Important and How to Develop it." LifeHack.org. At http://bit.ly/2DsPzQe

◊   Molokhia,Dalia, May 24, 2018. "The Importance Of Being Curious." Harvard Business Publishing Corporate Learning. At https://s.hbr.org/2UuX1jg

◊   Minion andrew P., May 24, 2017. "The Importance of Curiosity and Questions in 21st Century Learning." Global Learning. At http://bit.ly/2ZobwJm

◊   Shikin, Basil, October 19, 2017. "The Importance Of Hiring Curious People." At Forbes.

◊   http://bit.ly/2GoWs5L

Collaboration

◊ Cross, Rob, Rebele, Reb, Grant, Adam. January 2016. "Collaborative Overload," Harvard Business Review. At http://bit.ly/2ItyBVT

◊ Nixon, Natalie. "August 15, 2014. "5 Reasons Why Collaboration is Essential in Today's Business Environment." Inc. At http://bit.ly/2GvsGgW

◊ Jones, Benjamin F. September 6, 2017. "The Science Behind the Growing Importance of Collaboration." Kellogg Insight. At http://bit.ly/2GzUQrf

Adaptation

◊ Mehmedova, Filiz. "Why Do You Need to Adapt To Change?" Lifehack. org. At http://bit.ly/2BclnHV

◊ Satell, Greg. Febuary 21, 2016. "To Adapt, You Need to Evolve." Forbes. com. At http://bit.ly/2BssRqv

◊ Edgar, James. March 28, 2017. "Working in the Future: How Humans Need to Adapt." Euronews.com. At http://bit.ly/2BjZjv4

◊ Massey, Nathanael. September 25, 2013. "Humans May Be the Most Adaptive Species." ScientificAmerican.com. At http://bit.ly/2BjCE1K

◊ Brooks, Cassandra. January 16, 2009. "Adaptation is Key in Human Evolution." Stanford.edu. At https://stanford.io/2BknEAP

Intensity

◊ MVP Romania. July 22, 2017. "Stephen Curry—Intense Workout & Practice Mix." Youtube.com. At http://bit.ly/2TuxUO2

◊ Smith, Jacquelyn. "The Insane Work Ethic of Mark Cuban, Jeff Bezos and 14 Other Powerful Leaders." Inc.com. At http://bit.ly/2TvyaMD

◊ Nisen, Max. October 11, 2013. "18 People Whose Extraordinary Work Ethic Got them To The Top." Aol.com. At https://aol.it/2TqLhOZ

◊ Stillman, Jessica. "The Productivity Secret Behind Bill Gates's Incredible Success." Inc.com. At http://bit.ly/2TvyuuP

Adulthood

◊   Munsey, Christopher. June 2006. "Emerging Adults: The in-between age." APA.org. At http://bit.ly/2TvKso8

Going the Extra Mile

◊   Personal Finance Literacy. July 16, 2015. "The Habit of Going the Extra Mile Napoleon Hill." Youtube.com. At http://bit.ly/2TsIu81

Consumerism

◊   Gary Vaynerchuk Fan Page. December 3, 2018. "How to Escape the Rat Race—Gary Vaynerchuk Motivation Part 2." Youtube.com. At http://bit.ly/2TsOii0

◊   Etzioni, Amitai. September 04, 2012. "The Crisis of American Consumerism." Huffingtonpost.com. At http://bit.ly/2Tpzxwi

◊   Heinberg, Richard. April 14, 2015. "The Brief, Tragic Rein of Consumerism—and the birth of a happy alternative." Postcarbon.com. At http://bit.ly/2Tu6d85

Balance/Harmony

◊   Caramela, Sammi. March 22, 2018. "5 Ways to Improve your Work-Life Balance Today." Businessnewsdaily.com. At http://bit.ly/2Tt0ejN

◊   "Work Life Balance." Mentalhealthamerica.com. At http://bit.ly/2TzTXTD

◊   Jeffries, Stuart. November 7, 2014. "Ten Tips For a Better Work-life Balance." The guardian.com. At http://bit.ly/2TvyStc

◊   "Student Readiness Inventory: Tool Shop." Mtu.edu. At http://bit.ly/2TrKD3S

Health

◊   Calloway, Allison Brett. June 14, 2018. "9 Great Reasons to Drink Water." Facebook.com. At http://bit.ly/2TvUohp

◊   TED. June 19, 2018. "The Brain-Changing Effects of Exercise." Facebook.com. At http://bit.ly/2Tu7fkt

Money

◊ Top Trending. June 9, 2018. "10 Billionaires That Are Cheaper Than You." Youtube.com. At http://bit.ly/2TqN9qZ

◊ Advexon TV. March 3, 2017. "Warren Buffett HBO Documentary." Youtube.com. At http://bit.ly/2TukP7t

◊ Steinberg, Stephanie. August 13, 2014. "10 smart ways to spend $1,000." Usnews.com. At http://bit.ly/2Tu6dVr

Don't Be a Victim

◊ George, Cylon. September 25, 2015. "10 Ways to Stop Feeling Like a Victim Once and for All." Huffingtonpost.com. At http://bit.ly/2Ty6aYW

◊ Firestone, Robert W. September 30, 2009. "Don't Play the Victim Game." Psychologytoday.com. At http://bit.ly/2Tv01ww

◊ Cabelly, Harriet. "How to Stop Being a Victim and Start Creating Your Life." Tinybuddha.com. At http://bit.ly/2TwcgJj

Live

◊ Vincent, John. "28 Inspirational Quotes about Enjoying Life." Inspiringtips. com. At http://bit.ly/2Tv0aA4

◊ Deschene, Lori. "30 Ways to Live Life to the Fullest." Tinybuddha.com. At http://bit.ly/2TrV7jW

Spend Time Alone

◊ Carter, Sherrie Bourg. January 31, 2012. "6 Reasons You Should Spend More Time Alone." Psychologytoday.com. At http://bit.ly/2TroDGp

◊ Weingus, Leigh. December 6, 2017. "8 Reasons Why Spending Time Alone Is Actually Really Good for You." Huffpost.com. At http://bit.ly/2TuM7KF

Happiness

◊ Gregoire, Carolyn. August 23, 2013. "The 75-Year Study That Found the Secrets to a Fulfilling Life." Huffpost.com. At http://bit.ly/2TrVvyU

◊ Stossel, Scott. May 2013. "What Makes Us Happy, Revisited." Theatlantic. com. At http://bit.ly/2TrVBGM

◊ Slater, Dan. November 07, 2012. "What Harvard's Grant Study Reveals about Happiness and Life." Thedailybeast.com. At http://bit.ly/2Tu5sf2

YOUR SWORD

Your Brain Is A Double-Edged Sword

◊ Carey, Benedict. July 31, 2007. "Who's Minding the Mind?" nytimes.com. At https://nyti.ms/2BnLrzI

◊ Baraniuk, Chris. March 16, 2016. "The Enormous Power of the Unconscious Brain." Bbc.com. At https://bbc.in/2BlIBvj

◊ Pomeroy, Steven Ross. February 19, 2013. "How to Instill False Memories." Scientificamerican.com. At http://bit.ly/2Bl4vP7

The Age of Reason

◊ Sather, Rita and Shelat, Amit. "Understanding the Teen Brain." URMC. Rochester.edu. At http://bit.ly/2Bm0Mkt

◊ Stasney, Shelly. April 26, 2018. "7 Facts About Your Child's Prefrontal Cortex that Are Game Changers." Thisnthatparenting.com. At http://bit. ly/2Bl5XB3

◊ February 18, 2015. "At What Age Is the Brain Fully Developed?" Mentalhealthdaily.com. At http://bit.ly/2Bm9Cih

Perspective

◊ Kennedy, Terri. October 18, 2011. "The Power of Perspective." Huffpost. com. At http://bit.ly/2BlNK6y

◊ Robertson, Colin. April 02, 2015. "The Extraordinary Power of Perspective—How Your Point of View Affects Your Willpower." Willpowered.co. At http://bit.ly/2BfGBEP

◊ Berg, Monica. August 4, 2017. "The Power of Perspective." Rethinklife. today. At http://bit.ly/2Bj6FyQ

Perception

◊ Koch, Christof. July 1, 2010. "Looks Can Deceive: Why Perception and Reality Don't Always Match Up." Scientificamerican.com. At http://bit. ly/2BfGPf9

◊ Claus-Christian, Carbon. July 31, 2014. "Understanding human perception by human-made illusions." Ncbi.nlm.nih.gov. At http://bit.ly/2BlwHkR

Tribalism

◊ Subliminal: How Your Unconscious Mind Rules Your Behavior. At https://amzn.to/2Bnm9C2

◊ Sullivan andrew. September 2017. "America Wasn't Built for Humans." NYMag.com. At https://nym.ag/2BlP9dk

◊ Stalder, Daniel R. June 2018. "Tribalism in Politics." Psychologytoday.com. At http://bit.ly/2Bk6of9

◊ Chua, Amy. March 1, 2018. "How America's identity politics went from inclusion to division." Theguardian.com. At http://bit.ly/2BhYEdq

Groupthink

◊ McLeod, Saul. 2008. "Social Identity Theory." Simplypsychology.org. At http://bit.ly/2Bk8D1K

Cognitive Dissonance

◊ Festinger, Leon. "Cognitive Dissonance." Instructionaldesign.org. At http://bit.ly/2BlSvNc

◊ "Cognitive Dissonance." Psychologytoday.com. At http://bit.ly/2Bp9QVH

Motivated Reasoning

◊ "Subliminal: How Your Unconscious Mind Rules Your Behavior." At https://amzn.to/2Ble1lo

◊ Talks at Google. May 24, 2012. "Leonard Mlodinow: Subliminal: How Your Unconscious Mind Rules Your Behavior." Youtube.com. At http://bit.ly/2BnFTFx

◊ "Motivated Reasoning." Psychologytoday.com. At http://bit.ly/2Bno4GK

◊ Spitfire Strategies. November 20, 2012. "Yale Professor Dan Kahan on Motivated Reasoning." Youtube.com. At http://bit.ly/2BvXuLJ

◊ Complexity Labs. April 8, 2017. "Motivated reasoning." Youtube.com. At http://bit.ly/2BnnJDN

Manipulation

◊ Lanau, Kate. September 14, 2016. "A 'Memory Hacker' Explains How to Plant False Memories in People's Minds." Vice.com. At http://bit.ly/2BjjvgE

◊ Hrala, Josh. January 24, 2017. "Scientists Claim They've Developed a Psychological 'Vaccine' Against Fake News." Sciencealert.com. At http://bit.ly/2BlVu8m

◊ LaFrance, Adrienne. December 7, 2015. "What Makes Tom Hanks Look Like Tom Hanks." Theantlantic.com. At http://bit.ly/2Bjk4XO

◊ LaFrance, Adrienne. July 11, 2017. "The Technology That Will Make It Impossible for You to Believe What You See." Theantlantic.com. At http://bit.ly/2Bno6hF

Milgram's Obedience Study

◊ McLeod, Saul. 2017. "The Milgram Experiment." Simplypsychology.com. At http://bit.ly/2Tt1pzH

◊ Khan Academy. "Milgram Experiment on Obedience." Khanacademy.org. At http://bit.ly/2Twe8S5

◊ Encina, Gregorio Billikopf. 2014. "Milgram's Experiment on Obedience to Authority." Berkeley.edu. At http://bit.ly/2TwGYlu

Delusion and Entitlement

◊ Top5Central. April 5, 2017. "Top 5 Most Spoiled Kids Reacting to Expensive Cars!" Youtube.com. At http://bit.ly/2TtMnd6

◊ Fox News Insider. February 4, 2016. "Dr. Phil: We've Created a Generation of Entitled, Narcissistic People." Youtube.com. At http://bit.ly/2TvFk3q

◊ CBC News: The National. February 20, 2017. "Millennials: Coddled, entitled, narcissistic and lazy?" Youtube.com. At http://bit.ly/2TzGATo

◊ Denver 7: The Denver Channel. May 8, 2018. "'My Dad's The Mayor!' Video Shows Denver Mayor's Son Using Slur Against Officer During Traffic Stop." Youtube.com. At http://bit.ly/2TuumuV

◊ Skykel. January 22, 2017. "Passengers Cheer as Liberal Hag is Thrown Off Airplane for Berating Trump Supporter." Youtube.com. At http://bit.ly/2Tt23ND

◊ Inside Edition. May 22, 2017. "Man in Trump Hat Gets Escorted Off United Flight." Youtube.com. At http://bit.ly/2TwQPHZ

◊ Barrel Tap. November 19, 2018. "Dine and Dash is the New Black Entitlement at Chipotle in St Paul." Youtube.com. At http://bit.ly/2TAmvw4

◊ Cardone, Grant. August 29, 2011. "Lazy is an Entitlement Concept." Huffingtonpost.com. At http://bit.ly/2Tyk514

The Dunning-Kruger Effect

◊ TED. February 15, 2018. "Why Incompetent People Think They're Amazing." Facebook.com. At http://bit.ly/2TwLLTR

◊ Murphy, Mark. January 24, 2017. "The Dunning-Kruger Effect Shows Why Some People Think They're Great Even When Their Work Is Terrible." Forbes.com. At http://bit.ly/2TtQoyc

◊ Poundstone, William. January 21, 2017. "The Dunning-Kruger President." Psychologytoday.com. At http://bit.ly/2TxQuol

SHARPENING YOUR SWORD

Lifelong Learning

◊ Simmons, Michael. January 16, 2018. "The Secret to Lifelong Success is Lifelong Learning." Weforum.org. At http://bit.ly/2TtePvw

◊ January 12, 2017. "Lifelong Learning is Becoming an Economic Imperative." Economist.com. At https://econ.st/2TwjAol

◊ Coleman, John. January 24, 2017. "Make Learning a Lifelong Habit." Hbr. org. At http://bit.ly/2TxnwoL

Neuroplasticity

◊ "What is Neuroplasticity?" Brainworksneurotherapy.com. At http://bit. ly/2TzKMT8

◊ Hampton, Debbie. October 28, 2015. "Neuroplasticity: The 10 Fundamentals of Rewiring Your Brain." Reset.me. At http://bit.ly/2TzKRWW

◊ July 25, 2018. "What is Neuroplasticity? Definition + 14 Brain Plasticity Exercises." Positivepsychologyprogram.com. At http://bit.ly/2TCmlVa

Mindfulness

◊ "Mindfulness." The Centre for Mindfulness Studies. At http://bit. ly/2TzL5xg

◊ Bertin, Mark. November 9, 2015. "Mindfulness Meditation: Guided Practices." Mindful.org. At http://bit.ly/2TzGY3Z

◊ Congleton, Christina, Hölzel, Britta K. and Lazar, Sara W. January 08, 2015. "Mindfulness Can Literally Change Your Brain." Hbr.org. At http:// bit.ly/2TCoMHi

Meditation

◊ Smart is the New Sexy. October 12, 2017. "How Does Silence Affect the Brain?" Facebook.com. At http://bit.ly/2BpqWmu

◊ Roth, Bob and Peltz, Perri. 2016. "The Science of Meditation." Aspenideas. org. At http://bit.ly/2BlXi1t

◊ Reynolds, Gretchen. February 18, 2016. "How Meditation Changes the Brain and Body." Nytimes. At https://nyti.ms/2BobMOp

◊ Corliss, Julie. January 08, 2014. "Mindfulness Meditation May Ease Anxiety, Mental Stress." Harvard.edu. At http://bit.ly/2BoHkn2

Learn a Foreign Language

◊ December 2007. "The Benefits of Second Language Study." At http://bit. ly/2BnJeo6

◊ February 18, 2011. "Juggling languages can build better brains." PSU.Edu. At http://bit.ly/2Bm0zgY

◊ Marian, Viorica and Shook, Anthony. October 31, 2012. "The Cognitive Benefits of Being Bilingual." Ncbi.nlm.nih.gov. At http://bit.ly/2Bps89s

◊ Czekala, Bartosz. "80 Amazing Advantages and Benefits of Language Learning (Part 1)." Universeofmemory.com. At http://bit.ly/2Bm1EW4

Learn to Play a Musical Instrument

◊ TedED. "How Playing an Instrument Benefits Your Brain—Anita Collins." Thekidsshouldseethis.com. At http://bit.ly/2TxOah6

◊ Bergland, Christopher. June 25, 2014. "Does Playing a Musical Instrument Make You Smarter?" Psychologytoday.com. At http://bit.ly/2TxOs7G

◊ Rampton, John. "The Benefits of Playing Music Help Your Brain More Than Any Other Activity." Inc.com. At http://bit.ly/2TBuZTA

Practice and Repetition

◊ Shen, Jason. "Why Practice Actually Makes Perfect: How to Rewire Your Brain for Better Performance." Bufferapp.com. At http://bit.ly/2TvgbG6

◊ Weibell, C.J. 2011. "Repetition." Wordpress.com. At http://bit.ly/2TzuBoP

Creativity

◊ Naiman, Linda. February 17, 2014. "What is Creativity? (And Why is it a Crucial Factor for Business Success?)" Creativityatwork.com. At http://bit. ly/2TBqzfx

◊ Friedrich, Tamara. November 23, 2015. "Google Spills its Work Secrets and Gives Lessons in Boosting Creativity." Theconversation.com. At http://bit. ly/2TBRQyC

◊ Talbot-Zorn, Justin and Marz, Leigh. March 17, 2017. "The Busier You Are, the More You Need Quiet Time." Hbr.org. At http://bit.ly/2TzSjBj

◊ Wong, May. April 24, 2014. "Stanford Study Finds Walking Improves Creativity." Stanford.edu. At https://stanford.io/2Tw0Sgw

◊ Schuler, Matthew. November 3, 2013. "Why Creative People Sometimes Make No Sense." Matthewschuler.co. At http://bit.ly/2Tvhh4G

◊ December 1, 2015. "Red Bull High Performance Team Unveils Largest Study of Creative Styles and Invites the Public to Participate." Prnewswire. com. At https://prn.to/2THm96I

◊ April 19, 2010. "Brief Meditative Exercise Helps Cognition." Sciencedaily. com. At http://bit.ly/2TBRhoc

◊ "This is the Way Google & IDEO Foster Creativity." Ideou.com. At http:// bit.ly/2TzUTqZ

Learn to Code

◊ Bradford, Laurence. November 5, 2018. "10 Life-Changing Reasons You Should Learn to Code." Skillcrush.com. At http://bit.ly/2TyKE67

◊ Frost, Aja. "4 Major Reasons You Need Coding Skills Even If You Don't Want to Be an Engineer." Themuse.com. At https://muse.cm/2TBO08n

◊ Bradford, Laurence. June 20, 2016. "Why Every Millennial Should Learn Some Code." Forbes.com. At http://bit.ly/2Tvk5yK

Read

◊ Lebowitz, Shana. February 26, 2016. "The 100 Best Leadership and Success Books to Read in Your Lifetime, According to Amazon." Businessinsider. com. At https://read.bi/2TzJ5VF

◊ "50 Books Every Man Should Read Once in His Life." Coolmaterial.com. At http://bit.ly/2TCuwAO

The Socratic Method

◊ Garrett, Elizabeth. 1998. "The Socratic Method." Uchicago.edu. At http://bit.ly/2TBjvQ6

◊ Reis, Rick. "The Socratic Method: What it is and How to Use it in the Classroom." Stanford.edu. At https://stanford.io/2TziiZt

RELATIONSHIPS

Why Relationships Are Important

◊ Mineo, Liz. April 11, 2017. "Good Genes Are Nice, but Joy is Better." Harvard.edu. At http://bit.ly/2TAod0B

◊ Waldinger, Robert. "What Makes a Good Life? Lessons From the Longest Study on Happiness." Ted.com. At http://bit.ly/2TBXu3B

◊ Umberson, Debra and Montez, Jennifer Karas. August 2011. "Social Relationships and Health: A Flashpoint for Health Policy." Ncbi.nlm.nih. gov. At http://bit.ly/2TzIqUc

Love

◊ Raghunathan, Raj. January 08, 2014. "The Need to Love." Psychologytoday. com. At http://bit.ly/2TAZ6uy

◊ December 09, 2014. "Why is Love So Important?" Economictimes. indiatimes.com. At http://bit.ly/2TzjpZ9

Lifelong Relationships

◊ Fuller, Kristen. October 02, 2017. "Why Do We Need Friends? Six Benefits of Healthy Friendships." Psychologytoday.com. At http://bit.ly/2BnUKzC

Friends

◊ Brenner, Abigail. May 29, 2016. "The Importance of Friends." Psychologytoday.com. At http://bit.ly/2TGLBJX

◊ Crook, Lawrence and Ford, Dana. September 22, 2015. "10 More People Charged in Connection With Hazing Death." Cnn.com. At https://cnn.it/2TAoP6p

◊ "The Hunting Ground." Cnn.com. At https://cnn.it/2TAK3Rr

The Golden Rule

◊ MacLaclan, Maria. October 2007. "The Golden Rule." Thinkhumanism.com. At http://bit.ly/2Bn6Hpy

◊ Kalman, Izzy. February 20, 2010. "The True Meaning of the Golden Rule: Love Your Bullies." Psychologytoday.com. At http://bit.ly/2BmF3c8

Criticism

◊ Cardone, Grant. December 06, 2017. "Why Criticism is Important to Success." Huffingtonpost.com. At http://bit.ly/2BqAZaI

◊ Neese, Brian. March 29, 2017. "A Manager's Guide to Providing Constructive Criticism in the Workplace." Alvernia.com. At http://bit.ly/2Bo98YX

◊ Hill, Linda and Lineback, Kent. April 05, 2011. "Why Does Criticism Seem More Effective Than Praise?" hbr.org. At http://bit.ly/2Bt1gVX

Apologize

◊ Lerner, Harriet. March/April 2018. "The Power of Apologizing." Psychotherapynetworker.org. At http://bit.ly/2TxsdyN

◊ Stevenson, Herb. April 25, 2016. "The Power of Apologies." Clevelandconsultinggroup.com. At http://bit.ly/2TEhFy2

◊ Brody, Jane E. January 30, 2017. "The Right Way to Say 'I'm Sorry.'" Nytimes.com. At https://nyti.ms/2TCnU5n

Intelligence

◊ Walker, Aaron. October 03, 2018. "How Humour Can Help Reduce Workplace Stress." Anu.edu.au. At http://bit.ly/2TIzbBj

◊ Riggio, Ronald E. March 05, 2012. "Why Intelligence Alone Won't Lead to Success." Psychologytoday.com. At http://bit.ly/2TDW5cH

◊ Jensen, Keld. April 12, 2012. "Intelligence is Overrated: What You Really Need to Succeed." Forbes.com. At http://bit.ly/2TB51j5

Communication

◊ Grohol, John M. July 8, 2018. "9 Steps to Better Communication Today." Psychcentral.com. At http://bit.ly/2TDHGgL

◊ Ohlin, Birgit. August 25, 2017. "How to Improve Communication in Relationships: 7 Essential Skills." Positivepsychologyprogram.com. At http://bit.ly/2Tz6sOV

◊ "Communication tips for Parents." Apa.org. At http://bit.ly/2TIAznv

◊ "Communication." Hbr.org. At http://bit.ly/2TBriNS

◊ Stanford Graduate School of Business. December 4, 2014. "Think Fast, Talk Smart: Communication Techniques." Youtube.com. At http://bit.ly/2TB5lhN

Meaningful Conversations

◊ Hall, John. "13 Simple Ways You Can Have More Meaningful Conversations." Forbes.com. At http://bit.ly/2TB8le1

◊ Granneman, Jenn. June 20, 2017. "Why We Need to Have Deeper Conversations." Psychologytoday.com. At http://bit.ly/2TDIP83

◊ Lebowitz, Shana. March 21, 2018. "14 Ways to Skip the Shallow Small Talk and Have Deep Conversations." Businessinsider.com. At https://read.bi/2TCvLQh

Listen

◊ August 17, 2011. "How to Improve Listening Skills & Conversations." Eruptingmind.com. At http://bit.ly/2TDh3Zp

◊   Zetlin, Minda. February 11, 2016. "7 Smart Reasons You Should Talk Less and Listen More." Inc.com. At http://bit.ly/2BthWwz

◊   Schilling, Dianne. November 09, 2012. "10 Steps to Effective Listening." Forbes.com. At http://bit.ly/2BpOc3N

◊   "Top 10 Tips for Listening First Conversations." Listenfirstproject.org. At http://bit.ly/2BteJ06

Silence

◊   Price-Mitchell, Marilyn. December 09, 2013. "The Importance of Silence in a Noisy World." Psychologytoday.com. At http://bit.ly/2Btid2z

◊   Drexler, Peggy. June 4, 2018. "The Importance of Silence in an Age of Speaking Out." Thriveglobal.com. At http://bit.ly/2BrE3DH

Words Matter

◊   Pilkington, Ed. April 14, 2008. "Obama Angers Midwest Voters with Guns and Religion Remark." Theguardian.com. At http://bit.ly/2BrsqfY

◊   Reilly, Katie. August 31, 2016. "Here Are All the Times Donald Trump Insulted Mexico." Time.com. At http://bit.ly/2BnG43C

In Business, Be Brief

◊   Edwards, Jim. May 26, 2017. "This Memo from Winston Churchill on 'Brevity' is All You Need to Improve Your Writing." Businessinsider.com. At https://read.bi/2BpPrjt

◊   Boyle, Pete. August 2014. "The Power of Precision Writing—Why Brevity is Important." Have-a-word.com. At http://bit.ly/2BrsLiK

◊   "Brevity is Beautiful." Betterexplained.com. At http://bit.ly/2BuS1Vf

Nonverbal Cues

◊   Mlodinaow, Leonard. February 12, 2013. "Subliminal: How Your Unconscious Mind Rules Your Behavior." Penguinrandomhouse.com. At http://bit.ly/2BrQ0ZM

◊   "Mehrabian's Communication Theory—Verbal, Non-verbal, Body Language." Businessballs.com. At http://bit.ly/2BrXKLD

◊   Farnsworth, Bryn. December 6, 2016. "Facial Action Coding System (FACS)—A Visual Guidebook." Imotions.com. At http://bit.ly/2TEvXi5

◊   "The Definitive Guide to Reading Microexpressions." Scienceofpeople. com. At http://bit.ly/2TFSvyL

Compliment Others

◊ Marano, Hara Estroff. March 1, 2004. "The Art of the Compliment." Psychologytoday.com. At http://bit.ly/2TG4lJg

◊ Blatchford, Emily. June 20, 2017. "Compliments Are Good for Your Health, But Not If They're Fake." Huffingtonpost.com.au. At http://bit.ly/2TzL4Jw

◊ Berger, Marcia Naomi. July 08, 2018. "Why Compliments Are Powerful." Psychcentral.com. At http://bit.ly/2TEaNRd

Kindness

◊ Pourmoradi, Melody. December 06, 2017. "13 Reasons Why Kindness Counts." Huffingtonpost.com. At http://bit.ly/2TIk9va

◊ Miscov, Teodora. January 26, 2018. "Kill Them With Kindness: The Importance of Kindness In the Workplace." Digitaldoughnut.com. At http://bit.ly/2TEvn3H

Touch

◊ Chillot, Rick. March 11, 2013. "The Power of Touch." Psychologytoday. com. At http://bit.ly/2THEr8e

Smile

◊ Hall, Alena. February 08, 2015. "11 Surprising Reasons You Should Smile Every Day." Huffpost.com. At http://bit.ly/2THfedQ

◊ Smith, Jennifer. "7 Benefits of Smiling and Laughing that You Didn't Know about." Lifehack.org. At http://bit.ly/2THfVns

◊ Widrich, Leo. "The Science of Smiling: A Guide to The World's Most Powerful Gesture." Bufferapp.com. At http://bit.ly/2TNaZgM

◊ Pinker, Susan. April 05, 2018. "Smiles Hide Many Messages—Some Unfriendly." Wsj.com. At https://on.wsj.com/2TGwuQy

Networking

◊ Stahl, Ashley. March 29, 2018. "3 Tips to Improve Your Networking Skills." Forbes.com. At http://bit.ly/2TBCFFC

◊ Doyle, Alison. December 10, 2018. "The Importance of Career Networking." Thebalancecareers.com. At http://bit.ly/2THooaj

Community

◊ Steinberg Amy, January 23, 2018, What is Community and Why is it Important? Biobridges.com http://bit.ly/2Gvnt8G

◊ Spero, Harper, April 1, 2015, "The Importance of Community." Huffington Post http://bit.ly/2VWKruS

Volunteering

◊ Ready Citizen Corps; goabroad.com; gooverseas.com; govoluntouring. com; grassrootsvolunteering.com; mrc.hhs.gov; nvoad.org; wwoof.net; buildabroad.org; fullercenter.org; solutions.org; globalvolunteers.org; unitedplanet.org; workaway.info; seeds.is

◊ Project Helping. "Wellness Benefits of Volunteering." Projecthelping.com. At http://bit.ly/2TFRfMn

◊ Fritz, Joanne. July 03, 2018. "15 Unexpected Benefits of Volunteering That Will Inspire You." Thebalancesmb.com. At http://bit.ly/2THmzKq

Help

◊ "The Lost Art of Asking for Help." Amanet.com. At http://bit.ly/2BusHyA

◊ Zetlin, Minda. "5 Reasons You Must Learn to Ask for Help." Inc.com. At http://bit.ly/2BDevDN

◊ Boyes, Alice. October 31, 2016. "7 Effective Ways to ask for Help (and Get It)." Psychologytoday.com. At http://bit.ly/2Bnc5ZJ

Mentors

◊ Caprino, Kathy. September 21, 2014. "How to Find a Great Mentor—First, Don't Ever Ask a Stranger." Forbes.com. At http://bit.ly/2BrhzCC

◊ Jackson, Amy Elisa. October 09, 2015. "8 Successful People Share How Not to Find a Mentor." Fastcompany.com. At http://bit.ly/2E3sGUe

◊ D'Angelo, Matt. November 4, 2018. "How to Find a Mentor." Businessnewsdaily.com. At http://bit.ly/2Brwe0w

◊ Pearce, Kyle. February 12, 2018. "How to Find a Mentor or Apprenticeship Opportunity in 2018." Diygenius.com. At http://bit.ly/2BrVkg0

Respect

◊ Jackson, Shawn. 2014. "How to Respect Yourself and Others." Goodchoicesgoodlife.org. At http://bit.ly/2BtkY3I

◊ "The Power of Respect." Ccl.org. At http://bit.ly/2BrluPQ

◊ Williams, Debbie. July 13, 2017. "Respect for Others: The Foundation of Every Relationship." Bizlibrary.com. At http://bit.ly/2BwEgp3

How to Deal with Authority

◊ NowThis. June 8, 2016. "Missouri Teen Tased into a Coma." Facebook. com. At http://bit.ly/2BqgVp2

◊ "Kevin Ferguson (Police Officer)." Everpedia.org. At http://bit.ly/2Bv1Fay

◊ ABC News. September 22, 2016. "Video Shows 15-Year-Old Girl Being Pepper Sprayed by Police." Facebook.com. At http://bit.ly/2BsXXOy

◊ Schar, Reid J. September 17, 2015. "What Constitutes a 'Lawful Order'?" thehill.com. At http://bit.ly/2Bp1hKn

◊ Kerr, Orin. July 23, 2015. "Sandra Bland and the 'Lawful Order' Problem." Washingtonpost.com. At https://wapo.st/2BsKYfH

◊ Romero, Dennis. September 17, 2014. "Can You Refuse to Identify Yourself to Police?" laweekly.com. At http://bit.ly/2BsL1rT

Parenting 101

◊ Ted-ed. February 03, 2016. "How Stress Affects the Brain." Facebook.com. At http://bit.ly/2BsYbFo

◊ Gopnik, Adam. May 16, 2016. "Feel Me." Newyorker.com. At http://bit. ly/2Bs6Ec6

◊ Chillot, Rick. March 11, 2013. "The Power of Touch." Psychologytoday. com. At http://bit.ly/2THEr8e

◊ Konnikova, Maria. March 4, 2015. "The Power of Touch." Newyorker.com. At http://bit.ly/2BqOirW

How to Be a Good Father

◊   Taibbi, Robert. March 01, 2011. "Fathers & Sons: How to Be a Great Dad." Psychologytoday.com. At http://bit.ly/2BszI2Q

◊   Kelby, Scott. "10 Ways to Be a Great Dad." Parents.com. At http://bit.ly/2Bo5YEv

◊   Robinson, Bruce. "Top Ten Tips for Being a Great Dad." Thefatheringproject.org. At http://bit.ly/2Bufjue

◊   Firchau, Nick. September 10, 2018. "How to Be a Good Dad Even If You Never Had One." Lifehacker.com. At http://bit.ly/2Buiwdz

Respect Your Elders

◊   A Source Book in Chinese Philosophy by Wing-Tsit Chan. https://amzn.to/2GxiZyj

◊   February 02, 2014. "7 Cultures that Celebrate Aging and Respect Their Elders." Huffpost.com. At http://bit.ly/2BsyjcT

◊   Spears, Libby. February 16, 2016. "What is Respect to a Millennial, a Boomer and a Gen X'er?" uschamber.com. At https://uscham.com/2BtCfKd

◊   Reeves, Richard V. "The Respect Deficit." Aeon.com. At http://bit.ly/2BvTquS

◊   "Abuse of the elderly." Who.int. At http://bit.ly/2BqeEKs

ACTION IS MAGIC

Action

◊   Cardone, Grant. July 28, 2015. "You'll Only Achieve Success by Taking Massive Levels of Action." Entrepreneur.com. At http://bit.ly/2TLJjcw

◊   Sutevski, Dragan. "Willingness to Take Entrepreneurial Action." Entrepreneurshipinabox.com. At http://bit.ly/2TH31pJ

◊   Gdixonfitness. December 15, 2013. "To Be Successful Take Action Motivational Video." youtube.com. At http://bit.ly/2TNyN4x

◊   Bernat, Dragos. January 6, 2015. "9 Effective Practices that Will Drive You to Take Action Immediately." Thoughtcatalog.com. At http://bit.ly/2THgg9X

Delegation

◊ "Why Delegation Is Important." Ncsu.edu. At http://bit.ly/2TIFfJI

◊ "Importance of Delegation for the Smooth Functioning of a Business." Businessmanagementideas.com. At http://bit.ly/2TNyXsF

◊ Craven, Jack. February 21, 2018. "Great Leaders Perfect the Art of Delegation." Forbes.com. At http://bit.ly/2THlgeL

◊ Schleckser, Jim. "The 5 Levels of Delegation You Need to Know to Lead Well." Inc.com. At http://bit.ly/2THlLFF

Grit and a Growth Mindset

◊ Illumeably. July 27, 2017. "Why Some Students Fail and Other Students Succeed." Facebook.com. At http://bit.ly/2THClVH

◊ Duckworth, Angela, "Grit: The Power of Passion and Perseverance". https://amzn.to/2XyBUib

◊ Stanford Alumni. October 9, 2014. "Developing a Growth Mindset with Carol Dweck." Youtube.com. At http://bit.ly/2THlXET

◊ Dweck, Carol S., Mindset: The New Psychology of Success, Ballantine Books, 2016, https://amzn.to/2IMUcrF

Touch Things Once

◊ Umoh, Ruth. June 21, 2018. "Skyrocket Your Productivity With the 'Touch it Once' Rule." Cnbc.com. At https://cnb.cx/2TLKA3i

◊ Earnest, Laura. May 14, 2012. "Increase Your Productivity by Touching it Once." Lauraearnest.com. At http://bit.ly/2TIOXfc

To-Do Lists

◊ Parikh, Devi. April 25, 2018. "Calendar. Not to-Do Lists." usejournal.com. At http://bit.ly/2TG71Xj

◊ Markovitx, Daniel. January 24, 2012. "To-Do Lists Don't Work." Hbr.org. At http://bit.ly/2TOORTe

Prioritize

◊ Cooper, Belle. June 2, 2017. "How to Ruthlessly Prioritize Your Task List to Get More Done." Zapier.com. At http://bit.ly/2THqyqy

◊ "Get Ahead at Work With These Task Prioritization Tips." Asana.com. At http://bit.ly/2TF034U

Speed

◊ ForfunTV. May 20, 2018. "Fast Workers vs. Slow 'Lazy' Workers—Funny Compilation 2018." Youtube.com. At http://bit.ly/2TGejKH

◊ Knightgamer. November 20, 2016. "Motivation to Slow Workers." Youtube.com. At http://bit.ly/2TF0fBa

◊ Brox, Denene. October 2010. "Fast Food Fast." Qsrmagazine.com. At http://bit.ly/2TCA6my

◊ Bagley, Rebecca O. May 1, 2013. "Speed to Market: An Entrepreneur's View." Forbes.com. At http://bit.ly/2THnsmv

◊ O'Hara, Carolyn. January 03, 2017. "How to Get an Employee to Work Faster." Hbr.org. At http://bit.ly/2TH4PPx

Time

◊ Maidment, Paul. February 29, 2008. "The Price of Time." Forbes.com. At http://bit.ly/2TI2L9U

The 80/20 Rule

◊ Kruse, Kevin. March 07, 2016. "The 80/20 Rule and How It Can Change Your Life." Forbes.com. At http://bit.ly/2THj5b3

◊ The Awesome Life. September 28, 2015. "Improve Your Productivity With the 80/20 Rule." Youtube.com. At http://bit.ly/2TNCcAl

Procrastination

◊ Swanson, Ana. April 27, 2016. "The Real Reasons You Procrastinate—and How to Stop." Washingtonpost.com. At https://wapo.st/2THEzEx

◊ Thompson, Derek. August 26, 2014. "The Procrastination Doom Loop—and How to Break It." Theatlantic.com. At http://bit.ly/2TJgdKO

Declutter

◊ Jonas, Jeff. January 1, 2018. "On Going Nomad." Medium.com. At http://bit.ly/2BvBCjh

◊ "There's Proof That Clutter Causes Anxiety; Removing These 20 Items Will Instantly Boost Your Mood." Wakeupyourmind.net. At http://bit.ly/2TF4lcw

Punctuality

◊ Zudeick, Peter. September 12, 2012. "Germans and Punctuality." Dw.com. At http://bit.ly/2TGlbYv

◊ Cohen, Jennifer. May 12, 2014. "One Trait That Can Make or Break Your Reputation In Business." Forbes.com. At http://bit.ly/2THfFoF

Be Organized and Prepared

◊ Mendoza, Charley. "20 Ways to Organize Your Life Now." Keepinspiring.me. At http://bit.ly/2THJiWN

◊ Scott, SJ. "21 Success Habits of Highly Organized People." Developgoodhabits.com. At http://bit.ly/2THsNu3

Cool Apps

◊ Corpuz, John and Moren, Dan. December 5, 2018. "Best Free Apps for iPhone." Tomsguide.com. At http://bit.ly/2BvDys3

◊ Muchmore, Michael. December 26, 2018. "The 100 Best iPhone Apps for 2019." Pcmag.com. At http://bit.ly/2Bqh3oj

◊ January 25, 2019. "The 30 Best iPhone Apps to Download Now." Popularmechanics.com. At http://bit.ly/2Bompkb

◊ Duffy, Jill. September 26, 2018. "The 25 Best Productivity Apps for iPhone in 2018." Zapier.com. At http://bit.ly/2BtneZ8

◊ Grannell, Craig. February 2019. "The best iPhone apps we've used in 2019." Techradar.com. At http://bit.ly/2BomwfB

◊ "Best iPhone Apps for 2019." Cnet.com. At https://cnet.co/2Bu3QuJ

Morning and Evening Routines

◊ Ambrosini, Melissa. "Magical Morning Routines: Why they are Important and How to Create one." Melissaambrosini.Com. At http://bit.ly/2BsQ5g7

◊ Treneva, Ralitza. December 15, 2017. "The Importance of Morning Routines: How Routines Boost Mental Health." Inpathybulletin.com. At http://bit.ly/2Bv9AVf

◊ Brokaw, Ken. May 30, 2018. "The Importance of Establishing a Morning Routine." Forbes.com. At http://bit.ly/2BonubJ

◊ Toren, Matthew. "The 24-Minute Morning Routine That Will Make You an Entrepreneurial Rock Star." Entrepreneur.com. At http://bit.ly/2BtoLym

FEAR AND FAILURE

Understanding Fear

◊ Goalcast. November 10, 2017. "Walt Disney's Inspiring Story." Facebook. com. At http://bit.ly/2TLVTbK

◊ Campbell, Sherrie. March 26, 2015. "7 Ways to Think Differently About Fear." Entrepreneur.com. At http://bit.ly/2TGUgvN

◊ McGauran, Debbie. January 7, 2019. "The 10 Most Common Fear Motives." Activebeat.co. At http://bit.ly/2THAcJR

◊ Adolphs, Ralph. January 21, 2013. "The Biology of Fear." Ncbi.nlm.nih. gov. At http://bit.ly/2TDkeAo

Overcoming Fear

◊ Lahti, Emilia. September 15, 2016. "How to Cultivate the Courage to Achieve Your Goals." Fulfillmentdaily.com. At http://bit.ly/2TCKwTc

◊ Byrd, Ian. "On Nervousness & Understanding Fear." Birdseed.com. At http://bit.ly/2TFc8qM. Ian@byrdseed.com

◊ "Phobias and Irrational Fears." Helpguide.org. At http://bit.ly/2THtDa9

◊ Scott, Ben Lionel. July 22, 2018. "FEAR-Best Motivational Video." Youtube. com. At http://bit.ly/2THQn9P

◊ Hesmotivation. May 7, 2017. "Don't Let Fear Kill Your Dreams— Best Motivational Videos Compilation." Youtube.com. At http://bit. ly/2TGmPJO

◊ Beyondthepine. January 2, 2014. "Fear—Motivational Video 2014." Youtube.com. At http://bit.ly/2TIZOFY

Failure

◊ Top List. July 06, 2015. "25 People Who Failed Before Becoming Famous." Youtube.com. At http://bit.ly/2TIdjWy

◊ "Overcoming Fear of Failure." Mindtools.com. At http://bit.ly/2TIT8rm

◊ August 25, 2016. "Why Failure is Good for Success." Success.com. At http://bit.ly/2TIUZfM

◊ Fuentes, Agustin. October 10, 2013. "Failure is Good." Psychologytoday. com. At http://bit.ly/2THQUsl

◊ MotivatingSuccess. May 15, 2012. "Famous Failures." Youtube.com. At http://bit.ly/2TGwcJl

◊ Mashed. December 13, 2018. "The Tragic Real-Life Story of Colonel Sanders." Youtube.com. At http://bit.ly/2TGnY44

Mistakes

◊ Kalhorn, Renita. August 27, 2018. "Mistakes are Inevitable: How to Minimize the Pain, Maximize the Opportunity." Forbes.com. At http:// bit.ly/2THvltn

◊ Schulz, Kathryn. March 2011. "On being wrong." Ted.com. At http://bit. ly/2THvITv

◊ Morin, Amy. July 17, 2017. "5 Ways to Turn Your Mistake into a Valuable Life Lesson." Forbes.com. At http://bit.ly/2TCLWNw

◊ October 25, 2018. "10 Lessons I Learned from Making Many Mistakes In My 20s." dariusforoux.com. At http://bit.ly/2TJ1gIq

◊ McKay, Brett and Kate. February 19, 2013. "Personal Responsibility 102: The Importance of Owning Up to Your Mistakes and How to Do It." Artofmanliness.com. At http://bit.ly/2TJ67JJ

◊ Wax, Dustin. "How to Admit Your Mistakes." Lifehack.org. At http://bit. ly/2TNNUuN

Stress

◊ "50 Common Signs and Symptoms of Stress." Stress.org. At http://bit. ly/2BCN1xN

Flying Taxis

◊ Newcomb, Alyssa. January 10, 2019. "Flying cars could take off as soon as 2023." Nbcnews.com. At https://nbcnews.to/2BAbMLe

Opportunity in Adversity

◊ Ringer, Robert. June 21, 2012. "Identifying Opportunity in Adversity." Earlytorise.com. At http://bit.ly/2TLXHS4

◊ Laux, Chris. April 09, 2017. "How Moments of Adversity Are Your Greatest Opportunities." Goalcast.com. At http://bit.ly/2THCwR0

◊ DiNardo, Nick. "Bounce Back and Thrive: The Secret to Turning Adversity into Opportunity." Tinybuddha.com. At http://bit.ly/2TJtmUa

Never Quit

◊ Business Insider. May 13, 2017. "A Navy SEAL Commander Explains How He Learned to Never Give Up." Youtube.com. At http://bit.ly/2BwsVW3

◊ Scott, Ben Lionel. July 29, 2018. "I Will Not Stop—Best Motivational Video." Youtube.com. At http://bit.ly/2BrIX3u

◊ MotivationGrid. January 13, 2014. "Never Quit-Motivational Video." Youtube.com. At http://bit.ly/2By4OWZ

◊ Team Fearless. February 29, 2016. "Never Quit! An Uplifting Speech Featuring Walter Bond." Youtube.com. At http://bit.ly/2BsUWO4

Avoid Negativity

◊ Ted-ed. February 03, 2016. "How Stress Affects the Brain." Facebook.com. At http://bit.ly/2BsYbFo

◊ Baum, Isadora. August 1, 2016. "13 Ways to Avoid Negativity & Feel Happier." Bustle.com. At http://bit.ly/2BybOmJ

◊ Chernoff, Angel. August 08, 2012. "10 Ways to Defend Yourself Against Negativity." Marcandangel.com. At http://bit.ly/2BwhRIr

◊ Holik, Chase. August 02, 2015. "7 Ways to Avoid Negativity in Your Life." Iheartintelligence.com. At http://bit.ly/2BvW5ED

Drama Queens

◊   Sanders, Jillian. "7 Ways to Avoid Drama & Have Healthy Friendships." Mindbodygreen.com. At http://bit.ly/2BycQz7

◊   West, Nicole Leigh. July 02, 2014. "How to Avoid Unnecessary Drama in Your Life." Huffpost.com. At http://bit.ly/2Bum9zX.

◊   Hayes, Julian. "Avoid Life Dramas with These Tips." Lifehack.com. At http://bit.ly/2BuR2EC

Forgive

◊   Howes, Ryan. March 31, 2013. "Forgiveness vs. Reconciliation." Psychologytoday.com. At http://bit.ly/2BtDKIC

◊   November 04, 2017. "Forgiveness: Letting Go of Grudges and Bitterness." Mayoclinic.org. At https://mayocl.in/2Bt66mf

◊   Radford, Nancy. April 11, 2016. "Forgiveness: The Key to a Happier Future." Positivepsychologyprogram.com. At http://bit.ly/2Bunjvj

Don't Worry

◊   Morin, Amy. May 09, 2017. "How to Stop Worrying About Things You Can't Change." Psychologytoday.com. At http://bit.ly/2Bu885n

◊   Taylor, Jim. April 16, 2013. "What, me worry? Why worrying does more harm than good." Psychologytoday.com. At http://bit.ly/2BuRzGC

◊   Mann, Denise. "9 Steps to End Chronic Worrying." Webmd.com. At https://wb.md/2BvoevH

◊   Chan, Amanda L. April 14, 2014. "11 Habits of People Who Never Worry." Huffpost.com. At http://bit.ly/2Bws47U

YOUR ONE AND ONLY LIFE

Discover Your Purpose in Life

◊   MotivationHub. September 11, 2018. "One of the Greatest Speeches Ever." Youtube. At http://bit.ly/2Bsf57e

◊   Heart of Champions. May 13, 2018. "Actors Give Advice on Success." Youtube.com. At http://bit.ly/2BwAb4f

◊   Canfield, Jack. "10 Life Purpose Tips to Help You Find Your Passion." Jackcanfield.com. At http://bit.ly/2BuoM4N

◊   Fox, MeiMei. May 31, 2016. "Six Ways to Discover Your Life Purpose." Forbes.com. At http://bit.ly/2BvVJOk

Ikigai

◊   World Economic Forum. December 31, 2017. "This Japanese Concept Could Change Your Life." Facebook.com. At http://bit.ly/2Bugzxu

◊   Nescafe Arabia. February 22, 2015. "#Iwakeupfor The Ikigai Concept." Youtube.com. At http://bit.ly/2Bu5Bbo

◊   Big Think. April 14, 2018. "How to Reboot Your Life with the Japanese Philosophy of Ikigai." Youtube.com. At http://bit.ly/2BFWCEn

◊   Ikigai Wisdom. June 23, 2017. "The 10 Laws of Ikigai (Ikigai Wisdom 1)." Youtube.com. At http://bit.ly/2BzlcXf

Philotimo

◊   "Philotomo: A Greek Word Packed With So Much Meaning, it Can't Be Defined." En.protothema.gr. At http://bit.ly/2Buw7S2

◊   Philotimo Foundation. August 26, 2014. "The Greek Secret of Philotimo." Youtube.com. At http://bit.ly/2BuTbQG

◊   "The Greek Word Philotimo." Ellopos.com. At http://bit.ly/2BvXMSv

Dharma

◊   Thorp, Tris. "How to Explore Your Spiritual Dharma." Chopra.com. At http://bit.ly/2BxFqRd

◊   Biddle, Tabby. January 24, 2013. "10 Tips to Discover Your Personal Dharma." Huffpost.com. At http://bit.ly/2BxJhhg

◊   Philosophy of Spirituality. January 12, 2017. "What is Dharma and the Philosophy behind it?" Youtube.com. At http://bit.ly/2BuktXt

Strengths and Weaknesses

◊   "Strengths and Weaknesses Analysis." 123test.com. At http://bit.ly/2Bt1zjC

◊   Pillay, Hyma. March 24, 2014. "Why It's Important to Know Your Strengths and Weaknesses." Leadernomics.com. At http://bit.ly/2Bux8tq

Designing Your Future

◊ Arruda, William. February 02, 2014. "Five Ways to Learn What People Really Think About You." Forbes.com. At http://bit.ly/2BtqV0U

◊ Ludden, David. September 10, 2016. "How Others See You." Psychologytoday.com. At http://bit.ly/2BpVowL

◊ Hedges, Kristi. December 19, 2017. "How Are You Perceived at Work? Here's an Exercise to Find Out." Hbr.org. At http://bit.ly/2BwgJop

◊ "Self-Perception Assessment." Garfinkleexecutivecoacing.com. At http://bit.ly/2BrIvC7

The MAPP Career Test

◊ https://www.assessment.com/

How Are You Perceived

◊ Hedges, Kristi, December 19, 2017, How Are You Perceived at Work? Here's an Exercise to Find Out," Harvard Business Review. http://bit.ly/2VYRdjG

◊ Sudden, David, Ph.D., September 2016, "How Others See You," Psychology Today.

◊ http://bit.ly/2UvXPo0

◊ Arruda, William, February 25, 2014, "Five Ways to Learn What People Really Think About You." Forbes. http://bit.ly/2ZqQY3d

YOUR OPPORTUNITIES ARE UNLIMITED

Opportunity

◊ July 23, 2007. "7 Ways to Help Yourself Recognize Opportunity." Steveolsen.com. At http://bit.ly/2Buy0hG

◊ "Strengthening Your Ability to Recognize Opportunity." Experisjobs.us. At http://bit.ly/2BumdzZ

◊ Rainey, Don. November 19, 2010. "4 Ways to Recognize Opportunity When It Knocks." Businessinsider.com. At https://read.bi/2BvYsrf

◊ Daum, Kevin. "5 Ways to Recognize a Great Opportunity." Inc.com. At http://bit.ly/2BrWOXu

The Value of Work

◊ Ramsey, Dave. "Why Kids Need to Experience the Value of Hard Work." Daveramsey.com. At http://bit.ly/2BuOiHs

◊ December 25, 2015. "Teaching the Value of Hard Work." Exploringyourmind.com. At http://bit.ly/2BrXvA4

Crowdfunding

◊ Daly, Alex, "The Crowd-Sourceress: Get Smart, Get Funded and Kickstart Your Next Big Idea." https://amzn.to/2Uuo9yZ

Becoming an Online Sensation

◊ "Ingenious Storage Hack Guide Becomes the Most Popular Facebook Video of All Time Wwith a Whopping 333 Million Views." Dailymail. co.uk. At https://dailym.ai/2Bzq4vv

◊ Brass, Kevin. January 26, 2015. "How to Become an Online Celebrity— and Get Paid for It." Wsj.com. At https://on.wsj.com/2BrO5o3

◊ Simon, Denise. June 23, 2016. "How to Become a YouTube Sensation." Backstage.com. At http://bit.ly/2BvHfhw

◊ Urbaniak, Magdalena. May 25, 2017. "How to Become a Social Media Influencer in Ten Simple Steps." Forbes.com. At http://bit.ly/2Bs1YCQ

Google's Top Seven Skills

◊ Glazer, Lou. January 5, 2018. "Google finds STEM Skills Aren't the Most Important Skills." Michiganfuture.org. At http://bit.ly/2BwnKpf

Digital Nomads

◊ "Digital Nomadism: A Rising Trend." Mbopartners.com. At http://bit. ly/2BrOCGz

◊ Pofeldt, Elaine. August 30, 2018. "Digital Nomadism Goes Mainstream." Forbes.com. At http://bit.ly/2BunDu0

◊ Monroe, Rachel. April 24, 2017. "#Vanlife, The Bohemian Social-Media Movement." Newyorker.com. At http://bit.ly/2BzrmGR

eSPORTS

◊ eSports Earnings, http://bit.ly/2vfHAkI

Fablabs

◊ "What is a Fab Lab?" fabfoundation.org. At http://bit.ly/2Bq0wkv

◊ Thompson, Clive. March 2018. "Made to Order—The Future of Fab Labs." Wired.

◊ Fab Lab Connect. At http://bit.ly/2Bw2oIx

◊ "Fab Central." Mit.edu. At http://bit.ly/2BxcQzh

ISSUES THAT MATTER

Public Corruption

◊ RepresentUs. March 1, 2018. "Jennifer Lawrence Teaches Students How Government Really Works." Facebook.com. At http://bit.ly/2BxRNwK

Economic Inequality

◊ 2011. "20 Facts About U.S. Inequality that Everyone Should Know." Stanford.edu. At https://stanford.io/2BvAgoF

◊ Eidelson, Josh. March 01. 2018. "U.S. Income Inequality Hits a Disturbing New Threshold." Bloomberg.com. At https://bloom.bg/2Bxe9yb

◊ Reinicke, Carmen. July 19, 2018. "U.S. Income inequality continues to grow." Cnbc.com. At https://cnb.cx/2BusJGX

◊ Amadeo, Kimberly. November 07, 2018. "Income Inequality in America." Thebalance.com. At http://bit.ly/2BuT7k2

◊ Kain, Erik. October 05, 2011. "Could a Debt Jubilee Help Kickstart the American Economy?" forbes.com. At http://bit.ly/2Budmy2

Student Debt

◊ U.S. Senator Bernie Sanders. January 13, 2018. "How Millennials Are Getting Screwed by the Economy." Facebook.com. At http://bit.ly/2BrUGyP

◊ Smith, Noah. November 5, 2018. "Student-loan Debt is Crushing Millennials and Stressing Them Out." Denverpost.com. At https://dpo.st/2Bxu9jN

◊ Llorente, Elizabeth. "Students, Families Struggle to Repay Billions in Crushing Loan Debts." Foxnews.com. At https://fxn.ws/2Bw5ImG

◊ Pry, Alyssa and Ahn, Jeanie. September 21, 2018. "Student Debt is Forcing Millennials to Delay Life Milestones." Yahoo.com. At https://yhoo.it/2BxWmqS

Social Media

◊ Ehmke, Rachel. "How Using Social Media Affects Teenagers." Childmind.org. At http://bit.ly/2Bs7fKE

◊ Ramasubbu, Suren. May 26, 2015. "Influence of Social Media on Teenagers." Huffpost.com At http://bit.ly/2BuxccH

◊ "Royal Society for Public Health (RSPH) Submission to Inquiry on the Impact of Cyberbullying on Social Media on Children and Young People's Mental Health." Rsph.org.uk. At http://bit.ly/2BGbe6H

◊ May 19, 2017. "Instagram Ranked Worst for Young People's Mental Health." Rsph.org.uk. At http://bit.ly/2Bw6xvM

Racism

◊ Jerome, Fred. September 01, 2005. "Einstein and Racism in America." Physicstoday.com. At http://bit.ly/2Bthq1C

◊ "Racism in America." Apa.org. At http://bit.ly/2BxWFSr

◊ Fieseler, Robert. "Exposing Bias: Race and Racism in America." Harvard.edu. At http://bit.ly/2BthIpe

◊ Jacoby, Jeff. January 18, 2019. "As MLK Foresaw, Racism in America Has Been Largely Overcome." Bostonglobe.com. At http://bit.ly/2BuxJvd

◊ Glaude, Eddie S. September 6, 2018. "Don't Let the Loud Bigots Distract You. America's Real Problem with Race Cuts Far Deeper." Time.com. At http://bit.ly/2Bs8J7G

Incarceration

◊ Schoenherr, Neil. September 07, 2016. "Cost of Incarceration in the U.S. More Than $1 Trillion." Wustl.edu. At http://bit.ly/2BxX9bd

◊ Ferner, Matt. September 13, 2016. "The Full Cost of Incarceration in the U.S. Is Over $1 Trillion, Study Finds." Huffingtonpost.com. At http://bit.ly/2BvIkWt

◊ Fieseler, Robert. "Exposing Bias: Race and Racism in America." Harvard.edu. At http://bit.ly/2BthIpe

Global Warming

◊ "Climate Change: How Do We know?" nasa.gov. At https://go.nasa.gov/2BvuLq5

◊ https://nyti.ms/2VgseLu

◊ "Global Warming." Sciencedaily.com. At http://bit.ly/2Buyd4v

◊ Nunez, Christina. "Cause and Effects of Climate Change." Nationalgeographic.com. At https://on.natgeo.com/2BydxZ8

◊ "Is Global Warming a Myth?" scientificamerican.com. At http://bit.ly/2BrW6t9

The Second Amendment

◊ Chanos, George. February 15, 2018. "Understanding the Second Amendment." Georgejchanos.com. At http://bit.ly/2TKZtCG

◊ Willingham, AJ. March 28, 2018. "27 Words: Deconstructing the Second Amendment." Cnn.com. At https://cnn.it/2TINGF5

◊ Lund, Nelson and Winkler, Adam. "The Second Amendment." Constitutioncenter.com. At http://bit.ly/2TJAoIl

◊ "Do we really understand the Second Amendment anymore?" Washingtonpost.com. At https://wapo.st/2TKvD14

Hunger

- ◊ "India" thp.org. At http://bit.ly/2Bwithk
- ◊ "Hunger in America." Feedingamerica.org. At http://bit.ly/2Bs2MYf
- ◊ McMillan, Tracie. "New Face of Hunger." Nationalgeographic.com. At https://on.natgeo.com/2BsdIVW
- ◊ Resnikoff, Ned. July 19, 2016. "The Return of American Hunger." Theatlantic.com. At http://bit.ly/2BtIhuA
- ◊ Grameen Foundation. At http://bit.ly/2BwiKkm

Water

- ◊ Zhang, Sarah. June 03, 2014. "The Cutting-Edge Tech that Will Finally Bring Desalination to the U.S." Gizmodo.com. At http://bit.ly/2Bs34yj
- ◊ Bradley, Ryan. March 08, 2018. "Can Humans Survive on Water Vapor Alone?" wired.com. At http://bit.ly/2BzELyF
- ◊ Welch, Craig. March 5, 2018. "How Cape Town is Coping with Its Worst Drought on Record." Nationalgeographic.com. At http://bit.ly/2BvzXu5
- ◊ Thomasy, Hannah. January 10, 2019. "Scientists are Using Bacteria to Remove Harmful Contaminants From Our Water. Here's How." Ehn.org. At http://bit.ly/2BqdxKT
- ◊ Coren, Ora. January 11. 2019. "Israel Playing Catch-up in Expanding Its Water Infrastructure." Haaretz.com. At http://bit.ly/2By5Imn
- ◊ Schleifer, Leah. August 24, 2017. "7 Reasons We're Facing a Global Water Crisis." Wri.org. At http://bit.ly/2BuFh11
- ◊ Leahy, Stephen. March 22, 2018. "From Not Enough to Too Much, the World's Water Crisis Explained." Nationalgeographic.com At http://bit.ly/2BvAZGt

Loneliness

◊ "A Connected Society." Assets.publishing.service.gov.uk. At http://bit. ly/2TLhTTQ

◊ Solly, Meilan. November 08, 2018. "British Doctors May Soon Prescribe Art, Music, Dance, Singing Lessons." Smithsonianmag.com. At http://bit. ly/2TJV2bj

◊ King, Brendan. June 09, 2015. "Homeshare proposal matches young people with elderly in exchange for cooking and cleaning." Abc.net.au. At https:// ab.co/2BzZpi9

◊ Ali, Shainna. July 12, 2018. "What You Need to Know About the Loneliness Epidemic." Psychologytoday.com. At http://bit.ly/2Bv5PiE

Mental Illness

◊ Snow, Kate and McFadden, Cynthia. December 10, 2017. "Generation at risk: America's youngest facing mental health crisis." Nbcnews.com. At https://nbcnews.to/2BqsYmj

◊ Cahalan, Susannah. July 7, 2018. "The Shocking Truth About America's Mental Health Crisis." Nypost.com. At https://nyp.st/2BwRd2l

◊ Roth, Alisa. March 31, 2018. "A 'Hellish world': The Mental Health Crisis Overwhelming America's Prisons." The Guardian.com. At http://bit. ly/2BuHvNI

◊ Barnett, Brian. June 22, 2018. "America Can't Incarcerate Away Our Mental Health Crisis." Huffingtonpost.com. At http://bit.ly/2Bsk6ML

◊ "New Study Reveals Lack of Access as Root Cause for Mental Health Crisis in America." Thenationalcouncil.org. At http://bit.ly/2Bu3moI

◊ Henriques, Gregg. February 15, 2014. "The College Student Mental Health Crisis." Psychologytoday.com. At http://bit.ly/2Bv0IPx

◊ Mahnken, Kevin. November 7, 2017. "The Hidden Mental Health Crisis in America's Schools: Millions of Kids Not Receiving Services They Need." 74million.org. At http://bit.ly/2BvkmLk

EMDR

◊ Arkowitz, Hal, Lillenfeld, Scott O, "EMDR: Taking a Closer Look," Scientific American. August 1, 2012. http://bit.ly/2XwEx3J

◊ Khan, Olga, July 27, 2015, "Can Eye Movement Work Like Therapy?" The Atlantic.

◊ http://bit.ly/2IJxyAo

Suicide

◊ Lloyd, Noel. June 14, 2018. "Knowing How to Spot the Potential Warning Signs of Suicide Could Save a Life." Mhamd.org. At http://bit.ly/2BtGsxC

◊ http://bit.ly/2VaKZzX

◊ "Suicide." Psychologytoday.com. At http://bit.ly/2ByiZLJ

◊ Rosin, Hanna. December 2015. "The Silicon Valley Suicides." Theatlantic. com. At http://bit.ly/2Bqu7u7

Fake News

◊ Engadget. March 22, 2018. "Vicon Siren First Look." Facebook.com. At http://bit.ly/2BA2i2t

◊ Lanau, Kate. September 14, 2016. "A 'Memory Hacker' Explains How to Plant False Memories in People's Minds." Vice.com. At http://bit.ly/2BjjvgE

◊ Now You See TV. September 10, 2016. "Now You See? Exposing the Magic of the Media." Facebook.com. At http://bit.ly/2BfNeXJ

◊ LaFrance, Adrienne. July 11, 2017. "The Technology that Will Make It Impossible for You to Believe What You See." Theantlantic.com. At http://bit.ly/2Bno6hF

Technology and Employment

◊ Manyika, James. May 2017 "Technology, Jobs and the Future of Work." Mckinsey.com. At https://mck.co/2TLbIPC

◊ Rotman, David. June 12, 2013. "How Technology is Destroying Jobs." Technologyreview.com. At http://bit.ly/2TLprWG

◊ Vincent, James. November 30, 2017. "Automation Threatens 800 Million Jobs, but Technology Could Still Save Us, Says Report." Theverge.com. At http://bit.ly/2TMm4yQ

◊ Mabry, R.H. & Sharplin, A.D. March 18, 1986. "Does More Technology Create Unemployment?" Cato.org. At http://bit.ly/2TETb7H

◊ Rogoff, Kenneth. October 02, 2012. "The Impact of Technology on Employment." Weforum.org. At http://bit.ly/2TRj2cs

Political Dysfunction

◊ "Trust in Government." News.gallup.com. At http://bit.ly/2TO2F0E

◊ Wike, Richard, Simmons, Katie, Stokes, Bruce and Fetterolf, Janell. October 16, 2017. "Many Unhappy With Current Political System." Pewglobal.org. At https://pewrsr.ch/2TKwRto

◊ Ridge, Tom and Daschle, Tom. March 15, 2018. "America Has a Broken Political System Our Leaders Need to Fix." Thehill.com. At http://bit. ly/2TJD1dj

◊ Gehl, Katherine M. and Porter, Michael E. March 9, 2017. "Why Politics is Failing in America." Fortune.com. At http://bit.ly/2TJp1QL

◊ Gehl, Katherine M. and Porter, Michael E. September 2017. "Why Competition in the Politics Industry is Failing America." Hbs.edu. At https://hbs.me/2TEQH9k

◊ Mann, Thomas E. and Ornstein, Norman J. April 26, 2013. "Finding the Common Good in an Era of Dysfunction Governance." Brookings.edu. At https://brook.gs/2TIDE6J

◊ Mann, Thomas E. May 26, 2014. "Admit It, Political Scientists: Politics Really Is More Broken Than Ever." Theatlantic.com. At http://bit. ly/2TKVxll

The End of the Two-Party System

◊ Griffiths, Shawn. November 15, 2018. "Powerful Coalition Launches Campaign to challenge Two-Party Politics." Electionscience.org. At http://bit.ly/2Bz9prR

◊ Gallo, Alex. November 10, 2017. "The two-party system is dying—let's put it out of its misery." Thehill.com. At http://bit.ly/2BvBy3i

◊ Kindelan, Katie. February 25, 2018. "U.S. Could Be Witnessing 'End of a Two-Party System': Republican Governor." Abcnews.go.com. At https://abcn.ws/2BzyyCM

◊ Taibbi, Matt. March 30, 2018. "Is the Two-Party System Doomed?" Rollingstone.com At http://bit.ly/2BvDn08

Campaign Finance Reform

◊ Lessig, Lawrence. 2013. "We the People and the Republic we must reclaim." Ted.com. At http://bit.ly/2BsbdTF

◊ Lessig, Lawrence 2018, America, Compromised University of Chicago Press.

◊ Rowan, Beth. "Campaign Finance Reform: History and Timeline." Infoplease.com. At http://bit.ly/2ByifX7

◊ Ornstein, Norman and Mann, Thomas E. March 1, 2004. "So Far, So Good on Campaign Finance Reform." Brookings.edu. At https://brook.gs/2BtXknS

◊ Support Citizen-Funded Elections. http://bit.ly/2BwFlNN

◊ "Campaign Finance." Khan Academy. At http://bit.ly/2By0gA1

The Electoral College

◊ Rosenthal, Sean J. November 15, 2016. "The Electoral College is Genius." Intellectualtakeout.org. At http://bit.ly/2Bvb4yM

◊ November 1, 2004. "The Electoral College: Enlightened Democracy." Heritage.org. At https://herit.ag/2BxHXL3

◊ "The Genius of the Electoral College." Kingsmeadow.com. At http://bit.ly/2BwGEwb

◊ November 15, 2016. "Don't Trash the Electoral College—It Works." Investors.com. At http://bit.ly/2BwHj0D

American Exceptionalism

◊ December 06, 2018. "The Real Threat to American Exceptionalism." Wsj. com. At https://on.wsj.com/2Bzb7th

◊ Peterson, Paul. May 05, 2017. "American Exceptionalism Isn't a Modern Idea." Harvard.edu. At http://bit.ly/2BscJoP

◊ Tumulty, Karen. September 12, 2013. "American Exceptionalism Explained." Washingtonpost.com. At https://wapo.st/2TKvD14

◊ September 05, 2015. "American Exceptionalism and the Scars of the Past." Wsj.com. At https://on.wsj.com/2BxtdMh

The Bystander Effect

◊ "Bystander Effect." Psychologytoday.com. At http://bit.ly/2Bwxsrm

◊ January 09, 2017. "Who were Latane and Darley? AP Psychology Bystander Effect Review." Albert.io. At http://bit.ly/2BzuK4v

◊ Garcia, Stephen M., Weaver, Kim, Darley, John M. and Moskowitz, Gordon B. "Crowded Minds: The Implicit Bystander Effect." Umich.edu. At http://bit.ly/2BwNOk0

How to Build Consensus

◊ Binder, Sarah A. December 1, 2000. "Going Nowhere: A Gridlocked Congress." Brookings.edu. At https://brook.gs/2BxKC7v

◊ Boot, Max. October 03, 2017. "Political Gridlock is Killing Us, Literally." Thedailybeast.com. At http://bit.ly/2BwUu1E

◊ Bowman, Bryan. October 01, 2018. "Partisan Divide in U.S. Congress the Worst It's Ever Been." Theglobeposts.com. At http://bit.ly/2ByFUXj

◊ Jones, Bradley. May 08, 2018. "Most Americans Want to Limit Campaign Spending, Say Big Donors Have Greater Political Influence." Pewresearch. com. At https://pewrsr.ch/2Bsg3QP

◊ Zaidi, Syed. June 28, 2013. "Money in Politics This Week: Six Mind-Blowing Statistics About the 1 Percent of the 1 Percent." Brennancenter. org. At http://bit.ly/2BwzBDq

◊ Lloyd, John. January 03, 2018. "The Death of Political Parties." Tnp.sg. At http://bit.ly/2BIpXxZ

THE FUTURE IS HERE

Changes in Humanity

◊ Pontin, Jason. March 27, 2018. "Science is Getting Us Closer to the End of Infertility." Wired.com. At http://bit.ly/2BykklP

◊ Palmer, Katie M. September 18, 2018. "Why the Gene Editors of Tomorrow Need to Study Ethics Today." Wired.com. At http://bit.ly/2BwAxI2

◊ Testa, Sam and Tobia, Geoffrey. November 11, 2018. "Genetic Biomedics Outline." Tufts.edu. At http://bit.ly/2BzNfWs

◊ Regalado, Antonia. August 07, 2017. "A New Way to Reproduce." Technologyreview.com. At http://bit.ly/2BylqOt

◊ Ball, Philip. October 14, 2018. "Reproduction revolution: how our skin cells might be turned into sperm and eggs." Theguardian.com. At http://bit.ly/2BBS3e1

Artificial Intelligence

◊ "Benefits & Risks of Artificial Intelligence." Futureoflife.org. At http://bit.ly/2BxYE9b

◊ http://bit.ly/2DqALBx

◊ Davenport, Thomas H. and Ronanki, Rajeev. January 2018. "Artificial Intelligence for the Real World." Hbr.org. At http://bit.ly/2BAsWrU

◊ "Artificial Intelligence: Implications for Business Strategy." Mit.edu. At http://bit.ly/2BzJpwz

◊ Adams, R.L. October 1, 2017. "10 Powerful Examples of Artificial Intelligence in Use Today." Forbes.com. At http://bit.ly/2BzJpwz

The Singularity

◊ Gall, Richard. March 14, 2018. "5 Polarizing Quotes from Professor Stephen Hawking on artificial intelligence." Packthub.com. At http://bit.ly/2Bx1xHy

◊ November 07, 2017. "The Crystal Ball Musings of Ray Kurzweil— More Often Than Not, He is Dead On." 21stcentech.com. At http://bit.ly/2BwCunQ

◊ Big Think. April 28, 2009. "Ray Kurzweil: The Coming Singularity." Youtube.com. At http://bit.ly/2By0ozf

◊ Luckerson, Victor. December 02, 2014. "5 Very Smart People Who Think Artificial Intelligence Could Bring the Apocalypse." Time.com. At http://bit.ly/2BAuP7Y

Space Travel

◊ McNamara, Alexander. August 08, 2018. "10 future space missions to look forward to." Sciencefocus.com. At http://bit.ly/2TMPih9

◊ Kaku, Michio. "The Physics of Interstellar Travel." Mkaku.org. At http://bit.ly/2TMn0Dh

◊ "Future of Spaceflight." Nationalgeographic.com. At https://on.natgeo.com/2TP44Ea

The Wisdom of Crowds

◊ Emrani, Mahta. August 29, 2016. "Wisdom of Swarm." USC.edu. At http://bit.ly/2TNdTm1

◊ Whitfield, John. "The Wisdom of the Bees." Nature.com. At https://go.nature.com/2TMS71J

◊ "What is Swarm AI?" Unanimous.ai. At http://bit.ly/2TJ50Kc

◊ Rosenberg, Louis. July 20, 2015. "Human Swarming and the Future of Collective Intelligence." Singularityweblog.com. At http://bit.ly/2TPP3So

Glass Information Storage

◊ Futurism. "Glass is the future of data storage." Facebook.com. At http:// bit.ly/2TI6MuZ

◊ Vincent, James. February 16, 2016. "Five-dimensional Glass Discs Can Store Data for up to 13.8 Billion Years." Theverge.com. At http://bit. ly/2tnZWPy

Asteroid Mining

◊ "Asteroid Mining is the Key to our Future Expansion into Space." Planetaryresources.com. At http://bit.ly/2TNYHF8

◊ Foust, Jeff. October 31, 2018. "Asteroid Mining Company Planetary Resources Acquired by Blockchain Firm." Spacenews.com. At http://bit. ly/2TIpfrg

◊ Corbyn, Zoe. June 9, 2018. "The Asteroid Rush Sending 21st Century Prospectors in to Space." Theguardian.com. At http://bit.ly/2TIf5XH

Genomics

◊ September 26, 2010. "Longevity Escape Velocity May Be Closer Than We Think." Singularityweblong.com. At http://bit.ly/2TMZl5R

◊ "Deep Dive: Genetics and Genomics, Today and Tomorrow." Aspenideas. org. At http://bit.ly/2TPYv8k

◊ "Top 10 Innovations, Genetics and Genomics." The-scientist.com. At http://bit.ly/2TMZtST

◊ Kiara, Palmer. 2018. "DNA Day 2018: Celebrate 15 Ways Genomics Now Influences Our Lives." Genome.gov. At http://bit.ly/2TM6inG

Antibiotic-Resistant Superbugs

◊   Galey, Patrick. September 03, 2018. "Drug-resistant Superbug Spreading in Hospitals: study." Medicalxpress.com. At http://bit.ly/2TPZllu

◊   November 06, 2018. "Superbugs Killed 33,000 Europeans in 2015: Study." Medicalxpress.com. At http://bit.ly/2TMw3Ef

◊   Associated Press. April 03, 2018. "CDC: Drug-resistant Nightmare Bacteria' Pose Growing Threat." Statnews.com. At http://bit.ly/2TM5aAh

◊   Oaten, James. September 03, 2018. "Superbug Strains Resistant to All Known Antibiotics Discovered by Melbourne Researchers." Abc.net.au. At https://ab.co/2TKEmAs

◊   September 04, 2018. "Superbug Discovery Renews Hope for Antibiotic Treatment." Sciencedaily.com. At http://bit.ly/2TNn4mt

Cybersecurity

◊   "Information Technology Threats and Vulnerabilities." Nasa.gov. At https://go.nasa.gov/2TNyRBh

◊   "Cyber-attacks." Bbc.com. At https://bbc.in/2TPZLZ6

◊   Cimpanu, Catalin. September 27, 2018. "Port of San Diego Suffers Cyber-attack, Second Port in a Week after Barcelona." Zdnet.com. At https://zd.net/2TNcXhr

◊   Palmer, Danny. December 04, 2018. "Cyber Security: Hackers Step Out of the Shadows with Bigger, Bolder Attacks." Zdnet.com. At https://zd.net/2TOlKzu

◊   Mee, Paul and Schuermann, Til. September 14, 2018. "How a Cyber Attack Could Cause the Next Financial Crisis." Hbr.org. At http://bit.ly/2TO1Y7o

The Future of War

◊ Biryukov andrey and Anishchuk, Alexei. December 26, 2018. "Putin Says Latest Test of Hypersonic Warhead Successful." Bloomberg.com. At https://bloom.bg/2TM6Mdj

◊ Creighton, Jolene. March 26, 2018. "Some Powerful Predictions for the Future." Futurism.com. At http://bit.ly/2TO2pi2

◊ Watts, Anthony. September 13, 2018. "Google Video Leak Proves they are Evil After All." Wattsupwiththat.com. At http://bit.ly/2TTEZIh

◊ Powers, Benjamin. March 14, 2017. "How Intelligent Drones Are Shaping the Future of Warfare." Rollingstone.com. At http://bit.ly/2TREWwA

◊ Chamberlain, Craig. May 1, 2018. "How Are Drones Changing Warfare, Threatening Security?" Phys.org. At http://bit.ly/2TJTnCt

Other Worlds

◊ "TESS Science Support Center." Nasa.gov. At https://go.nasa.gov/2BA8ckl

◊ Guesgen, Mirjam. April 17, 2018. "Here Are the Necessary Ingredients for a Life-Supporting Exoplanet." Seeker.com. At http://bit.ly/2BA9snz

◊ Kowch 737. May 07, 2018. "CHaracterising ExOPlanet Satellite." Youtube. com. At http://bit.ly/2BzjKEd

◊ Library of Congress. March 02, 2016. "The Transiting Exoplanet Survey Satellite (TESS)." Youtube.com. At http://bit.ly/2BycAjA

The Merger of Man and Machine

◊ November 02, 2018. "Editor's Choice: Cognitive Neuroscience." Nature. com. At https://go.nature.com/2BBYuO6

◊ Forsythe, Chris, Berka, Chris, Matthews, Robert and Wagner, John. 2007. "Making the Giant Leap with Augmented Cognition Technologies: What Will Be the First 'Killer App'"? link.springer.com. At http://bit. ly/2BKfWAn

◊ St. John, Mark; Kobus, David A.; Morrison, Jeffrey G.; and Schmorrow, Dylan. 2004. "Overview of the DARPA Augmented Cognition Technical Integration Experiment." Mit.edu. At http://bit.ly/2BBFJuj

◊ Gallego, Jelor. December 25, 2016. "Becoming Borg: What Is a Hive Mind in Science and Could Humanity Get There?" Futurism.com. At http://bit. ly/2BxM8Xy

◊ Arthur, Isaac. December 07, 2017. "Hive Minds." Youtube.com. At http://bit.ly/2ByFujQ

You're Reading My Mind

◊ Begley, Sharon. November 15, 2018. "With Brain Implants, Scientists Hope to Translate Paralyzed Patients' Thoughts Into Speech." Statnews.com. At http://bit.ly/2ByFY9E

◊ "This Mind-Reading AI Tech Is Straight out of a Black Mirror Episode." Iflscience.com. At http://bit.ly/2BzSZ2F

◊ Begley, Sharon. November 20, 2018. "With Brain implants, Scientists Aim to Translate Thoughts into Speech." Scientificamerican.com. At http://bit.ly/2BucYjd

Archiving Your Mind

◊ The Human Connectome Project. At http://bit.ly/2BzVNwJ

◊ "Connectome Project." Harvard.edu. At http://bit.ly/2Bud3Dx

◊ "Advancing the Science and Technology of Memory." Nectome.com. At http://bit.ly/2Bytzm0

◊ Regalado, Antonio. March 13, 2018. "A Startup is Pitching a Mind-uploading Service that is '100 Percent Fatal.'" Technologyreview.com. At http://bit.ly/2ByE60z

◊ Letzler, Rafi. April 03, 2018. "Brain-Uploading Company Has No Immediate Plans to Upload Brains." Livescience.org. At http://bit.ly/2BDwXvP

Augmented Reality

◊ May 29, 2018. "The Future of Augmented Reality." Cnbc.com. At https://cnb.cx/2Byvkzy

◊ "The Ultimate Guide to Understanding Augmented Reality (AR) Technology." Realitytechnologies.com. At http://bit.ly/2BD3XEv

◊ Adobe. August 21, 2018. "How Artists are Shaping the Future of Augmented Reality." Youtube.com. At http://bit.ly/2BBEyLz

◊ Dezeen. August 19, 2014. "The future of augmented reality." Youtube.com. At http://bit.ly/2BBEZWd

◊ TED. January 10, 2018. "How Augmented Reality Could Change the Future of Surgery." Youtube.com. At http://bit.ly/2Bx27EX

Blockchain Technology

◊ February 09, 2018. "BlockChain in Retail: How Blockchain Will Change the Consumer Goods Supply." Redappletech.com. At http://bit.ly/2BLFeOz

◊ "Blockchain technologies: Business Innovation and Application." Mit.edu. At http://bit.ly/2BB3Edb

◊ Murray, Maryanne. June 15, 2018. "Blockchain Explained." Graphics. reuters.com. At https://tmsnrt.rs/2BzAuey

◊ YOcoin. December 23, 2016. "TED Talks: The Blockchain Explained Simply." Youtube.com. At http://bit.ly/2BEZZex

◊ Wilson, Steve. May 22, 2017. "Blockchain Explained in Plain English." Zdnet.com. At https://zd.net/2BBR39P

Miniaturized Computers

◊ Gent, Edd. March 26, 2018. "IBM's New Computer is the Size of a Grain of Salt and Costs Less Than 10 Cents." Singularityhub.com. At http://bit.ly/2BxruGQ

◊ Parrish, Kevin. June 22, 2018. "The 'World's Tiniest Computer' is Smaller Than a Grain of Rice. Much Smaller." Digitaltrends.com. At http://bit.ly/2Bywifa

3-D Printing

◊ "From Construction to Art, Here Are 25 Industries That 3-D Printing Could Disrupt." Cbinsights.com. At http://bit.ly/2TQ7rdI

◊ PBS NewsHour. March 21, 2018. "How 3-D Printing is Spurring Revolutionary Advances in manufacturing and Design." Youtube.com. At http://bit.ly/2TRLmeY

◊ U.S. Department of Energy. November 17, 2017. "Energy Talks: Recent Advances in Additive Manufacturing (3-D Printing)." Youtube.com. At http://bit.ly/2TTA4qM

◊ Digital Trends. January 12, 2018. "Ethereal Machines 'Halo' 5-Axis 3-D Printer at CES 2018." Youtube.com. At http://bit.ly/2TVlqzj

◊ DeSimone, Joseph. 2015. "What if 3-D Printing was 100x faster?" Ted.com. At http://bit.ly/2TONap5

The Internet of Things

◊ Burrus, Daniel. November 2014. "The Internet of Things is Far Bigger Than Anyone Realizes." Wired.com. At http://bit.ly/2TOZ4iN

◊ Morgan, Jacob. May 13, 2014. "A Simple Explanation of 'The Internet of Things.'" Forbes.com. At http://bit.ly/2TL6bZC

◊ Ranger, Steve. August 21, 2018. "What is the IoT? Everything you need to know about the Internet of Things right now." Zdnet.com. At https://zd.net/2TKgxJ4

◊ Burgess, Matt. February 16, 2018. "What is the Internet of Things? WIRED Explains." Wired.co.uk. At http://bit.ly/2TPbU0l

◊ Greenfield, Adam. June 06, 2017. "Rise of the machines: who is the 'internet of things' good for"? theguardian.com. At http://bit.ly/2BBZd1X

Invisible Checkout

◊ June 12, 2017. "'Just Walk out': The Invisible Payment Process." Ixtenso.com. At http://bit.ly/2BBrJ3P

◊ Leija, Joe. May 15, 2017. "PayThink Retailers Need 'Invisible' Mobile Pay for a Strong Brand Experience." Paymentsource.com. At http://bit.ly/2BDaqiL

◊ March 19, 2018. "No Cashier? No problem: The Checkout-Free Future of Grocery." Pyments.com. At http://bit.ly/2BDc0RJ

Medical Breakthroughs

◊ Tashobya, Athan. October 29, 2018. "Zipline to Start Assembling Drones in Rwanda." Newtimes.co.rw. At http://bit.ly/2BzWaXS

◊ Resources. Nanoscopetech.com. At http://bit.ly/2BA7un9

◊ June 27, 2017. "Drones as Humanitarian Tools." Doctorswithoutborders.org. At http://bit.ly/2BBcHLb

◊ Naik, Gautam. March 22, 2013. "Science Fiction Comes Alive as Researchers Grow Organs in Lab." WSJ.Com. At https://on.wsj.com/2BLQavB

◊ Comstock, Jonah. April 13, 2017. "The Qualcomm Tricorder X Prize has its winner, but work on tricorders will continue." Mobihealthnews.com. At http://bit.ly/2ByBJL6

◊ April 13, 2017. "Family-led Team Takes Top prize in Qualcomm Tricorder XPRIZE Competition for Consumer Medical Device Inspired by Star Trek." Tricorder.xprize.org. At http://bit.ly/2Bxxpvy

Longevity Escape Velocity

◊ "Ray Kurzweil Implies Rich People Have Already Reached Longevity Escape Velocity." Reddit.com. At http://bit.ly/2BvXX0j

◊ November 07, 2017. "The Crystal Ball Musings of Ray Kurzweil— More Often Than Not He is Dead On." 21stcentech.com. At http://bit.ly/2BwCunQ

◊ September 26, 2010. "Longevity Escape Velocity May Be Closer Than We Think." Singularityweblong.com. At http://bit.ly/2TMZl5R

Perfect Capitalism

◊ Kaku, Michio. "The Physics of Interstellar Travel." Mkaku.org. At http://bit.ly/2TMn0Dh

Massively Transformative Purpose

◊ Koulopoulos, Thomas. "According to Peter Diamandis and Ray Kurzweil, These Are the Most Dangerous and Disruptive Ideas." Inc.com. At http://bit.ly/2TLcT1K

◊ Sorenson, Peter. January 08, 2018. "Abundance Digital Massive Transformative Purpose." Youtube.com. At http://bit.ly/2TQjwj5

The Future of Food

◊ CTPCCPHET13. June 19, 2016. "Monsanto The Future of Food 2004." Youtube.com. At http://bit.ly/2TWQYo4

◊ Silverstein, Michael. "The Future of Food." Ted.com. At http://bit.ly/2TPe6oB

◊ Be Amazed. September 06, 2017. "Is THIS the Future of Food? Experts Say We'll Be Eating These 10 Foods by 2050." Youtube.com. At http://bit.ly/2BzIwUK

◊ Quartz. November 22, 2017. "Future of Food: Farming in the Age of Climate Change." Youtube.com. At http://bit.ly/2ByCtzS

◊ National Geographic. November 18, 2014. "The Future of Food." Youtube.com. At http://bit.ly/2BBtjCN

Eat Shit

◊ "Fecal Transplatation (Bacteriotherapy)." Hopkinsmedicine.org. At http://bit.ly/2BLSnan

◊ Gupta, Shaan, Allen-Vercoe, Emma and Petrof, Elaine O. March 2016. "Fecal Microbiota Transplantation: In Perspective." Ncbi.nlm.nih.gov. At http://bit.ly/2BDdkUH

◊ Tuft, Tracy. May 29, 2018. "I Had a Fecal Transplant and it Saved My Life." Huffingtonpost.com. At http://bit.ly/2BBQEEt

◊ "Fecal Microbiota Transplantation." Childrenscolorado.org. At http://bit.ly/2BzIJr0

◊ The Immorality Drive

◊ October 12, 2008. "American Game Designer Follows Father into Orbit." Abcnews.go.com. At https://abcn.ws/2BBevnr

Flying Taxis

◊ Moore, Clayton, January 7, 2019, Bell is Building a Self-flying Air Taxi and it Brought a Prototype to CES 2019. http://bit.ly/2IJNOSb

◊ Newcomb, Alyssa, January 10, 2019, "Flying Cars Could Take Off as Soon as 2023." At https://nbcnews.to/2Do85ct

Oumuamua

◊ Choitner, Isaac. January 16, 2019. "Have Aliens Found Us? A Harvard Astronomer on the Mysterious Interstellar Object 'Oumuamua.'" Newyorker.com. At http://bit.ly/2BBGP9c.

Made in the USA
Columbia, SC
04 September 2019